VIOLENT RELATIONSHIPS
BATTERING AND ABUSE AMONG ADULTS

INFORMATION PLUS®
WYLIE, TEXAS 75098
© **1981, 1983, 1985, 1987, 1989, 1991, 1993, 1995, 1997, 1999**
ALL RIGHTS RESERVED

EDITORS:
BARBARA A. KLIER, M.Ed.
NANCY R. JACOBS, M.A.
JACQUELYN QUIRAM, B.A.

CHAPTER I

ABUSE OF WOMEN — A WORLDWIDE TRADITION

A woman, a spaniel, and a walnut tree
The more they are beaten
The better they be. — Traditional Gloucester Ditty

Although seldom condoned in its more brutal forms, violence against wives has been tolerated throughout history. Based on ancient and commonly accepted beliefs of man's superiority over woman, values generally supported by economic, social, cultural, and religious institutions, the abuse of women has historically been seen as a natural consequence of the subordination of women to men. When beatings or floggings were society's accepted method of maintaining law and order, it was natural that men used violence to maintain law and order in their own families. Only when the use of violence began to be viewed as an unsatisfactory solution to problems did violence against wives begin to be seen as an unacceptable part of marriage. Nonetheless, the use of violence is still regarded as a man's right in many parts of the world.

EUROPEAN TRADITIONS

In Western civilization, the subservient role of women was well established by the Middle Ages. In fourteenth century France, a man could legally beat his wife for failure to obey reasonable commands, as long as he did not kill or permanently maim her. A tale of Geoffrey de la Tour de Landry in 1371 reflected contemporary attitudes toward the "wickedness of a nagging wife" and the proper punishment for such behavior:

Here is an example to every good woman that she suffer and endure patiently, nor strive with her husband nor answer him before strangers, as did once a woman who did answer her husband before strangers with short words: and he smote her with his fist down to earth; and then with his foot he struck her in her visage and broke her nose, and all her life after she had her nose crooked, which so shent [spoiled] and disfigured her visage after, that she might not for shame show her face, it was so foul blemished. And this she had for her language that she was wont to say to her husband, and therefore the wife ought to suffer, and let the husband have the words, and to be master, for that is her duty.

In 1427, Bernard of Sienna, Italy, advised husbands to show restraint and treat their wives with as much consideration as they did their fowl and livestock. This was probably not given much credence, however, in a city whose Rules on Marriage, prepared by Friar Cherubino, declared,

When you see your wife commit an offense, don't rush at her with insults and violent blows, rather, first correct the wrong lovingly. [If this does not work] scold her sharply, bully, and terrify her. And if this still doesn't work ... take up a stick and beat her soundly. It is better to punish the body and correct the soul than to damage the soul and spare the body.... You should beat [your wife] ... only when she commits a serious wrong.... Then readily beat her, not in rage, but out of charity and concern for her soul.

Wife beating was rarely viewed as a first alternative. Rather, societal and religious mores were designed to teach women that it was their religious and ethical duty to yield to the needs and desires of their husbands and it was in their spiritual best interests to have the badness beaten out of them. Only when an appeal to reason or to faith failed was the use of violence justified.

The "Rule of Thumb"

By the eighteenth century, in England and in the American colonies, violence against one's wife was legally unacceptable. It is commonly believed today that in the 1700s, the so-called "rule of thumb" applied to marital relations. This law allegedly permitted husbands to chastise their wives with a stick no bigger than the thumb. However, the *Oxford English Dictionary* (2nd edition, Clarendon Press, Oxford, England, 1989), the accepted authority on the origins and use of language, shows that the term did not apply to wife beating but has been used for over 300 years to mean measuring by practice or experience, especially for carpenters.

The "rule of thumb" is mistakenly attributed to English common law (the traditional source of American law) and the famous English legal commentator, Sir William Blackstone. Blackstone, however, never referred to a "rule of thumb" although he did refer to an ancient law that permitted domestic chastisement.

The husband ... by the old law, might give his wife moderate correction. For, as he is to answer for her misbehavior, the law thought it reasonable to entrust him with this power of chastisement, in the same moderation that a man is allowed to correct his apprentices or children.... But this power of correction was confined within reasonable bounds and the husband was prohibited from using any violence to his wife.

Blackstone admitted that the prohibitions against violence were not well enforced, especially among the lower classes. Not until 1829 was the husband's right to chastise his wife taken out of England's statutes. In practice, however, wife abuse has remained a reality to the present day.

Where did the myth of "rule of thumb" come from? Most likely, it derives from statements by two Southern judges, one from North Carolina and one from Mississippi. Both referred to an "ancient law" that reportedly permitted a man to beat his wife with a stick no wider than his thumb, although neither judge used the phrase "rule of thumb." A 1974 article (later republished in a 1975 anthology on domestic violence) reported these judges' decisions, giving the concept of a stick no wider than a thumb a wide audience, many of whom accepted the story as true.

THE AMERICAN TRADITION

In colonial America, the English common law tradition allowing physical "chastisement" prevailed, with the exception of the early Puritans, who forbade wife beating. The Massachusetts Bay Colony passed an edict stating, "No man shall strike his wife nor any woman her husband on penalty of such fine not exceeding ten pounds for one offense, or such corporal punishment as the County shall determine."

The first major American case to affirm "reasonable chastisement" was *Calvin Bradley v. The State* [of Mississippi] (156 Mississippi 1824). Bradley was convicted in a lower court of assault and battery against his wife. The court ruled that Bradley had gone to excessive lengths to chastise his wife. The court noted, "If the defendant now before us could shew from the record, in this case he confined himself within reasonable bounds, when he thought proper to chastise his wife, we would deliberate long before an affirmance of the judgment." Consequently, criticizing Bradley for having brought shame on his family, the court ruled,

Family broils and dissensions cannot be investigated before the tribunals of the country, without casting a shade over the character of those who are unfortunately engaged in the controversy. To screen from public reproach those who may be thus unhappily situated, let the husband be permitted to exercise the right of moderate chastisement in cases of great emergency and use salutary restraints in every case of misbehavior, without being subjected to vexatious prosecutions, resulting in mutual discredit and shame of all parties concerned.

Forty years later, in 1864, the North Carolina High Court ruled similarly in the *State v. Jesse Black* (1 Winston 266), a case in which a man abused his wife after she called him names. The court found that

A husband is responsible for the acts of his wife and he is required to govern his household, and for that purpose the law permits him to use towards his wife such a degree of force as is necessary to control an unruly temper and make her behave herself; and unless some permanent injury be inflicted, or there be an excess of violence, or such a degree of cruelty as shows that it is inflicted to gratify his own bad passions, the law will not invade the domestic forum, or go behind the curtain. It prefers to leave the parties to themselves, as the best mode of inducing them to make the matter up and live together as man and wife should.

Ten years later, in 1874, the North Carolina Court in *State v. Richard Oliver* (70 NC 60) once again expressed concern about excessive abuse, but still found that

From motives of public policy and in order to preserve the sanctity of the domestic circle, the Courts will not listen to trivial complaints.... If no permanent injury has been inflicted, nor malice, cruelty, nor dangerous violence shown by the husband, it is better to draw the curtain, shut out the public gaze, and leave the parties to forget and forgive.

A CHANGE IN DIRECTION

In 1871, an Alabama court reached a landmark decision denying the husband's right to physically abuse his wife even "moderately" or with "restraint." In *Fulgham v. The State* (46 Ala. 143-148), the court found "a married woman is as much under the protection of the law as any other member of the community. Her sex does not degrade her below the rank of the highest in the commonwealth." The court ruled,

A rod which may be drawn through the wedding ring is not now deemed necessary to teach the wife her duty and subjection to the husband. The husband is therefore not justified or allowed by law to use such a weapon, or any other, for her moderate correction. The wife is not to be considered as the husband's slave. And the privilege, ancient though it be, to beat her with a stick, to pull her hair, choke her, spit in her face or kick her about the floor, or to inflict upon her like indignities, is not now acknowledged by our law.

Finally, the justices concluded that "the rule of love has superseded the rule of force." A decade later, in 1882, Maryland enacted a law giving wife-beaters forty lashes with a whip or a year in jail (repealed in 1953).

CIVIL LIABILITY

While a husband could no longer legally beat his wife, the wife still had no civil recourse against her husband. In *Self v. Self* (376 P. 2nd 65, 1962), the Supreme Court of California agreed with earlier rulings that the right to sue "would destroy the peace and harmony of the house." The court, however, observed that this outdated assumption was based "on the bald theory that after a husband has beaten his wife there is a state of peace and harmony left to be disturbed." Therefore, "one spouse may maintain an action against the other" for physical abuse.

Although husbands can no longer legally beat their wives, and although wives can legally sue their husbands for damages, wife beating has not disappeared. It has remained a reality for far too many women who, despite the legal changes, feel trapped, with nowhere to go for help. Once "hidden behind curtains," the problem of wife abuse came into the open in the 1970s, as women became increasingly conscious of their rights. With expanded awareness and support, the increased alternatives for battered women offer them greater opportunities than they have ever had.

OTHER CULTURES

A wife married is like a pony bought; I'll ride her and whip her as I like. — Chinese proverb

"Wife beating is an accepted custom; we are wasting our time debating the issue." — parliamentary debate in Papua, New Guinea, 1987

Abuse against women is practiced all over the world in many forms and throughout all stages of life. Women everywhere risk victimization from acts such as forced abortion, genital mutilation, acid-throwing, wife beating, and elder abuse. (See Table 1.1.)

Bride Burning

Bride burning as a result of dowry disputes is a serious problem in India, Pakistan, and Bangladesh. A dowry is a form of payment, which includes money, property, and belongings, made by the wife and her family to the husband and his family. High inflation in India since 1960 has increased the desire for a dowry. The inability to meet dowry demands is often the cause of domestic violence in the first years of marriage. An estimated 5,000 women are killed annually over dowry dis-

---

TABLE 1.1

Gender violence throughout the life cycle

Phase	Type of violence present
Prebirth	Sex-selective abortion (China, India, Republic of Korea); battering during pregnancy (emotional and physical effects on the woman; effects on birth outcome); coerced pregnancy (for example, mass rape in war).
Infancy	Female infanticide; emotional and physical abuse; differential access to food and medical care for girl infants.
Girlhood	Child marriage; genital mutilation; sexual abuse by family members and strangers; differential access to food and medical care; child prostitution.
Adolescence	Dating and courtship violence (for example, acid throwing in Bangladesh, date rape in the United States); economically coerced sex (African secondary school girls having to take up with "sugar daddies" to afford school fees); sexual abuse in the workplace; rape; sexual harassment; forced prostitution; trafficking in women.
Reproductive age	Abuse of women by intimate male partners; marital rape; dowry abuse and murders; partner homicide; psychological abuse; sexual abuse in the workplace; sexual harassment; rape; abuse of women with disabilities.
Elderly	Abuse of widows; elder abuse (in the United States, the only country where data are now available, elder abuse affects mostly women).

Source: Lori Heise et al., *Violence Against Women: The Hidden Health Burden*, The International Bank for Reconstruction and Development/THE WORLD BANK, Washington, DC, 1994

putes. Many are victims of bride burning, a preplanned homicide inflicted by the husband and his family, often by the wife's mother-in-law.

The phenomenon of torching brides who are unable to meet exorbitant dowry demands is alarming. Women's organizations have estimated that one woman is burned every 12 hours in New Delhi alone. In the urban centers of Maharashtra state and greater Bombay, 19 percent of deaths to women 15 to 44 years old are due to "accidental burns" and for the younger age group of women 15 to 24, the rate is 1 in 4. In an eight-month period, the special New Delhi court assigned to deal with bride-burning tried only six defendants, all of whom were acquitted. India has had an anti-dowry law since 1961, but it is not enforced. Men merely need to claim that their wives died in a cooking accident or committed suicide to be excused of suspicion.

A Man's Duty

In Iran and much of the Middle East, wife beating is an accepted form of discipline. The Koran, the basis of Islamic law, states (in the Rashad Khalifa translation):

The men are placed in charge of the women, since God has endowed them with the necessary qualities and made them breadearners. The righteous women will accept this arrangement obediently, and will honor their husbands in their absence, in accordance with God's commands. As for the women who show rebellion, you shall first enlighten them, then desert them in bed, and you may beat them as a last resort. Once they obey you, you have no excuse to transgress against them. God is high and most powerful.

This passage of the Koran has allowed an Islamic husband to punish his wife physically whenever he determines that she has misbehaved.

A 1996 study by Egypt's National Population Council found that 86 percent of the 14,779 married women polled believed that men are justified in beating their wives for at least one of the following reasons: refusing sex, talking back to their husbands, talking to other men, neglecting their children, wasting money, or burning food. Agreeing with a man's right to beat his wife varied according to the respondents' age, education, employment, and place of residence. The study also found that 1 out of every 3 married women had been beaten at least once by her spouse. Thirty-two percent of pregnant women received a beating from their husbands; 44 percent of those say they were beaten as often or more often during pregnancy than before.

Virginity and sexual fidelity are also required of Islamic women. In Islamic countries, it is traditionally the role of the male relative to enforce chastity and chaste sexual conduct. The perpetrators of "honor killings," in which a man murders a female relative for her perceived lack of chastity, are generally given lighter sentences than those convicted in other types of murder cases.

Any Iraqi man who kills his own mother, sister, daughter, aunt, niece, or female cousin for adultery may receive immunity from prosecution under a 1990 law. A woman in Pakistan can be imprisoned for adultery if the man she accuses of rape is acquitted. Under the Hudood ordinances, enacted in 1979 to provide harsh punishments for violations of Islamic law, a female or non-Muslim witness is not accepted; consequently, if a man rapes a woman in the presence of several women, he cannot be convicted because female witnesses are not accepted. Punishments under the Hudood ordinances include death by stoning for unlawful sexual relations.

A wave of conservatism has been sweeping the Islamic world, forcing more and more women to wear headscarves, to undergo female circumcision (see below), and to avoid men in school and the workplace. The fundamentalist Taliban regime in Afghanistan bans women from any work outside the home and prevents girls from attending school. Women and girls may not appear outside the home unless accompanied by a male family member and

6

wearing a "burqa," a head-to-toe covering. A Cairo lawyer explained, "A man docsn't excite desire in a woman the way a woman does in a man. It's for their honor and their protection that they should be covered and kept in the house. Anything precious is always protected."

Rape

In many parts of the world, women who are raped have nowhere to turn for help. In Colombia, fewer than 0.5 percent of investigated rape cases in 1995 went to trial. Most cases, 95 percent according to Columbia's Institute for Legal Medicine, are never reported because the women know that nothing will be done if they complain. In poor families where parents and children sleep in the same bed, a woman has no place to go to remove her children from her partner's unwanted attention. (See Chapter V for a complete discussion of rape.)

The use of rape as a weapon of war has become evident in many parts of the world, such as the former Yugoslavia and Rwanda. During the Bosnian civil war, Serbs, knowing how important sexual purity is to the Muslims, allegedly raped more than 20,000 Muslim women, forcing many of them to bear Serbian children against their will. In Rwanda, thousands of ethnic Tutsi women were raped by the majority Hutu military during their bloody civil war. By one estimate, about 35 percent of the women became pregnant as a result. Abortion is illegal in Rwanda, leading many women to seek illegal abortions, to abandon babies, and even to commit infanticide. For those who have kept their babies, survival is precarious. Most of these women watched their husbands and families being murdered at the time they were raped. Now their Tutsi neighbors shun these mixed babies and blame their mothers for their existence.

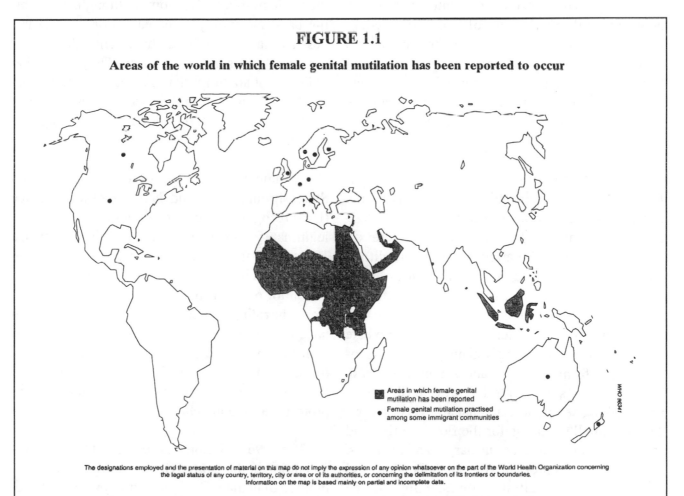

FIGURE 1.1

Areas of the world in which female genital mutilation has been reported to occur

■ Areas in which female genital mutilation has been reported
• Female genital mutilation practised among some immigrant communities

The designations employed and the presentation of material on this map do not imply the expression of any opinion whatsoever on the part of the World Health Organization concerning the legal status of any country, territory, city or area or of its authorities, or concerning the delimitation of its frontiers or boundaries. Information on the map is based mainly on partial and incomplete data.

Source: *Female Genital Mutilation: A Joint WHO/UNICEF/UNFPA Statement*, World Health Organization, Geneva, Switzerland, 1997

The United Nations established War Crimes Tribunals for Rwanda and the former Yugoslavia, though neither has had much success. In 1997, the Rwanda Tribunal filed its first indictment for rape and sexual abuse. At the present time, plans are being made within the international community to establish a permanent International Criminal Court for the prosecution of individuals who are accused of crimes against humanity, including sexual violence against women, but are not brought to justice in their own countries.

Female Circumcision

Female circumcision, also known as female genital mutilation (FGM), is practiced in many parts of Africa and in some parts of Asia and among immigrant communities in Europe, Australia, Canada, and the United States (Figure 1.1). Each year an estimated two million girls undergo genital cutting, with the total mutilated numbering about 150 million. Surveys of five African countries have provided reliable data showing that 93 percent of women in Mali and 89 percent of Sudanese women have been cut. Slightly less than half the women of the Central African Republic and the Ivory Coast and 12 percent of Togo's women have been circumcised.

Young girls are forced to submit to the mutilating surgery of their labia, vagina, and clitoris. Different societies practice different types of "circumcision," ranging from removing the foreskin of the clitoris to infibulation, in which the clitoris and labia are removed and the two sides of the vulva are sewn together, usually with catgut. These procedures are performed without anesthetic, often with primitive, unsterilized tools. Immediate risks include hemorrhage, tetanus, blood poisoning, shock from the pain, and sometimes death. Those who do survive are left with terrible scarring, making sex joyless and usually very painful. The too-small openings for the flow of urine and menstrual blood can cause urinary tract infections, kidney stones, reproductive tract infections, and even sterility, the ultimate disaster for women whose value is based on their ability to reproduce.

When they do give birth, infibulated women must be surgically reopened, only to be resewn after giving birth. In Somalia, a study of 33 infibulated women found that their final stage of labor was five times longer than normal, five of the babies died, and 21 babies suffered oxygen deprivation from the prolonged, obstructed labor (Lori Heise et al., *Violence Against Women: The Hidden Health Burden*, World Bank Discussion Papers no. 255, 1994).

Female circumcision stems from the male desire to control women's sexuality. Some Muslims mistakenly believe the Koran demands it; others see women's sexual organs as unclean and believe they are ritually purifying the woman. Men in these cultures will not marry uncircumcised women, believing them to be unclean, promiscuous, and sexually untrustworthy. Many women also do not object, seeing it as a tradition and a natural part of their role in life. Some women, though, are fighting back and trying to increase women's awareness so that they will be strong enough to resist the social pressure to conform. They insist that FGM is not an "important African tradition" that must be maintained in the face of Western influences but, rather, that it is violence directed against women.

In June 1996, for the first time, the United States Immigration and Naturalization Service (INS) recognized the fear of genital mutilation as legitimate grounds for asylum. Fauziya Kasinga, a 19-year-old from Togo who feared she would be circumcised if she returned home, was detained in prison for one year before the INS made its decision. The ruling quoted an INS report "that women have little legal recourse and may face threats to their freedom, threats or acts of physical violence, or social ostracization [sic] for refusing to undergo this harmful traditional practice, or attempting to protect their female children."

The 1996 U.S. Congress outlawed female genital cutting in the United States in the Federal Prohibition of Female Genital Mutilation Act of 1996, a part of the Omnibus Appropriations Act of 1997

(PL 104-208). Anyone found guilty of performing the surgery would face up to five years in jail. In addition, U.S. representatives to the World Bank and other international financial institutions are required to oppose loans to the 28 African countries where the practice exists if the country has not carried out educational programs to prevent it.

In Egypt, a 1995 government-supported study indicated that over 97 percent of the 14,770 never-married women interviewed had undergone circumcision. In 1997, in spite of a court decision overturning the health minister's ban on FGM on the grounds that it exceeded his authority, the Egyptian Supreme Court upheld the ban. Now, women's rights groups are working to change the traditions of Muslims in the villages, where midwives and barbers perform circumcision.

The Missing Women

In China, South Korea, India, Nepal, and other Asian countries, sons are favored over daughters for their economic value and for the dignity of carrying on a family name. Studies show that girls in these societies often receive inferior medical care and education and less food than their brothers do.

Human rights groups estimate that at least 10,000 cases of female infanticides occur yearly in India, primarily in poor rural areas. In India and China, many women use sonograms (an image of the fetus produced through ultrasound) and amniocentesis (a test done in early pregnancy to screen for birth defects, which also reveals the sex of the child) to learn if they are carrying a girl. If they are, the fetus is frequently aborted. One Chinese newspaper article quoted a doctor as saying that as many as 97.5 percent of abortions in his hospital were of female fetuses.

Based on a comparison of male-female sex ratios, Princeton demographer Ansley Coale estimated that at least 60 million women are missing, mainly from Asia and North Africa. These are females who have been aborted, given inferior care in childhood, underfed, and subjected to various forms of gender violence that have resulted in death. In India, the male-female ratio has dropped to 92.7 females per 100 males, a large demographic difference. The World Health Organization estimated China's ratio of males to females to be 117 to 100, another huge difference. In the United States, the male-female ratio is 96 males to 100 females.

CHAPTER II

SPOUSAL ABUSE — WHO, WHAT, AND WHEN?

Wife abuse is not new, but the public has only focused on the issue over the past 25 years, largely a result of the women's movement. While child abuse was "discovered" in the 1960s, wife abuse was "revealed" in the 1970s. Most important studies on the subject are dated 1975 or later. Congressional hearings, an indicator of public attitudes, began in 1978. The United States Commission on Civil Rights held a well-attended conference titled "Battered Women — Issues of Public Policy" in January 1978.

Two decades later, however, the federal government has withdrawn from funding research into abuse, leaving experts to rely primarily on early studies and small surveys. In addition, spousal abuse has become a heavily politicized issue debated in the media, using poorly understood statistics or highly publicized cases like the O. J. Simpson murder trial.

DEFINITIONS OF ABUSE

Early definitions of abuse focused on physical harm. The report of the Colorado Committee of the Advisory Committee to the United States Commission on Civil Rights, *The Silent Victims: Denver's Battered Women* (Washington, DC, 1977), described a "battered wife" as "a woman who has received deliberate, severe, and repeated physical injury from her husband, the minimal injury being severe bruising." The study further observed, "A battered woman may or may not be a wife in the legal sense," i.e., the couple may not be married, and therefore, "battered woman is the more accurate term to employ than battered wife." A counselor for a Denver shelter defined a battered woman as "one who is physically abused by a husband or a boyfriend and who can expect continuance of this. The violence will increase in severity and frequency."

Drs. Murray Straus, Richard Gelles, and their colleagues, in the groundbreaking work based on their 1975 and 1985 *National Family Violence Surveys* (see below), defined "spousal violence" by specific acts. These acts, labeled the Conflict Tactics Scale (CTS), a measure that is commonly used in surveys of domestic violence, are:

1. Threw something at one's partner.

2. Pushed, grabbed, or shoved.

3. Slapped.

4. Kicked, bit, or hit with a fist.

5. Hit or tried to hit with something.

6. Beat up one's partner.

7. Threatened with a knife or a gun.

8. Used a knife or fired a gun.

More recently, the definition of abuse has shifted to emphasize issues of intent and power. The National Coalition Against Domestic Violence defines battering as

a pattern of behavior with the effect of establishing power and control over another person through fear and intimidation. Battering happens when batterers believe they are entitled to control their partners.

The coalition adds that battering includes "emotional abuse, economic abuse, sexual abuse, using chil-

FIGURE 2.1

DEFINITIONS OF VIOLENCE AGAINST WOMEN

Behavior by the man, adopted to control his victim, which results in physical, sexual and/or psychological damage, forced isolation, or economic deprivation or behavior which leaves a woman living in fear. (Australia 1991)

Any act involving use of force or coercion with an intent of perpetuating/promoting hierarchical gender relations. (Asia Pacific Forum on Women, Law and Development 1990)

Any act of gender-based violence that results in, or is likely to result in, physical, sexual or psychological harm or suffering to women, including threats of such acts, coercion or arbitrary deprivations of liberty, whether occurring in public or private life. Violence against women shall be understood to encompass but not be limited to:

Physical, sexual and psychological violence occurring in the family and in the community, including battering, sexual abuse of female children, dowry-related violence, marital rape, female genital mutilation and other traditional practices harmful to women, non-spousal violence, violence related to exploitation, sexual harassment and intimidation at work, in educational institutions and elsewhere, trafficking in women, forced prostitution, and violence perpetrated or condoned by the State. (UN Declaration against Violence against Women)

Any act, omission or conduct by means of which physical sexual or mental suffering is inflicted, directly or indirectly, through deceit, seduction, threat, coercion or any other means, on any woman with the purpose or effect of intimidating, punishing or humiliating her or of maintaining her in sex-stereotyped roles or of denying her human dignity, sexual self- determination, physical, mental and moral integrity or of undermining the security of her person, her self-respect or her personality, or of diminishing her physical or mental capacities. (Draft Pan American Treaty against Violence against Women)

Any act or omission which prejudices the life, the physical or psychological integrity or the liberty of a person or which seriously harms the development of his or her personality. (Council of Europe 1986)

Source: Lori L. Heise et al., *Violence Against Women: The Hidden Health Burden*, World Bank Discussion Papers, Washington, DC, 1994

battering usually escalates, and what might start with a slap or name-calling can escalate into life-threatening danger.

The World Bank's international look at violence (Lori L. Heise et al., *Violence Against Women: The Hidden Health Burden*, World Bank Discussion Papers, no. 255, Washington, DC, 1994) defines abuse in terms intended to be broad enough to include the wide variety of abuse that occurs the world over (see Chapter I). Lori Heise points out, "What distinguishes violence against women is force or coercion ... that is socially tolerated in part *because the victims are female*." For Heise, the definition must rest on the idea of physical and psychological harm rather than on the intent of the perpetrator.

For example, genital mutilation (see Chapter I) is an example of abuse that is not intended to harm (the intention is to guarantee marriage for the girl), and yet the effect is harm and suffering. Heise also cautions against the overbroad definitions that some organizations have proposed, which encompass gender inequalities such as unequal pay or lack of access to birth control. She labels this kind of behavior, discrimination. Heise defines abuse as

Any act of verbal or physical force, coercion, or life-threatening deprivation, directed at an individual woman or girl, that causes physical or psychological harm, humiliation or arbitrary deprivation of liberty and that perpetuates female subordination.

Figure 2.1 shows definitions of violence from different organizations around the world.

HOW MUCH ABUSE IS THERE?

Almost four million American women were physically abused by their husbands or boyfriends in the last year alone. — The Commonwealth Fund Survey of Women's Health, 1993

The 1985 estimate of 1.6 million beaten wives is hardly an indicator of domestic

dren, threats, using male privilege, intimidation, isolation, and a variety of other behaviors used to maintain fear, intimidation and power." Finally, it warns that

tranquillity. — The 1985 National Family Violence Survey

More than 50 percent of all women will experience some form of violence from their spouses during marriage. More than one-third [approximately 18 million women] are battered repeatedly every year. — National Coalition Against Domestic Violence fund-raising brochure, no date

Nearly 1 in 3 adult women experience at least one physical assault by a partner during adulthood. — American Psychological Association, Presidential Task Force on Violence and the Family, 1996

More than 960,000 incidents of violence against a current or former spouse, boyfriend, or girlfriend occur each year, and about 85 percent of the victims are women. — National Crime Victimization Survey, 1992-96

Estimates of abuse vary depending on the source, the type and purpose of survey, the definition of abuse used, and the political context. A closer look at some of these surveys follows.

The Commonwealth Fund Survey

In 1993, the Commonwealth Fund (a private foundation) hired Louis Harris and Associates to survey American women's health (*The Commonwealth Fund Survey of Women's Health*, New York, 1993). The survey interviewed more than 2,500 women on a broad range of subjects, including questions on the Conflict Tactics Scale, to determine levels of abuse. One-third of respondents (34 to 35 percent) reported that their partners either insulted or swore at them or stomped away in an argument. (See Table 2.1.) In total, the Commonwealth Fund found that 37 percent (or 20.7 million women) suffered what it defined as verbal or emotional abuse.

One out of 9 women (11 percent) reported that her partner threw, smashed, hit, or kicked something. When the poll asked how often women were the object of the violence, 5 percent reported their partners had pushed, grabbed, shoved, or slapped them; 3 percent of women had something thrown at them, and 2 percent said they had been hit with a fist or an object,

---

TABLE 2.1

No matter how well a couple gets along, there are times when they disagree, get annoyed with the other person or just have spats or fights because they're in a bad mood or tired or for some other reason. They also use many different ways of trying to settle their differences. I'm going to read some things that you and your partner might do when you have an argument. I would like you to tell me whether, in the past 12 months, your spouse/partner ever (READ LIST)?

DO NOT ROTATE	Yes	No	Not sure
1. Insulted you or swore at you....................(34(	34 -1	66 -2	* -3
2. Stomped out of the room or house or yard........(35(	34 -1	66 -2	* -3
3. Threatened to hit you or throw something at you.(36(	5 -1	95 -2	* -3
4. Threw or smashed or hit or kicked something.....(37(	11 -1	89 -2	* -3
5. Threw something at you..........................(38(	3 -1	97 -2	* -3
6. Pushed, grabbed, shoved, or slapped you.........(39(	5 -1	95 -2	* -3
7. Kicked, bit or hit you with a fist or some other object................................(40(	2 -1	98 -2	* -3
8. Beat you up.....................................(41(	* -1	100 -2	* -3
9. Choked you......................................(42(	* -1	99 -2	* -3
10. Threatened you with a knife or gun..............(43(	* -1	100 -2	* -3
11. Used a knife or gun.............................(44(	* -1	100 -2	* -3

Source: *The Commonwealth Fund Survey of Women's Health*, New York, 1993

kicked, or bitten. Less than 1 percent of respondents said they had been beaten up,
choked, threatened with a knife or gun, or had
a knife or gun used against them. Adding all the
forms of physical violence together, 7 percent
(3.9 million) of women who live with a male
partner were physically abused within the year
before the survey.

National Crime Victimization Survey

The Bureau of Justice Statistics (BJS) con-
ducts an annual poll, the *National Crime Victimization Survey* (NCVS), to determine the
amount of crime suffered by adults in the United
States. While the focus of this survey is crime
and not all women consider spousal violence a
crime, the survey has been extensively rede-
signed to produce more accurate reporting of
incidents of rape and sexual assault and of any kind of
crimes committed by intimates or family members. The
BJS, in *Violence by Intimates: Analysis of Data on
Crimes by Current or Former Spouses, Boyfriends,
and Girlfriends* (Lawrence A. Greenfeld, et al., Washington, DC, 1998), gathered data on the violence committed against intimates from 1992 through 1996.

Although women were significantly less likely to
be victims of violent crime, they were 5 to 8 times

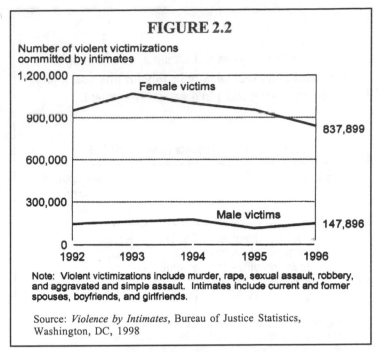

FIGURE 2.2

Number of violent victimizations
committed by intimates

Note: Violent victimizations include murder, rape, sexual assault, robbery,
and aggravated and simple assault. Intimates include current and former
spouses, boyfriends, and girlfriends.

Source: *Violence by Intimates*, Bureau of Justice Statistics,
Washington, DC, 1998

more likely than men to be victimized by intimates.
These estimates include murder, rape, robbery, and
assault; data on murder come from the FBI's *Supplementary Homicide Reports*. On average each year
from 1992 to 1996, women experienced nearly one
million violent victimizations by intimates compared to
about 150,000 incidents committed against men (Figure 2.2). One-fifth of the total violent crimes against
women were committed by an intimate, compared to
about 2 percent of men.

The NCVS found an average annual rate of assault by an intimate of 7.5 per 1,000 women, compared to 1.4 per 1,000 men. (See Figure 2.3.) About
half of the females who reported violence by an intimate (51 percent) were injured. Of those injured by
an intimate, 20 percent received treatment for physical injury. (See Table 2.2.) Table 2.3 indicates the types
of injuries suffered by female victims of intimate violence.

Black women experienced higher rates of nonlethal intimate violence (rape, sexual assault, robbery,
and aggravated and simple assault) than White women
or other minorities. The average rate each year from
1992 to 1996 was about 12 per 1,000 Black women,
compared to about 8 per 1,000 White women. White
and Black males experienced nonlethal intimate vio-

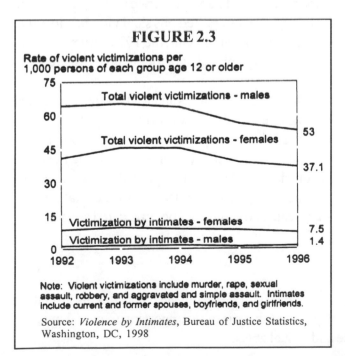

FIGURE 2.3

Rate of violent victimizations per
1,000 persons of each group age 12 or older

Note: Violent victimizations include murder, rape, sexual
assault, robbery, and aggravated and simple assault. Intimates
include current and former spouses, boyfriends, and girlfriends.

Source: *Violence by Intimates*, Bureau of Justice Statistics,
Washington, DC, 1998

13

TABLE 2.2
Among female victims of intimates, 1 in 10 sought treatment at a medical care facility for physical injury; among those injured 1 in 5 sought treatment.

Female victims of intimate violence, 1992-96

Physically injured 51%				No reported physical injury 49%
Not treated	Cared for at the scene or at home	Treated at doctor's office or clinic	Treated at an emergency room	Hospital-ized
32%	9%	3%	7%	<1%*

Note: Nonlethal violent victimizations include rape, sexual assault, robbery, and aggravated and simple assault. Intimates include current and former spouses, boyfriends, and girlfriends.
*Fewer than 10 sample cases in the source data from the NCVS.

TABLE 2.3
About half of the female victims of violence by an intimate were injured.

Female victims of intimate violence, 1992-96

Injured 51%			Not injured 49%
Rape or sexual assault 6%	Gun, knife or stab wound 0.5%	Other serious injury* 4%	Other injury* 41%

*Categories of injuries: Serious injuries include broken bones, internal injuries, being knocked unconscious, and any injuries requiring 2 or more days in a hospital. Other injuries include bruises, black eyes, cuts, swelling, chipped teeth, and unspecified injuries requiring less than 2 days' hospitalization.

Source of both tables: *Violence by Intimates*, Bureau of Justice Statistics, Washington, DC, 1998

lence at about the same rate, which was about one-fifth the rate for women. (See Figure 2.4.)

Women ages 16 to 24 had the highest rates of intimate violence, about 20 nonlethal violent victimizations per 1,000 women (Table 2.4). About 70 percent of female victims of intimate violence reported physical attacks. The rest reported attempts or threats of violence. (See Table 2.5.)

Women in low-income households suffered higher rates of nonlethal violence from an intimate. Generally, the rate decreased as household income levels increased. The rates for females ranged from 21.3 per 1,000 in households with incomes less than $7,500 to 2.7 per 1,000 in households with incomes of $75,000 or more. For men, the rates of nonlethal intimate violence ranged from 2.7 per 1,000 in households with incomes less than $7,500 to 0.5 per 1,000 when the household income was $75,000 or more. (See Table 2.6.)

The 1985 *National Family Violence Survey*

In 1985, Louis Harris and Associates conducted the 1985 *National Family Violence Re-Survey* (NFVS) for the Family Research Laboratory at the University of New Hampshire, Durham, NH. (The first *Family Violence Survey* was conducted in 1975.) The *Survey* is considered by many to be the most important study of family violence yet to be conducted. The 1985 *Survey* studied physical violence in 6,002 households and, along with the 1975 survey of 2,143 families, has provided data for years of research.*

Drs. Murray A. Straus and Richard J. Gelles found that the rate of wife abuse dropped only slightly over the decade between the surveys — the overall rate of husband to wife abuse (the husband hitting the wife) declined from 121 instances per 1,000 couples to 113 instances per 1,000 couples. This is not statistically significant and should not be considered as showing a

---

*Because interview time was limited, the researchers chose to concentrate on physical abuse. This limitation does not imply, however, that Drs. Straus and Gelles think physical abuse is more important or more damaging than other types of abuse, such as psychological abuse and sexual abuse.

decline in wife abuse. However, the rate of severe violence (hitting, kicking, using a weapon) dropped from 38 to 30 per 1,000 couples, a 21 percent drop. Figure 2.5 shows that most of this decline occurred in slapping and in kicking, biting, and hitting.

The NFVS also found nearly equal levels of violence committed by women against men. Although Straus and Gelles noted that men's greater strength made their abuse potentially much more serious, they condemned violence by either partner. (See below for more on abuse by women.)

Straus and Glenda Kaufman Kantor, in a paper presented to the World Congress of Sociology ("Change in Spouse Assault Rates from 1975 to 1992: A Comparison of Three National Surveys in the United States," Family Research Laboratory, University of New Hampshire, 1994), compared the rates of abuse from the two *National Family Violence Surveys* and a 1992 survey conducted by Kaufman

FIGURE 2.4

Characteristics of Victims of Violence by Intimates

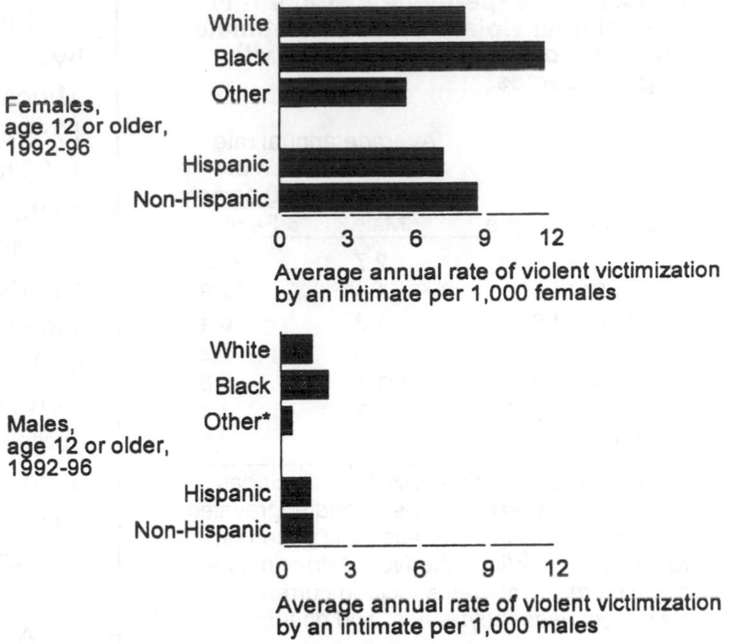

Note: Nonlethal violent victimizations include rape, sexual assault, robbery, and aggravated and simple assault. Intimates include current and former spouses, boyfriends, and girlfriends.
*Fewer than 10 sample cases.
"Other" denotes Asians, Native Hawaiians or other Pacific Islanders, Alaska Native, and American Indians. Hispanic can be of any race

Source: *Violence by Intimates*, Bureau of Justice Statistics, Washington, DC, 1998

TABLE 2.4

The highest rates of intimate violence affect women ages 16 to 24

Age of female victim	Average annual rate of nonlethal violent victimization by an intimate per 1,000 females
12-15	2.6
16-19	20.1
20-24	20.7
25-34	16.5
35-49	7.2
50-64	1.3
65 or older	.2

Note: Nonlethal intimate violence includes rape, sexual assault, robbery, and aggravated and simple assault. Because it is based on interviews with victims, the NCVS does not include murder. Intimates include current and former spouses, boyfriends, and girlfriends.

Source: BJS, National Crime Victimization Survey (NCVS), 1992-96.

Source of both tables: *Violence by Intimates*, Bureau of Justice Statistics, Washington, DC, 1998

TABLE 2.5

About 7 in 10 female victims of intimate violence reported that they were physically attacked.

For the remainder, the attack was attempted or threatened — nearly a third of these victims saying that the offender threatened to kill them.

Victim hit, knocked down, or attacked	70%
Attempted or threatened attack*	29

Offender —	
Threatened to kill	31%
Threatened to rape	1
Threatened other attack	53
Threatened with weapon	17
Threw object at victim	3
Followed/surrounded victim	5
Tried to hit, slap, or knock down victim	13

*Victims may report more than one type of threat.

TABLE 2.6

Women in low-income households experience a higher rate of nonlethal violence from an intimate than do women in households with larger incomes

Household income	Average annual rate of nonlethal intimate violence per 1,000 persons	
	Male	Female
Less than $7,500	2.7	21.3
$7,500-$14,999	1.4	12.3
$15,000-$24,999	1.8	10.4
$25,000-$34,999	1.8	7.2
$35,000-$49,999	1.1	5.8
$50,000-$74,999	1.5	4.4
$75,000 or more	0.5	2.7

Note: Nonlethal intimate violence includes rape, sexual assault, robbery, and aggravated and simple assault. Because it is based on interviews with victims, the NCVS does not include murder. Intimates include current and former spouses, boyfriends, and girlfriends.

Source: *Violence by Intimates*, Bureau of Justice Statistics, Washington, DC, 1998

Kantor. Pushing, grabbing, shoving, slapping, and throwing something were classified as minor assaults because they were less likely than severe abuse to cause an injury that would require medical attention. A severe assault was behavior that would be likely to cause serious injury — kicking, hitting with an object, biting, punching, beating up, and threatening with or using a knife or gun.

Figure 2.6 combines the assault data as reported by both spouses. Minor assaults by husbands decreased between the 1975 and 1985 surveys while it remained steady for wives. From 1985 to 1992, minor assaults increased for both husbands and wives. Severe assaults by wives remained fairly steady over the 18-year period, while the rate of severe assaults by husbands against their wives decreased steadily from 38 per 1,000 women in 1975 to 19 per 1,000 in 1992, a 50 percent decrease.

Straus and Kaufman Kantor hypothesized that reports of severe abuse by men may have declined so steeply because men have become aware that battering is a crime, and they are reluctant to admit battering. On the other hand, women have been encour-

aged not to tolerate abuse and to report it, which would tend to increase the rate.

Figure 2.7 shows the rates of abuse perpetrated by men as reported by men and women separately. Minor assaults by husbands decreased from 1975 to 1985 according to both husbands and wives. From 1985 to 1992, the rates based on husbands' reports continued to decrease; on the other hand, the rate as reported by wives increased. For severe abuse, men reported a decrease in rates of abuse between 1975 and 1985, while women reported no change. In contrast, between 1985 and 1992, men reported a slight increase, but women registered a sharp drop of 43 percent. This would tend to contradict the authors' hypothesis that the changes in rates are the result of men's reluctance to admit to abuse and women's greater freedom to report abuse.

As reported by wives, minor abuse by wives against their husbands decreased from 1975 to 1985, but the rate increased substantially from 1985 to 1992. According to husbands, the rate of minor assault increased over both time periods. Severe assault by wives as reported by wives stayed essentially the same in the first decade and then increased between 1985 and 1992. Husbands reported a steady decrease of severe abuse by their wives over the entire period. (See Figure 2.8.)

Conclusions

Straus and Kaufman Kantor noted that the large decrease in severe assaults by husbands was supported by the FBI's finding of an 18 percent decrease in the rate of homicides of wives by husbands over this same time period. The data suggest a genuine drop in severe abuse, rather than inconsistencies in reporting. Straus and Kaufman Kantor speculate that steps taken in the past 18 years to punish assaultive husbands and the greater availability of shelters and restraining orders for women have played a role in the decrease of severe abuse. The lack of change in minor assaults by husbands, they feel, may reflect the emphasis that has understandably been given severe assault, leaving men to assume that an occasional slap or shove does not constitute abusive behavior.

To explain the increase in minor assaults by women, Straus and Kaufman Kantor suggested there has been no effort to condemn assault by wives, and with increased equality between the sexes, more women may feel entitled to hit as often as their men. The decrease in severe abuse by wives as reported by husbands, which is not matched by the wives' responses, could perhaps reflect the men's reluctance to admit they are being abused.

WHO HITS FIRST?

The NFVS data on the violence of women set off a firestorm of protest from some feminist scholars. They claimed that the surveys ignored the context of the violence and that women struck their husbands in self-defense. Philip W. Cook, in *Abused Men: The Hidden Side of Domestic Violence* (Praeger Publishers, Westport, Connecticut, 1997), investigated the existing research on the issue of male spousal abuse. Using the data from the 1985 NFVS and especially "Physical Assaults by Wives: A Major Social Problem" (*Current Controversies on Family Violence*, Sage Publications, Newbury Park, California, 1993), Cook maintains that abuse is mutual in most cases. About 50 percent of those surveyed for the NFVS reported both spouses to be violent. The remaining cases were nearly equally split, with the male reported as violent in 27 percent of the cases and the female in 24 percent of the cases. (See Figure 2.9.) Focusing only on severe violence, 35 percent of those surveyed said both were violent, 35.2 percent reported only the husband was violent, and 29.6 percent said only the wife was (Figure 2.10).

In "Physical Assaults by Wives," Straus commented that

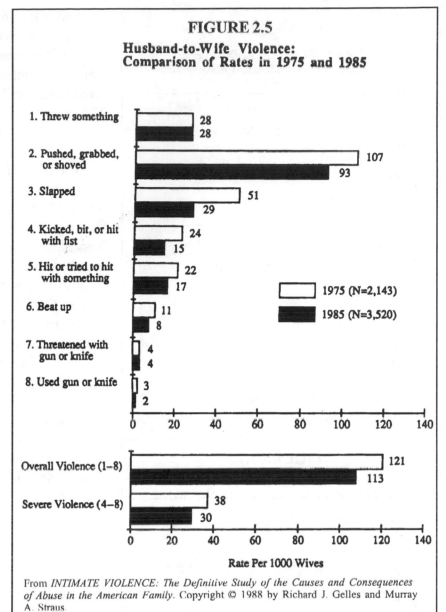

FIGURE 2.5

**Husband-to-Wife Violence:
Comparison of Rates in 1975 and 1985**

From *INTIMATE VIOLENCE: The Definitive Study of the Causes and Consequences of Abuse in the American Family.* Copyright © 1988 by Richard J. Gelles and Murray A. Straus.

Regardless of whether the analysis is based on all assaults or is focused on dangerous assaults, about as many women as men attacked spouses who had not hit them, during the one-year referent period. This is inconsistent with the self-defense explanation for the high rate of domestic assault by women.

However, it is possible that, among the couples where both assaulted, all the women were acting in self-defense. Even if that unlikely assumption were correct, it would still be true that 25-30 percent of violent marriages are violent solely because of attacks by the wife.

17

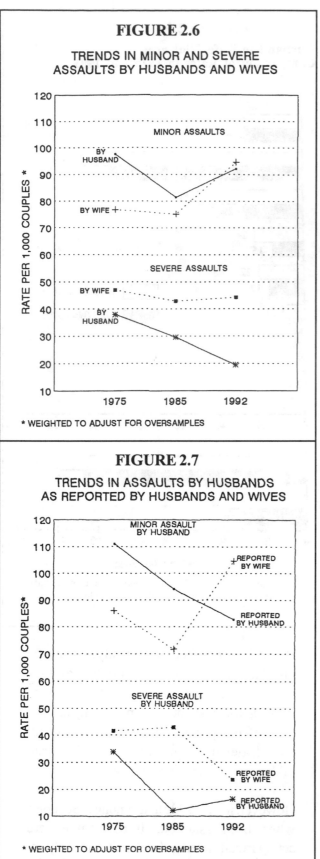

FIGURE 2.6

TRENDS IN MINOR AND SEVERE
ASSAULTS BY HUSBANDS AND WIVES

MINOR ASSAULTS

BY HUSBAND

BY WIFE

SEVERE ASSAULTS

BY WIFE

BY HUSBAND

RATE PER 1,000 COUPLES *

1975   1985   1992

* WEIGHTED TO ADJUST FOR OVERSAMPLES

FIGURE 2.7

TRENDS IN ASSAULTS BY HUSBANDS
AS REPORTED BY HUSBANDS AND WIVES

MINOR ASSAULT
BY HUSBAND

REPORTED
BY WIFE

REPORTED
BY HUSBAND

SEVERE ASSAULT
BY HUSBAND

REPORTED
BY WIFE

REPORTED
BY HUSBAND

RATE PER 1,000 COUPLES*

1975   1985   1992

* WEIGHTED TO ADJUST FOR OVERSAMPLES

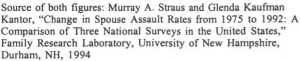

Source of both figures: Murray A. Straus and Glenda Kaufman Kantor, "Change in Spouse Assault Rates from 1975 to 1992: A Comparison of Three National Surveys in the United States," Family Research Laboratory, University of New Hampshire, Durham, NH, 1994

Following up on a large sample of wives from the mutually violent couples, the women reported that they hit first 53 percent of the time, while their partners hit first 42 percent of the time. Three percent could not remember. (See Figure 2.11.)

Abuse by Women

The Family Research Laboratory has been widely criticized for presenting data that shows that women are equally as violent as men (with the understanding that men, because of their strength and size, are far more likely to cause injury). Family violence researchers (those who study violence in all members of the family, not just men) attribute many factors to the causes of violence (see Chapter III), including sexism in patriarchal societies. Some feminist researchers, however, interpret factors such as violence in society and stressful living conditions as factors that are controlled by the overriding problem of male dominance.

Demie Kurz and Kersti Yllö debated the feminist viewpoint with Murray Straus and Richard Gelles in *Current Controversies on Family Violence*. Kurz's article, "Physical Assaults by Husbands: A Major Social Problem," defined the feminist viewpoint:

For feminists, gender is one of the fundamental organizing principles of society. It is a social relation that enters into and partially constitutes all other social relations and activities, and pervades the entire social context in which a person lives. Thus feminists criticize family violence researchers for equating "spouse abuse," elder abuse, and child abuse, because from that perspective women constitute just one group among a number of kinds of victims. Feminists believe that wife abuse should be compared with related types of violence against women, such as rape, marital rape, sexual harassment, and incest, all of which are also products of male dominance.

For these feminists, violence is an issue of power, and in society and marriage, power is in the hands of men. They warn that a family violence approach can have several negative repercussions for women. First,

18

it reinforces the popular idea that women cause their victimization by provoking their partners. Second, the research leads to policy decisions that are harmful to women, such as reduced funding for women's shelters or testimony against battered women in court. Third, this perspective encourages counselors to focus on clients' individual and personal problems without identifying the inequality between men and women that, feminists contend, is the context for battering. Finally, if a "battered husband syndrome" exists, it will encourage the police who operate under mandatory arrest statutes to arrest women in "domestic disputes."

A Critique of the Conflict Tactics Scale

Kurz argues that Straus's Conflict Tactics Scale (CTS) is not valid because the "continuum of violence in the scales is so broad that it fails to discriminate among different kinds of violence." A bite from a woman, she argues, cannot be compared to a kick from a man. Furthermore, she claims, it focuses on individual acts of violence and "draws attention away from related patterns of control and abuse in relationships" including psychological, sexual, and verbal abuse (verbal abuse is, in fact, often included in the CTS).

Kersti Yllö questions whether violence can be measured as a conflict tactic. Rather, "it is better conceptualized as a tactic of coercive control to maintain the husband's power." Furthermore, for Yllö, the CTS excludes information on economic deprivation, sexual abuse, intimidation, isolation, stalking, and terrorizing, "all common elements of wife battering and all rarely perpetrated by women."

According to Yllö, when women are asked about their use of violence, most report it is in self-defense or that they were fighting back. Some feminist scholars contend that by asking the single question, "Who initiated the violence," researchers are excluding the context of the situation. Women's advocates claim the violence has often been preceded by name-calling and other psychological abuse. Women may view these behaviors as early warning signs of violence and hit first in hopes of preventing their partners from using violence. "Thus, even when women do initiate violence, it may very well be an act of self-defense." Re-

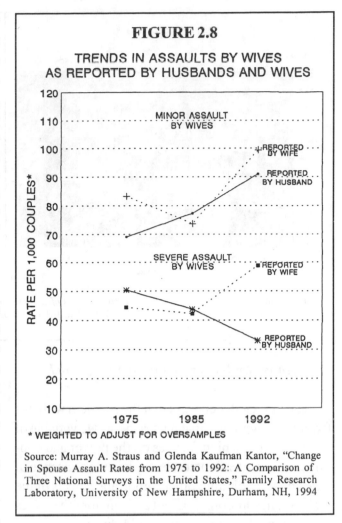

FIGURE 2.8

TRENDS IN ASSAULTS BY WIVES
AS REPORTED BY HUSBANDS AND WIVES

* WEIGHTED TO ADJUST FOR OVERSAMPLES

Source: Murray A. Straus and Glenda Kaufman Kantor, "Change in Spouse Assault Rates from 1975 to 1992: A Comparison of Three National Surveys in the United States," Family Research Laboratory, University of New Hampshire, Durham, NH, 1994

search has found that wives report their violence was in self-defense or for retaliatory reasons. Violent men, however, attribute their aggression to external causes or for coercive and controlling reasons.

Dobash et al., in "Separate and Intersecting Realities: A Comparison of Men's and Women's Accounts of Violence Against Women" (*Violence Against Women*, vol. 4, no. 4, August 1998), also criticizes the findings that result from the CTS. They dispute the assumption that CTS accounts of violence, whether from men or women or about their own violent behavior or that of their partner, are unbiased and reliable. Comparing accounts of male violence given by men with those given by women, the researchers found an overall pattern of obvious inconsistencies between the reports of men and women. (See Figure 2.12.) An even greater difference is seen in reports of the frequency of violent acts (Figure 2.13).

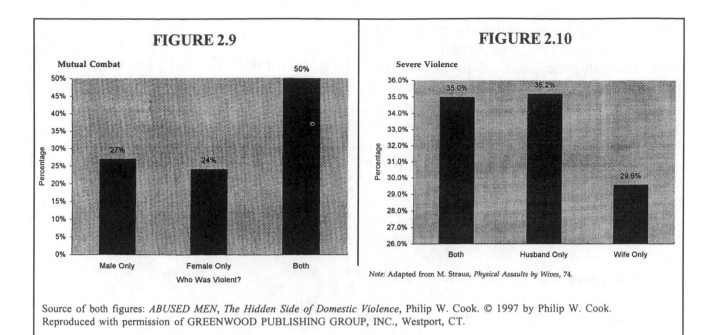

FIGURE 2.9

Mutual Combat

FIGURE 2.10

Severe Violence

Note: Adapted from M. Straus, *Physical Assaults by Wives*, 74.

Source of both figures: *ABUSED MEN*, *The Hidden Side of Domestic Violence*, Philip W. Cook. © 1997 by Philip W. Cook. Reproduced with permission of GREENWOOD PUBLISHING GROUP, INC., Westport, CT.

Abuse by Women Cannot Be Ignored

Richard Gelles charges that the problem with this feminist viewpoint is that it uses the single variable of the patriarchy, which focuses on the power and control of males over females, to explain the existence of wife abuse, excluding other important aspects of the problem. In addition, it cannot account for other types of abuse and therefore ignores child abuse, sibling abuse, elderly abuse, and violence by women.

In some cases, Straus charges, data on assaults by women have intentionally been suppressed. The *Survey of Spousal Violence Against Women in Kentucky* (Washington, DC, 1979), one of the first, issue-defining studies, did not publish the information that was gathered on the violence committed by women. But when other researchers obtained the computer tape, they reported that, among violent couples, 38 percent of the attacks were committed by women against men who, as reported by the women themselves, had not attacked them. The Commonwealth Fund survey, while it interviewed 1,000 men on many health issues, did not include men in the data on adult violence.

Straus and Gelles have always emphasized that the greater average size, strength, and greater aggressiveness of men means that the same act by a man (for example, a punch) is likely to be very different in the amount of pain or injury inflicted than when a woman strikes. In addition, some portion of the violence by women against their husbands is in retaliation or self-defense (how much depends on the point of view).

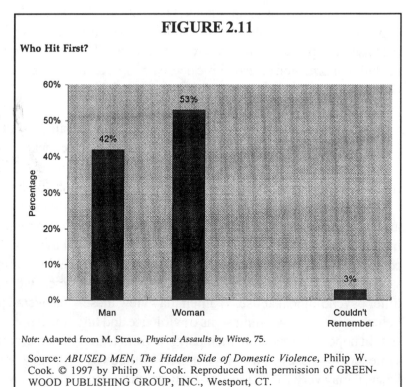

FIGURE 2.11

Who Hit First?

Note: Adapted from M. Straus, *Physical Assaults by Wives*, 75.

Source: *ABUSED MEN*, *The Hidden Side of Domestic Violence*, Philip W. Cook. © 1997 by Philip W. Cook. Reproduced with permission of GREENWOOD PUBLISHING GROUP, INC., Westport, CT.

Nevertheless, violence by women cannot be ignored, and according to Straus and Gelles, efforts to prevent it are needed for several reasons.

Perhaps the most fundamental reason is the intrinsic moral wrong of assaulting a spouse, as expressed in the fact that such assaults are criminal acts, even when no injury occurs. A second reason is the unintended validation of traditional cultural norms tolerating a certain level of violence between spouses. A third reason is the danger of escalation when wives engage in "harmless" minor violence. Finally, assault of a spouse "models" violence for children. This effect is as strong for assaults by wives as it is for assaults by husbands.

When women hit, they are legitimizing the abuse they receive from men. If she slapped him, she has provided the justification for him to hit her when he does not like her behavior. "Unless women also forsake violence in their relationships with male partners and children," Straus notes, "they are unlikely to be free of the risk of being assaulted."

The 1985 *National Family Violence Survey* found a physical rate of injury of 3 percent for females and 0.5 percent for men. Straus gives three reasons, however, against using injury as a criterion in the definition of abuse ("Conceptualization and Measurement of Battering: Implications for Public Policy," published in *Woman Battering: Policy Responses*, Michael Steinman, ed., Anderson Publishing, Cincinnati, Ohio, 1991). First, the effect on legislation would be detrimental to women who need the police to be able to make arrests without visible evidence of injury. Second, injury-based rates would eliminate from the data 97 percent of the assaults by men that did not result in injury but that are still a serious problem. Using the data from the 1985 survey, the rate of women abused would fall from over 6 million women a year to 189,000. Finally, focusing only on an in-

jury rate would make it too easy to ignore the high rate of abuse by women.

Redefining Battering

Neil S. Jacobson, known for his research on the physical responses to violence (See Chapters IV and VI), has redefined the definition of battering beyond the physical to include the abuse of control and power ("Contextualism Is Dead: Long Live Contextualism," *Family Process*, vol. 33, 1994). While women may hit or shove their partners, men are not terrorized by this violence.

"Battering" is not just physical aggression. Rather, battering constitutes the systematic use of violence and threat of violence in order to control, subjugate, and intimidate women. Without fear, there can be no battering. In 20

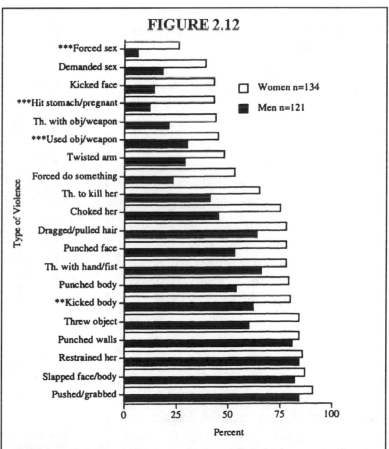

FIGURE 2.12

Type of Violence (top to bottom): ***Forced sex, Demanded sex, Kicked face, ***Hit stomach/pregnant, Th. with obj/weapon, ***Used obj/weapon, Twisted arm, Forced do something, Th. to kill her, Choked her, Dragged/pulled hair, Punched face, Th. with hand/fist, Punched body, **Kicked body, Threw object, Punched walls, Restrained her, Slapped face/body, Pushed/grabbed

Legend: □ Women n=134 ■ Men n=121

X-axis: Percent (0, 25, 50, 75, 100)

Prevalence of violence (at least once during relationship) — reports of women and men compared
*p < .05 **p < .01 *** p< .001

Source: Russell P. Dobash et al., "Separate and Intersecting Realities: A Comparison of Men's and Women's Accounts of Violence Against Women, *Violence Against Women*, vol. 4, no. 4, August 1998

years of research with couples ..., I have yet to encounter a man battered by a woman. However, I have encountered plenty of women who push, shove or hit men, usually in self-defense, often out of frustration, but seldom if ever as a method of control.

Violence Re-examined

The *National Youth Survey* (NYS) is a self-reported longitudinal study (a study following selected participants over an extended period of time) of problem behavior in a national sample of youth. The survey began in 1976 when the respondents were 11 to 17 years old. Barbara Morse used data from the 1983, 1986, 1989, and 1992 surveys to determine the level of violence between married or cohabiting partners ("Beyond the Conflict Tactics Scale: Assessing Gender Differences in Partner Violence," *Violence and Victims*, vol. 10, no. 4, Winter 1995). In 1983, the respondents were 18 to 24 years old; by 1992, they were 27 to 33 years old.

The survey found a high level of violence in these relationships. Over half (54.5 percent) of the partners reported some violence in 1983, declining to 32.4 percent by 1992. About one-quarter reported severe violence in the first survey, compared to 15.8 percent in 1992. This rate was nearly 3 to 4 times the rate reported by Straus. The major factor in the difference appeared to be the young age of the respondents in the NYS. This is supported by the decrease in violence reported in the later surveys. (See Table 2.7.)

The survey asked both males and females to report on violence either personally committed or committed by their partners. About 10 percent of couples reported at least one incident of severe male-to-female violence in the preceding year for the 1983 and 1986 surveys, decreasing to 5.7 percent in 1992 (Table 2.7) This is consistent with the 9 percent rate of severe violence found by the NFVS for men under 30 years old.

The NYS rates of female-to-male violence were remarkably high. Nearly half (48 percent) the NYS respondents reported one or more female-to-male assaults of any type in their relationships in 1983. This declined to 27.9 percent in 1992, still a high rate of violence. The rates of reported severe violence were also high. The rates ranged from 22.4 percent to 13.8 percent over the four years of study. (See Table 2.7.)

Who Was Responsible?

Morse noted that these rates are higher than most other studies and are at odds with common beliefs as well as police and hospital records. Some experts have explained that men tend to underreport their severe violence, not wishing to take responsibility for it, while

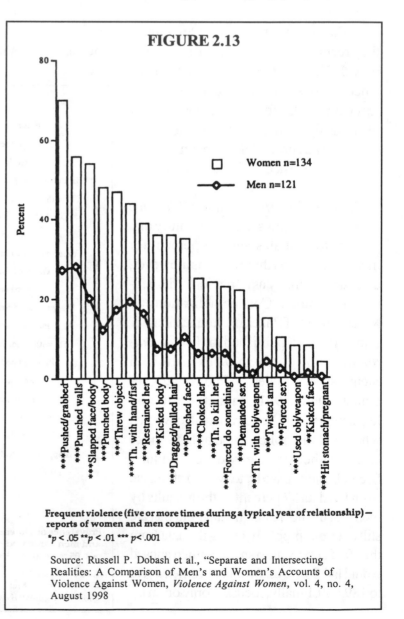

FIGURE 2.13

Frequent violence (five or more times during a typical year of relationship) — reports of women and men compared
*p < .05 **p < .01 *** p< .001

Source: Russell P. Dobash et al., "Separate and Intersecting Realities: A Comparison of Men's and Women's Accounts of Violence Against Women, *Violence Against Women*, vol. 4, no. 4, August 1998

women are more likely to be accurate. Analyzing the male and female reports in this survey, however, Morse found that both males and females underreported their violence in comparison to the reports of violence made by their partner. "Thus, there appears to be an 'offender effect' rather than a 'gender effect' in reporting violence, with each sex generally ... understating their own severe violence." In addition, each sex appeared to overstate its own severe violence victimization.

TABLE 2.7

Annual Prevalence Rates for Partner Violence: Percentage Reporting One or More Physical Assaults[a]

Type of Partner Violence	1983	1986	1989	1992
A. Couple violence				
Any violence	54.5	45.9	39.8	32.4
Severe violence	25.5	24.9	20.0	15.8
B. Male-to-female violence				
Any violence	36.7	31.4	27.9	20.2
Severe violence	10.1	9.5	7.6	5.7
C. Female-to-male violence				
Any violence	48.0	41.4	35.0	27.9
Severe violence	22.4	22.8	17.7	13.8
Number of cases	477	723	959	1001
Respondent ages	18–24	21–27	24–30	27–33

Note. [a]Among married or cohabitating respondents during target year.

Source: Barbara J. Morse, "Beyond the Conflict Tactics Scale: Assessing Gender Differences in Partner Violence," *Violence and Victims*, Winter 1995, Copyright © Springer Publishing Company, Inc., New York 10012. Used by permission.

Some experts have charged that the CTS obscures the difference between different violent acts and their repetitive nature. Table 2.8 shows that women in the NYS were significantly more likely than men to throw something at or slap their partners, as well as kick/bite/hit their partners with a fist or hit/try to hit with something. On the other hand, males were much more likely than females to "beat up" their partners. Among men who beat their wives, the reported frequency of

TABLE 2.8

Annual Prevalence and Mean Frequency Rates for Specific Acts of Partner Violence

Type of Violence	Male-to-Female 1983 Prev. (475)	Freq. (N)	1986 Prev. (723)	Freq. (N)	1989 Prev. (958)	Freq. (N)	1992 Prev. (1001)	Freq. (N)	Female-to-Male 1983 Prev. (475)	Freq. (N)	1986 Prev. (723)	Freq. (N)	1989 Prev. (958)	Freq. (N)	1992 Prev. (1001)	Freq. (N)
A. Minor violence	36.4	3.7 (254)	30.7	3.6 (327)	27.0	2.9 (373)	19.9	2.6 (315)	46.4	4.4 (254)	40.5	5.3 (327)	33.4	4.7 (373)	26.5	4.3 (315)
Threw something[b]	10.3	1.3 (140)	10.5	1.3 (190)	8.1	.9 (205)	6.0	.9 (173)	26.3	2.2 (140)	24.3	2.6 (190)	18.3	2.4 (205)	14.5	2.3 (173)
Pushed/grabbed/shoved	33.9	2.6 (204)	28.2	2.4 (272)	23.8	2.2[d] (302)	17.4	1.9[c] (246)	31.6	2.5 (204)	29.6	2.9 (272)	24.6	2.7 (302)	19.1	2.5 (246)
Slapped	16.6[b]	1.7[d] (141)	10.4[b]	1.6[b] (154)	8.8[b]	1.4[b] (174)	5.8[b]	1.4[b] (141)	23.2	2.3 (141)	17.4	2.8 (154)	15.8	2.7 (174)	12.0	2.3 (141)
B. Severe violence	10.1	2.5 (121)	9.5	2.9 (180)	7.6	1.7 (192)	5.7	2.1 (158)	22.4	3.8 (121)	41.4	4.9 (180)	35.0	3.6 (192)	13.8	4.5 (158)
Kicked/bit/hit with fist	6.7[b]	1.3[c] (91)	5.4[b]	1.6[b] (116)	4.1[b]	1.3[b] (119)	3.6[b]	1.2[b] (106)	15.8	2.4 (91)	15.2	3.9 (116)	11.0	2.9 (119)	8.7	2.6 (106)
Hit/tried with something[b]	5.7	1.1 (85)	6.0	1.4 (126)	4.0	.7 (123)	3.5	1.1 (104)	16.0	2.7 (85)	15.5	2.8 (126)	11.7	2.5 (123)	8.8	2.8 (104)
Beat up	4.6[b]	3.5[b] (23)	3.6[b]	3.5[c] (30)	2.0	2.8[b] (26)	2.0[b]	3.3 (26)	.4	.1 (23)	1.0	.6 (30)	1.1	.8 (26)	.9	1.3 (26)
Threatened with knife/gun[a]	1.3	.9 (14)	1.5[c]	.7 (32)	.9	.6 (25)	.7[b]	.5[d] (22)	1.7	.6 (14)	3.5	1.6 (32)	1.8	1.0 (25)	1.8	3.4 (22)
Used knife or gun[a]	.6	1.4 (5)	.8	3.7 (9)	.1	.5 (2)	.1	.1[d] (8)	.4	.4 (5)	.6	1.2 (9)	.1	1.0 (2)	.7	4.3 (8)
C. Any violence	36.7	4.8 (259)	31.4	5.1 (332)	27.9	3.7 (381)	20.2	3.6 (324)	48.0	6.1 (259)	22.8	7.9 (332)	17.7	6.4 (381)	27.9	6.3 (324)

Note. Prevalence rates reflect the proportion of all married or cohabitating respondents who reported involvement in a specific act during the target year. Mean frequency rates reflect the average number of specific acts experienced by those respondents who reported involvement in such act(s) during the target year.

[a]Although the significance level is indicated, the *N* for these items is small enough to require caution in interpretation. [b]*p* < .001. [c]*p* < .01. [d]*p* < .05 (two-tailed *t* tests for male-to-female and female-to-male differences). A superscript immediately following the item indicates significant differences in prevalence and frequency across all four survey years.

Source: Barbara J. Morse, "Beyond the Conflict Tactics Scale: Assessing Gender Differences in Partner Violence," *Violence and Victims*, Winter 1995, Copyright © Springer Publishing Company, Inc., New York 10012. Used by permission.

their beating up their partners was an average of three to four times per year, at least three times as often as women who engaged in this behavior.

In response to the charge that women use violence as a form of self-defense, the NYS found that the violence was mutual in about half the cases, and that in the remaining half, women accounted for about two-thirds of the nonreciprocal violence. This finding was supported by reports from both men and women. When asked who started the fight that led to the violence, men claimed both partners were responsible 44 percent of the time, men started the fight 26 percent of the time, and their partners initiated the fight 30 percent of the time. In contrast, women blamed their partners 46 percent of the time, took equal responsibility with their partners 36 percent of the time, and took responsibility 18 percent of the time.

About one-fifth of the female respondents in all three study years reported that violence led to personal injury. Twenty percent of men reported injuries in 1986, 10 percent in 1989, and 14 percent in 1992. Women were more likely to receive medical care for their injuries. Furthermore, approximately 30 percent of female NYS respondents reported being fearful of being injured, compared to 9.5 percent of male respondents.

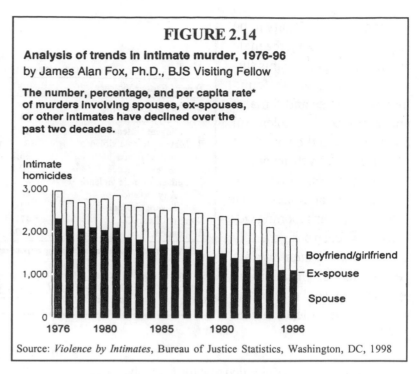

FIGURE 2.14

Analysis of trends in intimate murder, 1976-96
by James Alan Fox, Ph.D., BJS Visiting Fellow

The number, percentage, and per capita rate* of murders involving spouses, ex-spouses, or other intimates have declined over the past two decades.

Source: *Violence by Intimates*, Bureau of Justice Statistics, Washington, DC, 1998

ABUSED TO DEATH

In 1996, according to the Federal Bureau of Investigation (FBI) in its *Supplementary Homicide Reports, 1976-1996,* about 2,000 murders were attributed to intimate partners, down from 3,000 two decades earlier. (See Figure 2.14.) Thirty percent of all female murders were perpetrated by husbands, ex-husbands, or boyfriends, while just 3 percent of all male murder victims were killed by intimates (Figure 2.15). The rate of intimate murders dropped from 13.6 percent of all homicides in 1976 to 8.8 percent of all homicides in 1996. The total number of intimate murders fell 36 percent in the 20-year period. Spouse murders, the largest component of intimate murder, fell 52 percent (Figure 2.14).

Between 1976 and 1996, of the 20,311 male intimate murder victims, 3.7 percent were killed by wives, 0.2 percent by ex-wives, and 2 percent by nonmarital partners such as girlfriends. During the same period, 31,260 women were intimate murder victims; 19 percent were killed by husbands, 1.4 percent by ex-husbands, and 9.4 percent by nonmarital partners, such as boyfriends.

Intimate murder rates dropped far more rapidly among Blacks than among Whites, with the sharpest

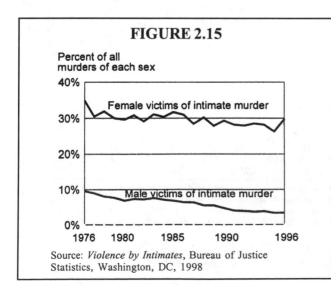

FIGURE 2.15

Source: *Violence by Intimates*, Bureau of Justice Statistics, Washington, DC, 1998

24

decrease among Black male victims (10 percent). Only one category, White girlfriends, increased over the 20-year period. (See Figure 2.16.) The female to male ratio has been increasing for both White and Black victims of intimate murder. (See Figure 2.17.) Females at every age are much more likely than males to be murdered by an intimate (Figure 2.18).

LESBIAN ABUSE

One aspect of abuse that has often treated as taboo is violence between lesbians. Just as many men have tried to ignore a subject they did not like, many women have responded the same way to violence among women. Barbara Hart (K. Lobel, ed., *Naming the Violence: Speaking Out About Lesbian Battering*, Seal Press, Seattle, Washington, 1986) wrote in her introduction, "[It] is painful. It challenges our dream of a lesbian utopia. It contradicts our belief in the inherent nonviolence of women."

Vernon R. Wiehe, in *Understanding Family Violence* (Sage Publications, Thousand Oaks, California, 1998), feels that the same forms of abuse (physical, emotional, or sexual) occur between same-sex couples as heterosexual partners. In addition, however, emotional abuse may also occur with threats to disclose a partner's homosexuality to family, friends, or employers.

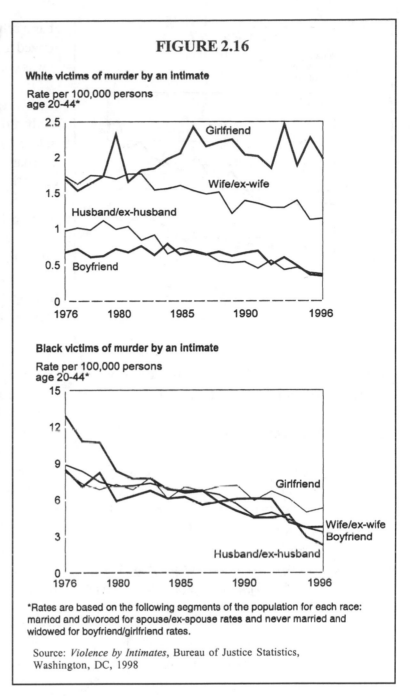

FIGURE 2.16

White victims of murder by an intimate

Rate per 100,000 persons age 20-44*

Black victims of murder by an intimate

Rate per 100,000 persons age 20-44*

*Rates are based on the following segments of the population for each race: married and divorced for spouse/ex-spouse rates and never married and widowed for boyfriend/girlfriend rates.

Source: *Violence by Intimates*, Bureau of Justice Statistics, Washington, DC, 1998

Comparisons of prevalence rates of partner abuse in same-sex relationships to abuse in heterosexual relationships are difficult to make and limited because researchers must rely on nonrandom, self-selected samples of same-sex relationships. As with other forms of partner abuse, same-sex partners may underreport violence in their relationships. Depending on the study, findings tend to indicate that abuse rates are about the same for both gay and lesbian relationships or that rates are higher in lesbian relationships.

How Abusive Are Lesbian Relationships?

There are few data on rates of lesbian violence. Gwat-Yong Lie and associates surveyed lesbian women in current aggressive relationships ("Lesbians in Currently Aggressive Relationships: How Frequently Do They Report Aggressive Past Relationships?" *Violence and Victims*, vol. 6, no. 2, Springer Publishing, New York, 1991). The participants (174) were asked to answer a questionnaire on abusive relationships they had been in or were presently in. Overall, nearly 9 out

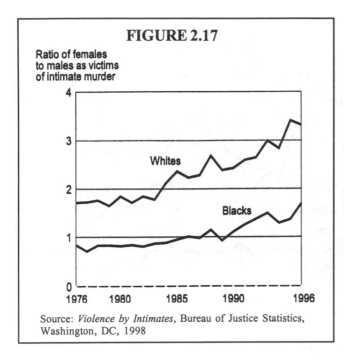

FIGURE 2.17

Ratio of females
to males as victims
of intimate murder

Whites

Blacks

1976   1980   1985   1990   1996

Source: *Violence by Intimates*, Bureau of Justice Statistics, Washington, DC, 1998

it as a self-defensive measure, 39.4 percent characterized it as mutual aggression, and 30.3 percent said it was both aggression and self-defense.

The researchers cautioned that the results of this study provided only a very preliminary look at abuse in lesbian relationships. The group was self-selective (the participants chose to take the survey perhaps because they had been abused and wanted to tell about it, or they declined because they were in an abusive relationship and did not want to discuss it), and there was no way to verify the statements that they made. Furthermore, the survey did not look at the intent for the aggression other than self-defined self-defense, making it impossible to draw any conclusions as to the motivations behind the abuse.

of 10 women reported either having observed or been the recipient of some form of aggression (physical, verbal, and sexual aggression were included) in their family of origin (where they grew up).

The respondents also revealed more aggression in past lesbian relationships than in their present relationships. Over half (51.5 percent) characterized a past relationship as "aggressive," and nearly three-quarters (73.4 percent) reported experiencing aggressive acts. Nearly 57 percent reported sexual aggression, 45 percent mentioned physical abuse, and 64.5 percent cited verbal/emotional aggression.

Only 9.6 percent of the current relationships were described as "aggressive." The researchers could not say whether the women had learned from past experience and were now able to avoid abusive partners or whether women in currently abusive relationships were unwilling to answer the survey. Aggression was still fairly common, with 8.9 percent reporting sexual aggression, 11.6 percent reporting physical aggression, and 24 percent citing verbal/emotional aggression. Sixty-eight percent of those surveyed reported both having used and experienced aggression in their lesbian relationships — 30.3 percent saw

Based on the scant research that has been done, risk factors for lesbian abuse appear similar to those for heterosexual wife assault. The main contributors to lesbian battering have been identified as dependency and jealousy. The dependency versus autonomy issue involves a balance of power, also called the fusion issue, and is especially significant for gay and lesbian relationships, where a lack of social acceptance and support is found. This causes couples to rely more intensively on each other. In addition to dependency and jealousy, clinical and anecdotal reports have indicated that lesbian batterers often abuse alcohol or drugs, feel powerless, and have low self-esteem.

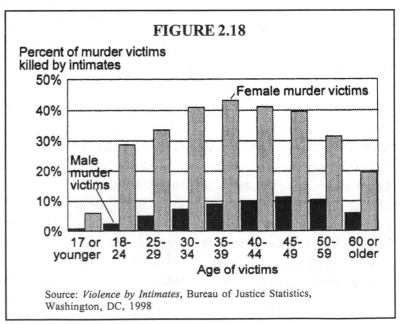

FIGURE 2.18

Percent of murder victims
killed by intimates

Female murder victims

Male murder victims

17 or   18-   25-   30-   35-   40-   45-   50-   60 or
younger 24   29   34   39   44   49   59   older

Age of victims

Source: *Violence by Intimates*, Bureau of Justice Statistics, Washington, DC, 1998

Lesbians who are battered are the most under-served population of the battered, often facing denial from other lesbians and homophobia from service providers. Two myths are often cited to justify the lack of services: the violence is mutual and the abuse is not as violent as man-to-woman abuse. In fact, according to Pam Elliott, coordinator of a lesbian abuse intervention project, the abuse is rarely mutual, and it can be just as harmful as heterosexual abuse.

GENDER ISSUES IN SAME-SEX RELATIONSHIPS

Lisa A. Waldner-Haugrud et al. (in "Victimization and Perpetration Rates of Violence in Gay and Lesbian Relationships: Gender Issues Explored," *Violence and Victims,* vol. 12, no. 2, 1997) studied a sample of 165 gays* and 118 lesbians to explore gender issues in homosexual relationships. A 15-page questionnaire, using a modified version of the Conflict Tactics Scale, was distributed to an all-White, highly educated sample. Data collected in the spring and summer of 1991 found that 47.5 percent of lesbians and 29.7 percent of gays reported being or having been the victim of relationship violence. Pushing and threatening were the most frequently used tactics, and using a weapon was the least frequent. (See Table 2.9.)

Thirty-eight percent of the lesbian respondents reported perpetrating violence, primarily pushing, slapping, and making threats. Both victimization and perpetration rates of lesbians were greater than those reported by gay men, with the exception of using a weapon. The only tactic showing a significant difference between lesbians and gays was pushing, or being pushed, with lesbians far more likely to report this tactic than gays. (See Table 2.9.)

TABLE 2.9

Percentage of Gays and Lesbians who have Perpetrated or Experienced Relationship Violence

	Lesbian		Gays	
Tactics	Perpetration	Victimized	Perpetration	Victimized
1. Threat	16.3	26.7	11.7	19.4
2. Pushed	29.3	37.9	11.7	18.1
3. Slapped	17.2	25.9	12.9	17.6
4. Punched	12.1	12.9	9.2	15.1
5. Struck with an object	3.5	7.8	3.1	6.7
6. Use of a weapon	0	2.6	.6	2.4
Total	38.0	47.5	21.8	29.7

Source: Lisa M. Waldner-Haugrud et al., "Victimization and Perpetration Rates of Violence in Gay and Lesbian Relationships: Gender Issues Explored, *Violence and Victims*, vol. 12, no. 2, Summer 1997

According to the researchers, several factors may increase the likelihood of relationship violence in lesbian couples: "prejudice-encouraged" social isolation of lesbian couples, overdependency of one partner on the other, the tendency of lesbians to create "closed" relationships, sexual orientation identity issues, and the underreporting of partner abuse by gay men. However, they recognize that the limitations of this study (all-White, well-educated, nonrandom sample) "require a cautious interpretation of the results." Still, the implications of their findings seem to indicate a need to move beyond the theories that use gender in defining victim and perpetrator.

EMOTIONAL AND VERBAL ABUSE

Most definitions of abuse focus on situations where violent physical abuse was either threatened or actually used. Most official definitions (as used by the courts or the police) do not include emotional or psychological abuse, which can, in many cases, hurt more and cause more long-term damage than many acts of physical violence. A woman with an abusive, alcoholic father remembered, "You know something, those cuts and bruises healed, but to this day I can still hear my father yelling at me. That's what really hurts, it was the yelling that really hurt." See Figure 2.19, prepared by the National Coalition Against Domestic Violence, for a list of ways in which partners use emotional abuse.

---

*While the term "gay" may apply to male or female homosexuals, increasingly the term "gay" has been applied to male homosexuals and the term "lesbian" to female homosexuals, hence the contemporary terms "gay and lesbian."

Emotional and psychological abuse is usually harder to define than physical abuse, where the scars often can be clearly seen. Almost all couples scream and shout things to hurt one another at some point in a relationship. Emotional and psychological abuse result, however, when the abuser uses words to project his or her power over his or her mate in a way meant to demean and cause harm. Lenore Walker, in *Terrifying Love* (Harper and Row, New York, 1989), equated it with Amnesty International's definition of psychological torture and cited it as a factor in paralyzing women in an abusive relationship. Amnesty's definition includes, "verbal degradation, denial of powers, isolation, monopolizing perceptions, occasional indulgences, and threats to kill."

FIGURE 2.19

How many of these things has your partner done to you?

- ignored your feelings
- ridiculed or insulted women as a group
- ridiculed or insulted your most valued beliefs, your religion, race, heritage, or class
- withheld approval, appreciation or affection as punishment
- continually criticized you, called you names, shouted at you
- humiliated you in private or public
- refused to socialize with you
- kept you from working, controlled your money, made all decisions
- refused to work or share money
- took car keys or money away from you
- regularly threatened to leave or told you to leave
- threatened to hurt you or your family
- punished or deprived the children when angry at you
- threatened to kidnap the children if you left
- abused, tortured, killed pets to hurt you
- harassed you about affairs your partner imagined you were having
- manipulated you with lies and contradictions
- destroyed furniture, punched holes in walls, broken appliances
- wielded a gun in a threatening way

Source: National Coalition Against Domestic Violence

A Study of Verbal Aggression

Murray Straus and Stephen Sweet returned to the data from the 1985 *National Family Violence Survey* to study verbal aggression ("Verbal/Symbolic Aggression in Couples: Incidence Rates and Relationships to Personal Characteristics," *Journal of Marriage and the Family*, vol. 54, 1992). They found no significant difference between man-to-woman and woman-to-man verbal aggression. Furthermore, when one partner engaged in verbal aggression, the other often responded in kind. Women reported more abuse regardless of who initiated it, but the researchers were unable to determine if men minimized the incidence of verbal abuse or if women exaggerated it.

This study found no correlation between race or socioeconomic status and verbal aggression (other studies have reported higher levels of verbal aggression among Black couples). There was, however, a link between age and levels of abuse. As couples aged,

their level of verbal aggression dropped regardless of how much conflict there was in the relationship.

The study also revealed a positive connection between the number of times either partner was drunk and the level of verbal aggression. The more often the man was drunk, the more often he was likely to be verbally abusive (Figure 2.20). Similarly, the more often a woman used drugs, the greater the probability of verbal abuse. For a man, however, drugs did not have a significant effect on the use of verbal abuse. The researchers cautioned that this study did not show which way the influence lies — do men and women drink to provide themselves with an excuse to be abusive, or is the drinking the reason for their aggression?

The United States Department of Health and Human Services, in its National Institute on Drug Abuse drug use survey (*National Household Survey on Drug Abuse: Main Findings, 1993*, Department of Health and Human Services, Rockville, Maryland, 1995),

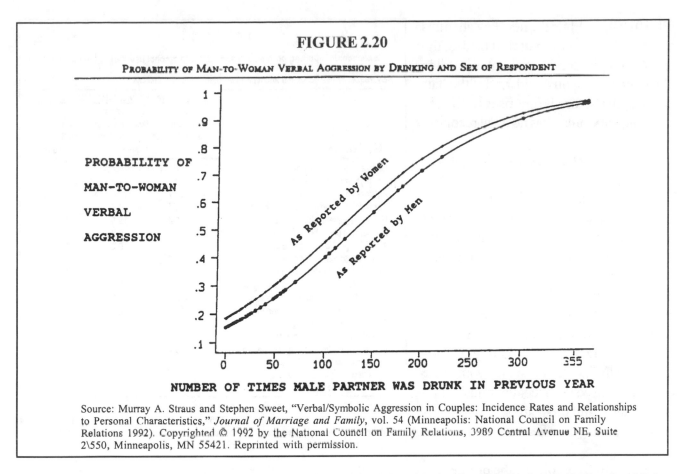

FIGURE 2.20

PROBABILITY OF MAN-TO-WOMAN VERBAL AGGRESSION BY DRINKING AND SEX OF RESPONDENT

PROBABILITY OF
MAN-TO-WOMAN
VERBAL
AGGRESSION

As Reported by Women

As Reported by Men

NUMBER OF TIMES MALE PARTNER WAS DRUNK IN PREVIOUS YEAR

Source: Murray A. Straus and Stephen Sweet, "Verbal/Symbolic Aggression in Couples: Incidence Rates and Relationships to Personal Characteristics," *Journal of Marriage and Family*, vol. 54 (Minneapolis: National Council on Family Relations 1992). Copyrighted © 1992 by the National Council on Family Relations, 3989 Central Avenue NE, Suite 2\550, Minneapolis, MN 55421. Reprinted with permission.

found that 41.7 percent of those who reported being drunk more than twice a month became aggressive and angry when they drank, and 35.4 percent had heated arguments when drunk. In contrast, those who did not use alcohol to become drunk rarely became argumentative while drinking. (See Table 2.10.)

IMMIGRANT ABUSE

Abuse of immigrant women is a growing problem in the United States. Immigrant women can be at risk for abuse because of the special circumstances of their lives. Some come from cultures where women are taught to defer to their husbands. Many cannot speak English and do not know their rights in the United States. They fear being deported, and they have no resources or support to turn to for help.

Asian Americans have become increasingly aware of abuse in their community. Some Asian women have been sent to this country as the result of an arranged marriage to live with a man they hardly know. In some cases, the husband takes the woman's money, jewelry, and passport, making her totally dependent on

him. Her abusive husband often tells her that if she leaves him, she will be deported. If she returns home, she will bring shame on her family, and in some traditional cultures, divorced women have no place in society.

The U.S. immigration laws unintentionally contributed to the problem of abuse. The Immigration Marriage Fraud Amendments (IMFA; PL 99-639) were passed in 1986 in an attempt to prevent immigrants from illegally attaining resident status through a sham marriage to a U.S. citizen. The IMFA requires that the spouse (usually the husband) of the immigrant petition for her conditional resident status. Conditional status has to last a minimum of two years, during which time the couple must remain married. If the marriage dissolves, the immigrant loses conditional status and can be deported. As a result, in some cases the wife becomes a prisoner of an abusive husband as long as he controls her conditional status.

In 1990, the law was amended to permit a waiver of conditional status if the immigrant could prove battery or extreme cruelty (the Immigration Act of 1990,

PL 101-649). While the new law attempts to provide relief for battered brides, the initial filing for conditional status is still in the hands of the husband, and if the battery begins before he chooses to file the petition, the woman has no legal recourse.

A Different Culture

Most recent immigrants from Asian countries have a culture radically different from the predominant American society. Although the Asian American community includes a wide variety of cultures (Chinese, Vietnamese, Indian, Korean, Cambodian, etc.), there is a common acceptance of male dominance and of the belief that the community and the family take priority over the individual. Asian women are generally raised to accept their husbands' dominance, and most are afraid to complain or leave.

Issues that complicate the problem of domestic abuse include familial identity, economic dependency, stigma of divorce, taboo of airing dirty laundry, fear of losing face and bringing shame upon the family, and a lack of awareness that wife battering is wrong. A Cambodian social worker explained (quoted by Kimberly Huisman in "Wife Battering in Asian American Communities," *Violence Against Women*, vol. 2, no. 3, September 1996),

The stigma of divorce and fear of bringing shame upon the family is especially hard for them to deal with. Everything belongs to the husband, is his property — assets, wife, and kids. These beliefs are ingrained in their upbringing and values. Women are expected to be submissive, passive, and dependent. They are taught to obey and not to say no. Violence is viewed as a means to control and is not seen as a problem.... When a woman is beaten it is thought of as maintaining control because she deserved it.

TABLE 2.10

Respondents reporting problems associated with alcohol use during the past year

By frequency of alcohol use and type of problem, United States, 1993[a]

Type of problem	Frequency of alcohol use		
	Drunk more than twice a month (N=1,469)	Drunk about twice a month or less often (N=5,507)	Not drunk in past year (N=8,264)
Unable to remember what happened	42.6%	20.4%	1.6%
Got high or tight while drinking alone	42.3	17.2	2.7
Aggressive or cross while drinking	41.7	20.0	2.2
Tossed down drinks fast to get effect	38.1	20.4	2.2
Heated argument while drinking	35.4	15.5	1.6
Partner told me I should cut down	32.2	12.2	1.6
Afraid I might be or become alcoholic	29.3	9.2	2.7
Relative told me I should cut down	29.2	7.5	1.0
Difficult for me to stop drinking	25.0	8.2	0.6
Kept on drinking after promising myself not to	23.9	7.0	1.1
High or tight on job or at school	20.7	5.2	0.5
Stayed drunk for more than one day	20.6	2.9	0.2
Stayed away from work or school	19.6	6.3	0.4
Friend told me I should cut down	17.0	3.5	0.6
Hands shook after drinking day before	16.4	3.0	0.2
Quick drink when no one was looking	14.1	4.7	1.1
Drink first thing in morning	7.9	1.2	0.1
Lost or nearly lost job	6.3	0.6	0.1

Note: "Drunk more than twice a month" includes respondents who reported getting very high or drunk on alcohol 25 or more days in the past 12 months. "Drunk about twice a month or less often" includes respondents who reported getting very high or drunk on alcohol at least once but not more than 24 days in the past 12 months.

[a]Only respondents who reported having at least one drink in the past 12 months and who reported their frequency of being drunk in the past year are included.

U.S. Department of Health and Human Services, Substance Abuse and Mental Health Services Administration, *National Household Survey on Drug Abuse: Main Findings 1993* (Rockville, MD: U.S. Department of Health and Human Services, 1995), p. 140. Table adapted by SOURCEBOOK staff.

Source: Kathleen Macguire and Ann L. Pastore, eds., *Sourcebook of Criminal Justice Statistics — 1995*, Bureau of Justice Statistics, Washington, DC, 1996

Language problems often make it harder to get help. Women who do not speak English generally do not know how to find help, cannot avail themselves of the help that does exist, and do not know their rights in the United States. Social workers report that interpreters (often male) do not always translate correctly, preferring to maintain the community values rather than support the battered wife. In addition, many Asian women do not know the law and are told by their partners that they will be deported or lose their children if they report abuse to authorities.

In September 1994, President Clinton signed the Violence Against Women Act (VAWA—part of the Violent Crime Control and Law Enforcement Act of 1994, PL 103-322) permitting undocumented battered women to obtain lawful permanent resident status through self-petitioning or suspension of deportation. In order to implement this law, however, immigrant women must hire a lawyer and enter a system many of them mistrust.

New policies and programs for recent immigrant victims are being implemented across the country, especially in cities with large immigrant populations. Multicultural criminal justice staff, special efforts to reach immigrant victims, police representatives at meetings of immigrant groups, informational materials printed in a variety of languages, and immigrant community representatives on citizen police committees are improving the communication between immigrants and the criminal justice system. A recent survey of immigrant victims in neighborhoods in New York and Philadelphia showed few problems with their encounters with the justice system and a high degree of satisfaction with the police and the courts. However, as is true in the native-born population, immigrant victims of domestic violence were less likely to report this type of victimization to the police than the victimization of other crimes.

CHAPTER III

THE CAUSES OF WIFE ABUSE*

WHO IS ABUSED?

Although wife abuse has been studied for about 25 years, researchers often differ on the origins of abuse. Sociologists interpret data differently from feminists; feminists see it differently from therapists; therapists see another picture than the one perceived by shelter workers; and the abused women themselves have their own point of view.

SOME ARE MORE LIKELY

When past observers, such as the English legal commentator Sir William Blackstone (see Chapter I), wrote about wife abuse, it was treated as a lower-class phenomenon. This was generally accepted until domestic violence became a public issue. When abuse began to be investigated, researchers warned that, while it appeared that lower-class women were the majority of the victims, this might be a misconception stemming from the fact that lower-class women were the ones who most often came to public attention.

Middle- and upper-class women were also abused, but they did not turn to emergency rooms and shelters for help; they used private facilities and were therefore largely unknown to the support community. Nonetheless, while women of any social class may be abused, general population studies have found that women with lower incomes and less education, as well as minority women, are more likely to be victims of domestic violence.

The Effect of Poverty

Murray Straus, director of the Family Research Laboratory at the University of New Hampshire, has found that serious physical acts of wife abuse are more likely in poorer homes. Straus observed,

> For the ordinary violence in family life, the pushing, slapping, shoving, there's not much difference by socioeconomic status or race. But when you come to the more serious kinds of violence, then the lower the socioeconomic status, the higher the level of violence, by very large amounts.

Gerald Hotaling and David Sugarman (see "Risk Markers," below) found that in 9 of 11 studies that looked at socioeconomic status (SES), low SES was found to be a consistent risk marker (sign) of wife assault. The authors proposed two interpretations for this finding. First, men who have a lower SES are exposed to greater stress and possess fewer resources (economic security or education) to cope with it. Second, the relationship between lower SES and wife abuse is due to a subculture of violence — these individuals are more

---

* This chapter focuses on the causes of wife abuse and the characteristics of abusive families. It is extremely important to remember that, regardless of the circumstances, the majority of husbands and wives do not beat each other. Even in families in which all the indicators show a significantly greater likelihood that abuse might occur, most husbands do not beat their wives.

likely to hold values that permit the abuse of women (see below).

The 1985 *National Family Violence Survey* (NFVS; see Chapter II), based on 6,002 nationally representative households, provided researchers with the primary data to test their observations against a database large enough to produce statistically valid findings. In the NFVS, families living at or below the poverty level had a rate of marital violence 500 percent greater than more well-to-do families.

A QUESTION OF POWER

Is abuse a manifestation of men insisting on their superiority over women, or is this just one piece of a much more complicated issue? (See also Chapter II.) Certainly, power in the relationship seems to play a major role in the causes of battering. Power can also be expressed through financial, social, and decision-making control.

Some researchers have theorized that because statistically lower socioeconomic status (SES) men are more likely to batter, they do it to assert the power that they lack economically. Violence becomes the power tactic that makes up for what these men lack in other areas.

The Balance of Power

Diane Coleman and Murray Straus, in "Marital Power, Conflict, and Violence in a Nationally Representative Sample of American Couples" (*Violence and Victims*, vol. 1, no. 2, 1986), used the first *National Family Violence Survey* to investigate the type of family most prone to violence. They asked the respondents to indicate "who has the final say" in buying a car, having children, what house or apartment to take, what job either partner should take, whether a partner should go to work or quit work, and how much money to spend each week on food. The response options were husband only, husband more than wife, husband and wife exactly the same, wife more than husband, and wife only.

They then arranged the responses to create four categories: male-dominant, female-dominant, equalitarian, and divided power. "The difference between the equalitarian and the divided power types was that the former was equal in the sense of making most decisions jointly, while the latter is equal in the sense of dividing responsibility for decisions, with the wife and husband each having the final say for different decisions." They found that the uneven relationships, female- and male-dominant, had the highest likelihood of violence, while equalitarian and divided responsibility marriages had the lowest likelihood of violence. They also found that equalitarian relationships could tolerate more conflict before violence erupted than other power relationships.

Coleman and Straus attributed most of the difference in violence to higher rates of marital conflict among unequal relationships than among equalitarian and divided ones. The more conflict, the more likely the violence. Inequality, the researchers believe, inevitably leads to attempts to even it out, which result in conflict and, perhaps, violence. Those in female-dominant relationships also have to contend with an "unusual" relationship in a traditionally male society, which adds to the tension. Coleman and Straus emphasized a major exception to this pattern — those who accept the legitimacy (accept it as right and proper) of male- or female-dominant relationships are likely to have low levels of conflict and violence.

A further elaboration of the balance of power is provided by J. E. Prince and I. Arias in "The Role of Perceived Control and the Desirability of Control Among Abusive and Nonabusive Husbands" (*American Journal of Family Therapy*, vol. 22, no. 2, 1994). Assessing the relationship between control and self-esteem, they found two patterns. In one, men who had high self-esteem but a poor sense of control over their lives (as in unemployment) used violence in an attempt to gain control. In the second pattern, men who had low self-esteem and felt powerless became violent in response to frustration. The researchers concluded that the lack of control over life events was a more significant predictor of wife assault than self-esteem.

Learned Gender Roles

Pointing to history, some researchers see wife abuse as a natural consequence of the woman's traditional second-class role in society. Among the first to express this point of view, Emerson and Russell Dobash (*Violence Against Wives*, Free Press, New York City, 1979) wrote, "men who assault their wives are actually living up to cultural prescriptions that are cherished in Western society — aggressiveness, male dominance, and female subordination — and they are using physical force as a means to enforce that dominance." Many believe that men are socialized to exert power and control over women. Some men may use both physical and emotional abuse to maintain their position of dominance in the spousal relationship.

Kersti Yllö agrees. In "Through a Feminist Lens: Gender, Power, and Violence" (*Current Controversies on Family Violence*, Gelles and Loseke, eds., Sage Publications, Newbury Park, California, 1994), she states that "violence grows out of inequality within marriage (and other intimate relations that are modeled on marriage) and reinforces male dominance and female subordination." Violence against women (in all its forms, including sexual harassment, date rape, etc.) is a tactic of male control. Domestic violence for Yllö is not conflict of interest; it is domination by men. Other researchers have found that higher levels of dominance were associated with higher levels of violence.

Murray Straus compared data on wife battering with indexes to measure gender equality, income, and social disorganization variables in all 50 states ("State-to-State Differences in Social Inequality and Social Bonds in Relation to Assaults on Wives in the United States," *Journal of Comparative Family Studies*, vol. 25, no. 1, Spring 1994). Gender equality was evaluated by measuring the extent to which women have parity with men in economic, political, and legal spheres of life (24 different indicators). Income inequality was based on the 1980 census data on family income. Social disorganization measured the level of societal instability, such as geographic mobility, divorce, lack of religious affiliation, female-headed households, households headed by males with no female present, and the ratio of tourists to residents in each state.

Among the 50 states, gender equality was the variable most closely related to the rate of wife assault — the higher the status of women, the lower the probability of that state having a high rate of wife abuse (Figure 3.1). Social disorganization was also related to abuse — the higher the degree of

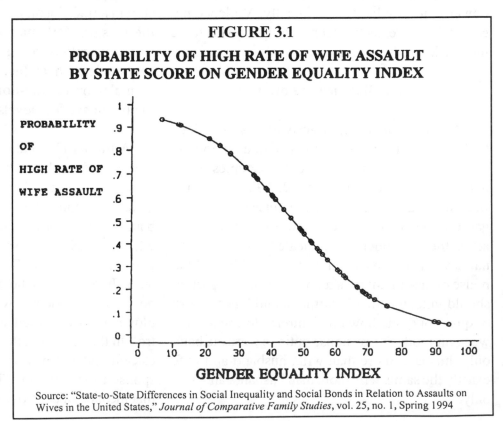

FIGURE 3.1

PROBABILITY OF HIGH RATE OF WIFE ASSAULT BY STATE SCORE ON GENDER EQUALITY INDEX

PROBABILITY OF HIGH RATE OF WIFE ASSAULT

GENDER EQUALITY INDEX

Source: "State-to-State Differences in Social Inequality and Social Bonds in Relation to Assaults on Wives in the United States," *Journal of Comparative Family Studies*, vol. 25, no. 1, Spring 1994

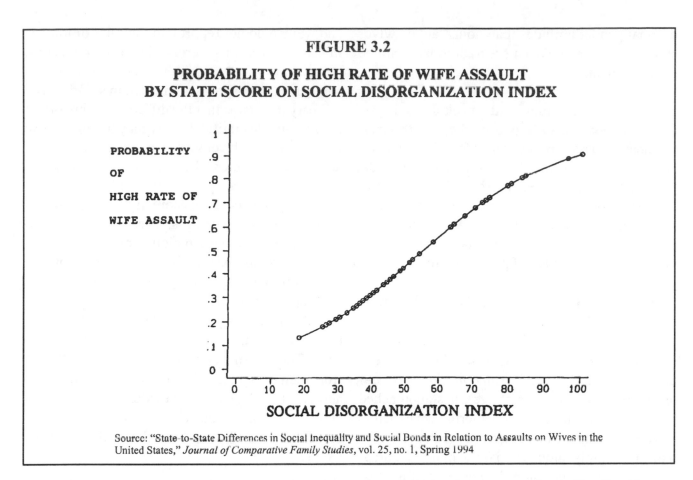

FIGURE 3.2

PROBABILITY OF HIGH RATE OF WIFE ASSAULT BY STATE SCORE ON SOCIAL DISORGANIZATION INDEX

PROBABILITY OF HIGH RATE OF WIFE ASSAULT

SOCIAL DISORGANIZATION INDEX

Source: "State-to-State Differences in Social Inequality and Social Bonds in Relation to Assaults on Wives in the United States," *Journal of Comparative Family Studies*, vol. 25, no. 1, Spring 1994

social disorganization, the higher the probability that the state would have a high rate of wife assault (Figure 3.2). On the other hand, economic inequality did not relate to wife abuse rates.

Evidence Against the Role of a Patriarchal Society

Donald Dutton, professor of psychology and director of a treatment program for batterers, questions the role of patriarchy (male domination), pointing out that different types of research offer other explanations for violence ("Patriarchy and Wife Assault: The Ecological Fallacy," *Violence and Victims*, vol. 9, no. 2, 1994). According to the patriarchal model, societies that place a high value on male dominance should be high in abuse. Dutton cites studies that contradict this premise.

Some research in the Hispanic community has found significantly lower rates of abuse among Hispanics than Whites. Coleman and Straus's research (above) found that in marriages where the spouses agreed that the husband should be domi-

nant, violence levels were low. Finally, Dutton points out, Straus and Gelles have found in surveys that only about 10 percent of husbands are abusive and even fewer are severely abusive or repeat batterers. How strong a factor can the patriarchal society be if so few men are influenced by it?

Other research has also discounted the weight of the patriarchal theory of abuse. David Sugarman and Susan Frankel, in "Patriarchal Ideology and Wife-Assault: A Meta-Analytical Review" (*Journal of Family Violence*, vol. 11, no. 1, 1996), examined studies for evidence of this theory. They measured whether violent husbands had a higher acceptance of violence than nonviolent men did and whether they believed that women should exhibit traditional gender roles of obedience, loyalty, and deference. They also measured whether assaultive men were more likely to possess a traditional "gender schema" (an individual's *internal* perception of his or her own levels of masculinity, femininity, or androgyny [having both male and female characteristics]). For women, the authors examined whether assaulted wives held more traditional gender attitudes than nonassaulted wives and whether they held a more traditional feminine gender schema.

Overall, Sugarman and Frankel's analysis found support for only two of the five theories. Predictably, assaultive husbands found marital violence more acceptable than nonviolent husbands, and assaulted wives were more likely to be classified as having a "traditional" feminine gender schema than nonassaulted wives. At best, they concluded these findings "give partial support for the ideological component of patriarchy theory...."

THE PSYCHOLOGICAL POINT OF VIEW

K. Daniel O'Leary, in "Through a Psychological Lens: Personality Traits, Personality Disorders, and Levels of Violence" (*Current Controversies on Family Violence;* see above), has approached the causes of violence by considering what factors in a relationship are most likely to predict violence. Not surprisingly, aggression is the major factor: a) acceptance of aggression, b) past use of aggression, c) relationship conflict, and d) partner's aggression.

Some experts believe that low levels of aggression (slapping and shoving) will escalate over time into more severe forms of abuse such as battering and threatening with weapons. Moreover, while most relationships characterized by severe violence began with milder forms of abuse, many partners limit their aggression to pushing and slapping. These behaviors occur in so many marriages that they are essentially normal. O'Leary believes that different levels of aggression (verbal, mild physical, and severe physical aggression) are three distinct, but related, sets of behaviors, and men who engage in the milder forms are not motivated by the same impulses as men who use severe abuse. (See also "Risk Markers and a Continuum of Aggression," below.)

As further evidence of the differences in levels of abuse, O'Leary notes that in marriages with low levels of physical violence, it is often mutual and women do not report that their use of force is in self-defense. In severely violent relationships, however, women do claim to have used violence, sometimes to the point of murder, in self-defense. O'Leary maintains that the difference is important because, while marital therapy may be appropriate for treating low-level violence, it is not for severe abuse. (See Chapter VI.)

Mildly abusive men score highly on personality tests for impulsiveness, a readiness to defend oneself, aggression, suspicion of others, and a tendency to take offense easily. Men in treatment programs for abuse (generally, highly abusive men) have been diagnosed with serious psychological disorders (including schizoid/borderline, narcissistic/antisocial, and possessive/dependent/compulsive). These men were also significantly different from men who were in bad marriages but were not abusive. For O'Leary, this evidence shows a psychological component to abuse rather than a social system that promotes the domination of women.

Researchers with a feminist viewpoint disagree with the concept of separate types of abuse. All violence against women is unacceptable, and they reject the idea that some men abuse because they are mentally deranged, thereby excusing their behavior. Feminists are often critical of psychological interpretations of violence that portray batterers as psychologically different from the rest of society. Feminist theory supports the concept that any man has the capability to be a batterer because he is a part of a patriarchal society.

THE SOCIOLOGICAL POINT OF VIEW

Richard Gelles, a sociologist at the Family Research Laboratory, believes it is risky to put too much emphasis on a psychological explanation of abuse. The picture of a mentally deranged, violent abuser focuses attention on only the most extreme cases of abuse stereotyped by a psychotic offender and an innocent victim. According to Gelles, only about 10 percent of abusive incidents are caused by mental illness; the rest cannot be explained by a psychological model.

Gelles believes a more complete understanding of the causes of abuse can be had through sociological models. There are four primary theories: general systems theory, resource theory, exchange/social control theory, and subculture of violence theory.

General Systems Theory

The general systems theory views violence as a system rather than as the result of individual mental disturbance. It describes the process of violence in families and explains how violence is managed. Gelles's colleague, Murray Straus, developed eight concepts to illustrate the general systems theory:

- Violence between family members has many causes and roots. Personality, stress, and conflicts are only some.

- More family violence occurs than is reported.

- Most family violence is either denied or ignored.

- Stereotyped family-violence imagery is learned in early childhood from other family members.

- The family-violence stereotypes are continually reaffirmed through ordinary social interactions and the mass media.

- Violent acts by violent persons may generate positive feedback; that is, these acts may produce desired results.

- Use of violence, when contrary to family norms, creates additional conflicts.

- Persons who are labeled violent may be encouraged to play out a violent role, either to live up to the expectations of others or to fulfill their own self-concepts of being violent or dangerous.

Resource Theory

The more resources — social, personal, and economic — a person can command, the more force he or she can muster. The more resources a person has, the less he or she needs to use force in an open manner. But a person with little education, low job prestige and income, and poor interpersonal skills may use violence to maintain dominance.

Exchange/Social Control Theory

Violence can be explained by the principle of costs and rewards. The private nature of the family, the reluctance of social institutions to intervene, and the low risk of other interventions reduce the cost (the risk of negative consequences) of abuse. The cultural approval of violence raises the potential rewards for violence.

Subculture of Violence Theory

The subculture of violence is perhaps the most widely accepted theory of violence. This theory states that some groups within society hold values that permit the use of violence, explaining why some portions of society and some cultures are more violent than others are.

Gelles supports the theory of gender inequality as a cause of violence, but he warns that it is wrong to make it the basic framework of abuse, as some feminists have done. For Gelles, it is only a part of the picture.

ALCOHOL

The role played by alcohol in family violence has been examined in many studies. From anecdotal evidence, alcohol appears to be a major factor in abuse ("When he gets drunk, he beats me"), and yet, in controlled studies, the connection between the two is not as clear. Some research has found that heavy, binge drinking is more predictive of abuse than daily consumption of alcohol.

Jerry Flanzer, in "Alcohol and Other Drugs Are Key Causal Agents of Violence" (*Current Con-*

troversies on Family Violence; see above), states that, while not all alcoholics are violent, alcoholism causes family violence. He notes that personality characteristics of alcoholics and abusers are remarkably similar, marked by behavior such as blaming others, being jealous and possessive, suffering from depression and low self-esteem, and "blacking out" (forgetting) critical incidents. Table 3.1 shows the similarities between the characteristics and family responses in abusive and alcoholic families.

Given the strong similarities between these two groups, Flanzer proposes that perhaps they are the same group of families that have been approached from two different directions — studies of physical abuse and studies of alcohol abuse. Not all alcoholic families are violent, and not all violent families are alcohol abusers, but Flanzer suspects that a careful examination of family histories would reveal that most are. Studies show that the link between alcohol and abuse does not apply only to the offender. Adults abused in childhood are more likely to be alcoholic, and children from alcoholic homes are more likely to be offenders.

Alcohol acts as a disinhibitor, permitting a person to act out anger that was previously held in check. Alcohol also hinders a person's understanding of a situation, and the drinker's limited comprehension may lead him or her to respond inappropriately with anger. Furthermore, the alcohol is frequently used as a rationalization for the violence. The alcoholic avoids responsibility for the violent behavior by blaming the effects of the al-

cohol. Finally, alcoholism distorts the family system by constantly forcing the family to accommodate to the short-term demands of the alcoholic to maintain some kind of stability. This restructuring of family life establishes an atmosphere that tolerates and accommodates violence.

An Excuse, Not a Cause

Richard Gelles ("Alcohol and Other Drugs Are Not the Cause of Violence," also in *Current Controversies*) disagrees with Flanzer. While substantial evidence links alcohol and drug use to violence, there is little scientific evidence that alcohol or

---

TABLE 3.1
Commonalities of Behavioral Response Among Family Members Experiencing Alcoholism and Family Violence

Response	Perpetrator	Victim	Family Function
Defense mechanisms	denial of the problem; minimizing, rationalizing, isolating	denial of the problem; minimizing, rationalizing, isolating	denial of the problem; rationalizing, isolating
Parenting	autocratic	enmeshed, infantilized	parentification
Tolerance	low frustration, increasingly aggressive, controlling	high frustration, increasingly hurt	increasing tolerance
Projection	blaming others	accepting blame, feeling shame	family inferiority
Loyalty	secretive	secretive, loyal	keeping the family intact
Communication	decreasing empathic communication	distancing to avoid abuse	minimizing pain through rigidifying communication patterns
Control	solidifying power	decreasing power	unequal power relationships
Affection	less intimate	less intimate	rigidifying affectionate relationships to avoid pain
Stress	increasingly provocative, restrictive	increasingly alarmed, timid	stress reduction
Depression	defending against depression, low self-esteem	building depression, lowering self-esteem	depression, eventual destabilization
Thought patterns	increasing impulsivity	increasing magical thinking	external rescue fantasies

Source: Richard J. Gelles and Donileen R. Loseke, *Current Controversies on Family Violence,* p. 173. © 1993 by Sage Publications, Inc. Reprinted by permission of Sage Publications, Inc.

other drugs, such as cocaine, have pharmacological properties that produce violent and abusive behavior. In fact, amphetamines have been, so far, the only drugs that appear to produce increased aggression. Gelles maintains that, although alcohol may be associated with intimate violence, it is not a primary cause of the violence.

If alcohol had the pharmacological property of inducing violence, it would do so in all cultures. Cross-cultural studies of drinking and violence, however, do not support this. In some cultures, individuals who drink become passive; in others, they become aggressive. In our culture, Gelles proposes, drinking disinhibits, permitting violent behavior without responsibility. "The social expectations about drinking and drinking behavior in our society teach people that if they want to avoid being held responsible for their violence, they can either drink before they are violent or at least say they were drunk."

Experiments with college students have found that if the students thought they were being given alcohol, they acted more aggressively than if they were told they were being given a nonalcoholic drink. It is the expectation of the effects of alcohol that influences behavior, not the actual liquor consumed.

Gelles also points out that, although abusive families may also abuse alcohol, an analysis of the drinking behavior at the time of the abuse has found that alcohol was not used immediately prior to the abuse in a majority of cases (see Straus and Kaufman Kantor, below).

The "Drunken Bum" Theory of Wife Beating

Drs. Glenda Kaufman Kantor and Murray Straus tested three commonly held beliefs — alcohol and wife abuse are related, wife abuse is more common in blue-collar than white-collar families, and the acceptance of violence contributes to spousal abuse. In "The 'Drunken Bum' Theory of Wife Beating" (Chapter 12 of *Physical Violence in American Families*, Transaction Publishers, 1990), Kaufman Kantor and Straus found that "the com-

bination of blue-collar occupational status, drinking, and approval of violence is associated with the highest likelihood of wife abuse." Men with these characteristics had a rate of abuse that was 7.8 times greater than the rate of white-collar men who drink little and disapprove of violence.

Kaufman Kantor and Straus emphasized that in three-quarters of the cases (76 percent), alcohol was not being drunk immediately before the instance of wife abuse. In about 14 percent of the instances, only the male was drinking, in 2 percent, only the female, and in 8 percent, they were both drinking. The researchers found a definite correlation between the amount of alcohol consumed and violence. Approximately 6.8 percent of abstainers abused their wives, while almost three times as many binge drinkers (19.2 percent) used violence. However, Kaufman Kantor and Straus stress, "it is extremely important not to overlook the substantial amount of wife abuse by abstainers and moderate drinkers."

Kaufman Kantor and Straus found the major factor that determined wife abuse was whether the individual approved the use of violence against women. Those who approved of a man hitting his wife were far more likely to have hit their wives than those who disapproved. The study concluded,

Finally, even though we found that the rate of wife abuse is seven times greater among binge-drinking blue-collar men who approve of violence, two-thirds of men with these characteristics did *not* assault their wives during the year of the study. Thus, although the results of this study show that there is more than a "kernel of truth" in the drunken bum theory of wife beating, the findings also provide the basis for demythologizing this stereotype.

Donald Dutton (above), in a survey of abusers, found that assaultive men, in general, have very high alcohol use scores (*The Batterer: A Psychological Profile*, Basic Books, New York City, 1995). Men who had an abusive profile were also depressed and anxious and, in response, used alcohol and anger to suppress these uncomfortable feelings. The result Dutton found was a dangerous combination of unhappy, angry men without inhibitions who are at high risk for violence.

Dutton warns, however, that alcohol use and violence do not cause each other — they are both aspects of an abusive personality. "Both are traced back to an earlier aspect of the self. One's personality is formed much sooner than one learns to use alcohol or to hit."

The Relationship Is Complex

In her more recent research ("Refining the Brushstrokes in Portraits of Alcohol and Wife Assaults," *Alcohol and Interpersonal Violence: Fostering Multidisciplinary Perspectives*, National Institute on Alcohol Abuse and Alcoholism Research, Rockville, Maryland, 1993), Glenda Kaufman Kantor warned that considering alcohol simply to be a disinhibitor of violence understates the complexity of the problem. Kaufman Kantor has found that heavy drinking by wives can increase their risk of abuse. She proposes that this may be because, by being intoxicated, the women violate the gender role norms. Furthermore, if they become verbally or physically aggressive under the influence of alcohol, they risk being beaten. Alcoholic women are more likely to initiate violence from their partners than nonalcoholic women are. Kaufman Kantor underscores that this is not to imply that the wife has brought on the abuse by her drinking. "We should not lose sight of the fact that violence is a property of the perpetrator's behavior and not of the victim or object of violence."

Kaufman Kantor and Nancy Asdigian, in "When Women Are Under the Influence: Does Drinking or Drug Use by Women Provoke Beatings by Men?" (*Recent Developments in Alcoholism*, M. Galanter, ed., Plenum Press, New York City, 1997), have found little evidence that women's drinking provokes or precedes aggression by husbands. The authors theorize that women drink or use drugs as a means of coping with violent partners. In households where the husband is a substance abuser and abuses his wife, the wife is also more likely to be a substance abuser. The authors propose that both excess drinking and spousal abuse have common roots in childhood experiences of physical and/or sexual abuse.

Can Treatment Help?

Timothy O'Farrell and Christopher Murphy, in "Marital Violence Before and After Alcoholism Treatment" (*Journal of Consulting and Clinical Psychology*, vol. 63, no. 2, 1995), examined whether behavioral marital therapy (BMT) was helpful in reducing violence in abusive relationships. The percentage of couples who experienced any violent act decreased from about 65 percent before treatment to about 25 percent after BMT. Severe violence dropped from 30 or 35 percent before to about 10 percent after.

After treatment, alcoholics in remittence (recovery) no longer had elevated violence levels. Alcoholics who had relapsed, however, did. Based on women's reports of their partners' violence, 2.6 percent of nondrinking alcoholics, compared to 12.8 percent of the nonalcoholic sample, were violent. In contrast, 34.7 percent of the relapsed alcoholics were violent. While the authors warn that the data do not permit stating that drinking caused the continued violence (other factors may have had an influence), they do indicate that recovery from alcoholism can reduce the risk of marital violence.

In O'Farrell and Murphy's sample, the wives of the men being treated for alcoholism were equally violent. The women's self-reports of violence within the relationship revealed twice the prevalence of violence, four times the prevalence of severe violence, and more frequent substantial violent acts than the wives of nonalcoholics.

PREGNANCY

A review of the research on abuse of pregnant women found studies reporting that between 1 and 20 percent of pregnant women were physically abused by their partners (Julie Gazmararian et al., "Prevalence of Violence Against Pregnant Women," *Journal of the American Medical Asso-*

ciation, vol. 275, no. 24, 1996). Higher abuse rates were reported later in pregnancy — 7.4 to 20 percent in the third trimester. The lowest rates were reported only in a study of women with higher socioeconomic status who were treated in a private clinic. The assailants were mainly intimate partners, former intimate partners, parents, or other family members. The two studies that also examined violence in the period after birth found that violence was more prevalent then than during pregnancy.

Research has not yet confirmed whether violence occurring during pregnancy is specific to the pregnancy or is, rather, a part of an ongoing pattern of violence, nor has research suggested the reasons why pregnant women appear to be at high risk for violence. Gazmararian et al., in an earlier study, found that women with unwanted pregnancies had 4.1 times the risk of experiencing physical violence by a husband or boyfriend during the months prior to delivery than did women with desired pregnancies. Other researchers have also found that violence during pregnancy was greater when the partner was unhappy about the pregnancy or when the pregnancy was unplanned.

Many researchers, including Gazmararian, point out that violence may be more common than the routinely screened physical complications of pregnancy, such as pre-eclampsia (high blood pressure caused by pregnancy), gestational diabetes (pregnancy-induced diabetes), and placenta previa (the placenta blocks the cervix). Screening for violence, at least once each trimester, should be just as routine.

INTERGENERATIONAL ABUSE

Does violence beget violence? Research shows that being the victim of violence is often related to being violent oneself. Dr. Murray Straus cautions against jumping to the conclusion, however, that once violence occurs in the family, it will automatically be passed on to the next generation. Far from all husbands who experienced violence at the hands of their parents grow up to hit their wives.

Not all abused children or abused wives abuse others. Conversely, some violent people grew up in nonviolent families.

Drs. Gelles and Straus, in *Intimate Violence* (Simon and Schuster, New York City, 1989), pointed out that "the learning experience of seeing your mother and father strike one another is more significant than being hit yourself." Experiencing and, more importantly, observing violence as a child teaches three lessons:

* Those who love you are also those who hit you, and those you love are people you can hit.

* Seeing and experiencing violence in your home establishes the moral rightness of hitting those you love.

* If other means of getting your way, dealing with stress, or expressing yourself do not work, violence is permissible.

Gerald T. Hotaling and David B. Sugarman, in ("An Analysis of Risk Markers in Husband to Wife Violence: The Current State of Knowledge," *Violence and Victims*, vol. 1, no. 2, 1989), considered 52 studies of domestic violence for 97 potential risk markers. A risk marker is "an attribute or characteristic that is associated with an increased probability to either the use of husband to wife violence, or the risk of being victimized by husband to wife violence. It is not necessarily a causal factor."

They found only one consistent risk for the victim in all the articles they reviewed. "Women who have been victimized physically by their husbands are more likely to have witnessed violence between parents/caregivers while growing up." Experiencing violence is a weaker predictor of severe husband-to-wife violence than is witnessing violence. Perhaps, the authors suggest, "the use of physical punishment in childrearing is so common in this society that it is no longer useful in predicting future abuse."

Shame

Donald Dutton (Dutton et al., "The Role of Shame and Guilt in the Intergenerational Transmission of Abusiveness," *Violence and Victims*, vol. 10, no. 2, Summer 1995) has developed a theory that being shamed in childhood leads to an assaultive adulthood. The difference between shame and guilt is that shame attacks the global self and produces disturbances in self-identity; guilt produces bad feelings about the condemned behavior, but not the self.

Using a series of psychological tests with 140 battering men, Dutton concluded that shaming experiences in childhood led to the formation of borderline personality organization (identity disturbances, temporary psychotic experiences, and the use of defenses such as projecting responsibility on someone else or "splitting" one's personality). According to Dutton, shaming experiences result in personality disturbances, while parental abusiveness contributes the model behavior for expressing anger. In addition, shame drives the contrition phase of the abuse cycle, leading the batterer to feel remorse and to attempt temporarily to atone for his bad behavior. (See also Chapter V.)

Beaten Child, Beaten Wife

Ronald Simons et al., in "Explaining Women's Double Jeopardy: Factors that Mediate the Association Between Harsh Treatment as a Child and Violence by a Husband" (*Journal of Marriage and the Family*, vol. 55, 1993), examined the link between women who received harsh treatment in childhood and who later married abusive husbands. Simons believes that women who were abused in childhood marry abusive husbands, not because they have learned that violence is permissible, but because they are apt to marry men from similar backgrounds.

Children raised in a violent environment are often noncompliant, defiant, and aggressive and perform poorly in school. Simons has found that the abusive behavior by adults who were abused in childhood is part of a pattern of interpersonal difficulties and antisocial behavior. Persons who have these behavior patterns tend to affiliate with similar individuals.

Simons studied single mothers (they have a much higher likelihood of having had an abusive marriage than women who remain married) and found that harsh treatment by a mother rather than a father was more likely to be associated with an abusive marriage. Simons did not find a connection between traditional gender beliefs (men are supposed to be dominant) or the level of control the women felt they had in their lives (mastery) and abuse. To the contrary, the women in abusive marriages were not submissive; they tended to have a history of aggressive, deviant behavior. Simons theorized that rebellious girls are more likely to date and marry equally antisocial, rebellious young men and end up in abusive relationships.

STRESS AND SPOUSE ABUSE

Murray Straus and Richard Gelles have found, based on the data in their *Family Violence Surveys,* that certain factors — employment status, income, number of children — were often associated with domestic violence in a given family. Families with the lowest incomes, the most children (at least up to five children), and the lowest level of employment of the husband (either unemployed or employed part-time) tended to be most at risk for spouse abuse.

Straus, Gelles, and Steinmetz constructed a scale to measure overall family stress. In addition to income, number of children, and employment, they included illness or death in the family, arrest or conviction of a family member, moving, sexual difficulties, and problems with in-laws. The researchers found a strong correlation between the number of stressful events experienced during the past year and the rate of wife and husband abuse. The greater the stress, the greater the likelihood of abuse.

Women were even more influenced by stress than men were. Families with 10 or more stressful events had a wife-abuse rate of 25 percent and a husband-abuse rate of 50 percent. The authors speculated that differences in family stress might be a major factor in the racial differences they found in family violence. Since minority families are more likely to have lower incomes, more unemployment, more children, and more experience of social discrimination and frustration in daily life, it is not surprising that they suffer from more domestic violence.

Murray Straus, in Chapter 11 of *Physical Violence in American Families*, wrote that stress does not directly cause violence. Stress can also be associated with hypertension, suicide, depression, alcoholism, and many other responses. Straus emphasized that stress and violence occurred because of the link to other factors already discussed in this chapter, such as intergenerational violence, attitudes towards violence and marriage, income, status, and social isolation.

VIOLENCE DECLINES
WITH INCREASING AGE

Murray Straus has observed that women under 31 years old were abused about twice as often as older women. Is this a tendency towards less violence among older people (noticeable also in crime statistics) that comes as a natural result of aging, or is the generation that is now older simply less violent (and always was) than the one that is now young and violent? If the greater violence among the younger age cohorts (groups) is specific to this younger generation, then that violence might continue as they age, contributing to a large overall increase in domestic violence.

Jill Suitor, Karl Pillemer, and Murray Straus, in "Marital Violence in a Life Course Perspective" (Chapter 18 in *Physical Violence in American Families*, Straus and Gelles, eds.), found that both marital conflict and verbal aggression dropped with every 10-year period. Using data from the 1975 and 1985 *Surveys of Family Violence*, they found that the rate of violence in the 18- to 29-year group dropped when they became the 30- to 39-year-old group. For those in the 30- to 39-year-old cohort, their rate dropped when they became the 40- to 49-

year-old group. This drop applied to both men and women in all four age cohorts between 18 and 65.

Suitor, Pillemer, and Straus concluded that marital conflict and verbal aggression decreased with age. They considered several different possible reasons for this, including greater pressure to conform, perhaps because of a greater stake in society, the greater cost of deviating from accepted patterns, and greater expectations. They observed, however, that "it appears that we cannot adequately explain the observed relationship between age and marital violence with the data currently available on this issue." Perhaps, they concluded, at some future time, researchers will find the answer in causes they had not even considered.

CHARACTERISTICS AND
RISK MARKERS

What signs are there to warn a woman that she is dating or living with a potentially violent man? The National Coalition Against Domestic Violence has published a list of predictive behaviors in men that signal violence ("Predictors of Domestic Violence"). The list includes the following:

- Did he grow up in a violent family? Those who come from violent homes have grown up learning that violence is normal behavior.

- Does he tend to use force or violence to "solve" his problems? Does he overreact to little problems and frustrations? Does he punch walls or throw things when he's upset? Is he cruel to animals? Cruelty to animals is a common behavior of men who are cruel to women and children.

- Does he abuse alcohol or other drugs? *Do not think that you can change him.*

- Does he have strong traditional ideas about what a man should be and what a woman should be? Does he think a woman should stay at home, take care of her husband, and follow his wishes and orders?

- Is he jealous of your other relationships — not just of other men that you may know but also of your girlfriends and your family? Does he want to know where you are at all times?

- Does he have access to guns, knives, or other lethal instruments? Does he talk of using them against people or threaten to use them to "get even"?

- Does he expect you to follow his orders or advice? Does he become angry if you do not fulfill his wishes or if you cannot anticipate what he wants?

- Does he go through extreme highs and lows, almost as though he is two different people? Is he extremely kind at one time and extremely cruel at another time?

- When he gets angry, do you fear him? Do you find that not making him angry has become a major part of your life?

- Does he treat you roughly? Does he physically force you to do what you do not want to do?

Risk Markers

Risk markers refer to characteristics that are associated with an increased likelihood of assault; they are not necessarily causes of abuse, although they can be. An analysis by Richard Gelles, Regina Lackner, and Glen Wolfner of men who batter found that homes with two of the following risk markers showed twice as much violence as those with none. In those with seven or more factors, the violence rate was 40 times higher.

- Male is unemployed.

- Male uses illicit drugs.

- Male and female have different religious backgrounds.

- Male saw father hit mother.

- Male and female cohabit and are not married.

- Male has blue-collar occupation, if employed.

- Male did not graduate from high school.

- Male is between 18 and 30 years of age.

- Male or female uses severe violence toward children in home.

- Total family income is below the poverty line.

Gerald Hotaling and David Sugarman looked at risk markers in over 400 studies for their analysis in "A Risk Marker Analysis of Assaulted Wives" (*Journal of Family Violence*, vol. 5, no. 1, 1990) and in "Prevention of Wife Assault" (*Treatment of Family Violence*, Ammerman and Hersen, eds., John Wiley and Sons, New York City, 1990). They found that abused women show no specific personality traits and are no different from nonabused women in terms of age, educational level, race, occupational status, length of time in the relationship, and number of children. A woman's poor self-esteem did not appear to be a risk factor, but rather a consequence of being abused.

Contrary to other researchers, Hotaling and Sugarman found that being abused as a child or seeing a parent abused *did not* associate a woman with being battered as a wife. Instead, severely assaultive males could be distinguished from nonassaultive and verbally abusive men, as well as men who committed minor abuse, by the greater likelihood of having witnessed violence between their parents. In addition, men who engaged in minor physical aggression were more likely to have experienced violence in the past than were men who were verbally abusive.

After careful analysis of the data, Sugarman and Hotaling concluded that the only factor that differentiated abused wives from nonabused wives was the level of marital conflict. Obviously, if a marriage has no conflict, there is no reason to hit one another. While there is some level of conflict in every relationship, it does not necessarily result in violence. Individuals in adequately functioning relationships negotiate their way through disagreements, while individuals in violent relationships lack these skills and resort to violence.

Four factors were most often associated with abuse — marital conflict, the frequency of the husband's drinking, expectations about the division of labor in the relationship, and a measure of educational incompatibility. Sugarman and Hotaling concluded that to understand wife abuse, researchers had to look at the perpetrator's behavior rather than the characteristics of the victim.

Risk Markers and a Continuum of Aggression

David Sugarman et al. used the analysis of risk markers to test the theory that there is a continuum of aggression in husband-to-wife violence that is linked to some of the risk markers ("Risk Marker Analysis of Husband-to-Wife Violence: A Continuum of Aggression," *Journal of Applied Social Psychology*, vol. 26, no. 4, 1996). The risk markers considered were marital conflict, depressive symptoms, alcohol usage, attitude toward interpersonal violence, violence in the family of origin, nonfamily violence level, and socioeconomic status.

Sugarman found that an increase in severity in husband-to-wife violence was associated with increased levels of the husband's depressive symptoms, his greater acceptance of marital violence, and a higher likelihood that he experienced and witnessed family-of-origin violence. In addition, greater alcohol usage and higher levels of nonfamily violence by the couple were linked to greater violence severity. The women's data was very similar to the men's. The same risk factors applied to increased severity of violence for both.

Three risk markers were unique in that they could be either causes or effects of marital violence. Research did not reveal whether depressive symptoms preceded the violence or whether they were the result of the violence. Similarly, the authors were unable to determine if marital discord caused violence or if marital discord increased with violence as an excuse for the behavior. Finally, alcohol can be used by men as an excuse, and women may use it as an escape from violence. On the other hand, drinking may add to the conflict, which increases the violence.

Sugarman concluded that there is a continuum of violence. Those who engage in minor violence do not necessarily use severe violence, but those who use severe violence almost always also use minor violence. The most important implication is that early intervention might prevent more severe abuse. Most battering programs are only initiated after a woman has suffered severe battering. She might be wiser to insist on treatment after suffering only minor slaps or pushing.

CHAPTER IV

THE EFFECTS OF ABUSE — WHY DOES SHE STAY?

One of the most often asked questions concerning abused women is, "Why do they stay?" Not all women do stay. Many leave an abusive situation without turning to the police or public or private support institutions. While their number is unknown, most who leave without asking for help usually have a strong personal support system of friends and family and/or a job so they are not economically dependent on their abusing husbands or companions.

Nonetheless, there can be little question that a large percentage of women remain with their abusers. There are many reasons why women stay, and there are many outcomes to their abusive relationships.

REASONS TO STAY

There are many reasons why women stay in abusive relationships. Some are strictly economic. Many women feel they are better off with a violent husband than facing the challenge of raising and housing children on their own. Some of these considerations include:

- Most women have at least one dependent child who must be taken care of.

- Many are not employed.

- Parents are either distant, unable, or unwilling to help.

- Many have no property that is solely their own.

- Some lack access to cash.

- If the woman leaves, she runs the risk both of being charged with desertion and of losing the children and joint assets.

- She faces a potential decline in living standard for both herself and her children. In fact, children, especially older ones, might resent this decrease in living standard.

- The woman or the children may be in poor health.

Some battered women have what experts have labeled a "traditional ideology," which can include:

- Many women do not believe divorce is a viable alternative; marriage is a permanent commitment.

- Some mothers feel that having both a mother and father is crucial for children, and as long as the husband beats only her, she can put up with it for the children's sake.

- Many women are emotionally dependent on their husbands. They have never relied on themselves, having left their fathers and gone directly to husbands "who took care of them."

- Many women have become isolated from friends and families. Some of this isolation may have been forced on them by jealous and possessive husbands who did not allow them any freedom. Some of it might be self-imposed by women ashamed that the visible signs of wife-beating might be seen by friends or family.

- Many women are trained to be helpless and dependent on a man and are unable to take the initiative to escape from their situation.

- Because many are trained to believe that a "successful marriage" depends on them, many women blame themselves for the abuse. They must have been bad or provocative and, therefore, deserve the physical abuse.

- Many victims have a very low sense of self-esteem and worth.

- Many women rationalize their situation, blaming the abuse on heavy stress, alcohol, problems at work, or unemployment.

- Spouse abuse usually comes in cycles. During the nonabusive periods, the husband is often exceedingly romantic, fulfilling some women's dreams of romantic love. This leads some women to believe that beneath it all she still loves him or that he is basically good or, if only he didn't drink, he would be okay.

The National Resource Center on Domestic Violence assembled an information packet (no date) including "Why She Stays, When She Leaves" (Barbara Hart, from the manual *Stopping the Violence X*, produced by the Pennsylvania Coalition Against Domestic Violence). According to the packet, battered women reported the following reasons for staying or leaving an abusive partner.

- Hope for change: Many abusive men become contrite after beating their spouse. The wife, who is in a committed relationship, often with children, hopes that this time her husband means it. "When the batterer acknowledges the error of his ways, when he breaks down and cries out his despair and concedes the need for dramatic change, hope is often born anew for battered women."

- Isolation: Men who batter are often highly possessive and extremely jealous. They believe they own their partners and are entitled to their exclusive attention and absolute obedience. Batterers isolate their spouses from potential support from family, friends, or institutions because they fear this support will threaten their control.

- Societal denial: Abused women discover that many institutions trivialize their complaints (doctors prescribe tranquilizers, priests recommend prayer, the police do not always remove the abusive husband from the home, etc.). In addition, many violent husbands hide their behavior behind closed doors and appear pleasant in public, leading the woman to fear no one will believe her if she leaves.

- Prevention by the batterer: Batterers may put up barricades to a woman leaving the home. He may threaten (or carry out his threats) to commit suicide, to keep the children from her, to withhold support, or to escalate the violence. In fact, many battered women who are killed by a partner are killed after they have left the relationship.

- Belief in batterer treatment: Many battered women are reluctant to leave a partner while he is in a treatment program. They assume the programs will help their spouses make the profound changes necessary to stop the use of violence. It is crucial that battered women receive full information about the success of treatment programs.

According to Hart, the most likely predictor of whether a separated woman will stay away is whether she has the economic resources to survive without him. It is important, therefore, that a woman learn about child support awards, job training, and other economic opportunities. In many cases, a woman leaves several times before finally separating from her abuser. She is usually testing the responses of the outside community and gathering information before the final break.

The Man's Response

A battered woman's fear of reprisal is very real and well-founded. Dr. Lenore Walker, author of three major books in the field of abuse, wrote in *Terrifying Love: Why Battered Women Kill and How Society Responds* (Harper and Row, New York City, 1989) that a batterer often panics when he thinks the woman is going to end the relationship. In the personal stories women told to Walker, women repeatedly related that after calling the police or asking for a divorce, their partners' violence was reactivated, often worse than before. Angela Browne, author of *When Battered Women Kill*, and Kirk Williams of the Family Research Laboratory, in "Resource Availability for Women at Risk and Partner Homicide" (*Law and Society*, University of New Hampshire, Durham, 1989), found that more than 50 percent of all women homicide victims were murdered by former abusive male partners. (See Chapter II for more recent statistics, from the FBI, on female victims of intimate murder.)

Walker points out that in an abusive relationship, it is not the woman who is crazy, but the man who is desperately dependent on this relationship. "Many battered women believe that they are the sole support of the batterer's emotional stability and sanity, the one link their men have to the normal world. Sensing the batterer's isolation and despair, they feel responsible for his well-being." Dr. Walker claims that almost 10 percent of abandoned batterers committed suicide when their women left them.

LEARNED HELPLESSNESS?

Do women learn to be helpless from their life experiences? Martin Seligman (*On Depression, Development, and Death*, 1975) conducted a famous experiment in which animals randomly shocked in their cages seemingly became totally passive, even when they were shown how to escape. On closer inspection, the researchers discovered that the animals had developed coping skills by lying in their own excrement (an insulator against electrical impulses) in the part of the cage with the least electrical stimulation.

Walker believes that this supports the behavior she has observed in her clients and concluded that "people lose the ability to predict whether their natural responses will protect them after they experience inescapable pain in what appear to be random and variable situations." When a person no longer controls his or her life and does not know what to expect, the person becomes helpless to stop it and takes on coping skills to try to minimize the pain. "Battered women don't attempt to leave the battering situation, even

when it may seem to outsiders that escape is possible, because they cannot predict their own safety; they believe that nothing they do or anyone else does will alter their terrible circumstances."

Based on her research (much of which has focused on women who have murdered their partners as a consequence of severe abuse), Dr. Walker has identified five factors in childhood and seven factors in adulthood that she believes contribute to learned helplessness. The childhood factors include physical or sexual abuse, traditional sex roles, health problems, and periods in the child's life where the child loses control of events, such as a death in the family or frequent moves. Adult factors include patterns of physical and sexual abuse, jealousy and threats of death from the batterer, psychological torture, seeing other abuse committed by the abuser, and drug and alcohol abuse by either partner.

Women Are Not Helpless

Lee Bowker ("A Battered Woman's Problems Are Social, Not Psychological," *Current Controversies on Family Violence*, Gelles and Loseke, eds., Sage Publications, Newbury Park, California, 1994) believes that women trapped in violent marriages are held by conditions in the social system rather than by psychological symptoms. According to Bowker, battered women are not as passive as they are portrayed in abuse literature — they are not always trapped, and they routinely take steps to make their lives safer and to free themselves. He sees "the length of time it took them to free themselves from abuse as a reflection of the intransigence of their husbands' penchant for domination and the lack of support from traditional social institutions."

Bowker analyzed questionnaire answers from 1,000 battered women and found that the women used seven major strategies to end the abuse. The women tried to extract promises from their partners that they would stop the abuse, threatened to call the police or file for divorce, avoided their partners or certain topics of conversations, hid or ran away, tried to talk the man out of it, covered their bodies to protect against blows, and, in some cases, tried to hit back. Of these, the promises to change, with a 54 percent positive reaction, was the most effective strategy, while self-defense was the least effective.

Because of the limited effectiveness of these strategies, most of the women turned to outside sources of help, first to informal sources such as other family members or friends. For most, this was also ineffective. Generally, these women then turned to formal sources of help such as the police, physicians, clergy, lawyers, counselors, women's groups, and shelters. Calling a lawyer or prosecutor was the most effective in ending the battering, followed by women's groups and social service agencies (such as shelters and counseling).

Bowker does not believe, as other experts have suggested, that the loss of self-esteem that appears to trap women in battering relationships paralyzes women. While abused women do lose self-esteem for a time, many escape from their abusive marriages. This fact suggests that when all seems hopeless (hitting bottom), an innate need to save themselves reemerges and propels them to seek escape from their situation. Bowker theorizes that the reason women's groups and shelters are effective in offering these women help is that they bolster personality growth and nurture the woman's return to strength.

Bowker asked the women he surveyed why some chose to stay with a batterer. They responded that there were situations they perceived to be worse than the abusive relationships they were in. Some of the situations the women feared would be worse than their present battering relationships included spousal threats made against other family members and pets, fear of being left homeless without financial resources, the shame of having a failed marriage, and a loss of social identity and one's way of life.

Bowker concluded that because women recover from their feelings of helplessness as they gain strength, battered woman syndrome (BWS) symptoms are fundamentally different from the long-lasting symptoms that characterize most psychiatric disorders. (See below for more on BWS.) Rather, in his interpretation,

[The battered woman syndrome] is a summary term for the many social, psychological, eco-nomic, and physical variables that tend to hold women in abusive relationships for extended periods of time. Learned helplessness arises in oppressive relationships from which the victims cannot easily escape. If some battered women appear to have been taught by their batterers to be helpless, it probably is a signal that they have not yet been taught how to resist this negative indoctrination and how to force abusers to become more egalitarian without necessarily having to leave them or to kill them.

The Battered Woman Syndrome (BWS)

In "The Battered Woman Syndrome Is a Psychological Consequence of Abuse" (also in *Current Controversies*), Lenore Walker claims that battered woman syndrome (BWS) is common among severely abused women and that it is part of the recognized pattern of psychological symptoms called post-traumatic stress disorder (PTSD). Women who suffer BWS learn that they cannot predict whether what they do will result in a particular outcome (learned helplessness). These women cannot reliably determine if a particular response will bring them safety. Walker emphasizes that they do not respond with total helplessness; rather, they narrow their choices, choosing the ones that seem to have the greatest likelihood of success.

Normally, fear and the responses to fear abate on their own when the feared object is removed. People who have suffered a traumatic event that has taken away their power or control often continue to respond to the fear with flashbacks and intrusive thoughts of violence after the event has passed. These symptoms of PTSD can affect anyone whether or not he or she suffers from other psychological problems. A normal person can develop them as a result of adapting to survive abnormal experiences.

Symptoms of PTSD involve changes in the mental state that are made to cope with severe trauma. Symptoms include difficulty in thinking clearly and a pessimistic outlook. The woman's outlook often improves, however, when she achieves some power and control in her life.

PTSD can lead to two forms of memory distortions:

- Intrusive memories of the trauma can magnify the woman's terror.

- Partial amnesia can cause her to forget many of the painful experiences.

Abused women frequently turn to drugs or alcohol to block out intrusive memories. Other symptoms of PTSD include sleep and eating disorders and medical problems associated with high stress.

A LARGER CONTEXT

Evan Stark and Anne Flitcraft, best known for their research on battered women who seek help in medical emergency rooms, see the question of traumatization in a larger context (*Women at Risk*, Sage Publications, Newbury Park, California, 1996). PTSD and BWS have been proposed as the special reactions to events outside the range of usual human experience. Symptoms included in the category of PTSD reactions cover nearly every possible (and contradictory) response to battering — chronic alertness, flashbacks, floods of emotion, detached calm, anger, inability to concentrate, sleep disturbances, indifference, profound passivity, and depression. Over time, the more aggressive symptoms diminish to be replaced by the more passive, constrictive symptoms, making the woman appear helpless.

Stark and Flitcraft question whether these severe psychological reactions are caused by the violence. They believe that the damage is done by the coercive control exercised by the abuser and the larger social institutions that ignore the woman's attempts to seek help. Traditional mental health treatment contributes to the coercion by assigning mutual responsibility or defining the issue in terms of the victim's behavioral problems (her apparent helplessness). Stark and Flitcraft charge that it is easier to undervalue the woman's attempts at autonomy and to suggest that she needs rescuing rather than to support her choices. It is easier to accept an abused woman as a dependent victim than as an aggressive individual with a history of persistent attempts to seek help.

[B]eneficence must be carefully managed with women who alternately feign dependence (as a means of survival), fear it (because it has put them at risk), desperately need genuine interdependence (to support self-esteem), and experience dependence as the antithesis of safety. Despite the frustration of witnessing a client failing to leave a situation we believe puts her in danger, "rescuing" such women only reinforces their sense of not being able to do so for themselves. Worse, when benign paternalism fails, therapists often behave like rejected lovers, alternately acting out in the treatment process or unwittingly identifying with the assailant's anger.

Neil S. Jacobson and colleagues, who have studied men's physical response to anger (see Chapter VI), have found that both men and women in violent relationships are angry, belligerent, and contemptuous ("Affect, Verbal Content, and Psychophysiology in the Arguments of Couples with a Violent Husband," *Journal of Consulting and Clinical Psychology*, vol. 62, no. 5, 1994). Control, however, appears to be a crucial factor. Men were more domineering and more defensive, while women showed more tension, fear, and sadness. In other words, the men were more controlling and less likely to acknowledge that there was anything wrong with them.

Jacobson theorized that the woman's intense anger, combined with fear and sadness, may be part of her apparent helplessness. These women are hostile to their husbands but, because of the physical abuse, they are afraid of them. "These results simply illustrate that the battered women in our sample, despite their history of being beaten, had not been beaten into submission."

The Battered Woman's Home Is Her Prison

Noga Avni of the Department of Criminology of Bar-Ilan University in Israel compared the battered woman's home to an institution which places physical barriers (locks, walls, etc.) between a person and the outside world, similar to nursing homes, orphanages, mental asylums, prisons, army and work camps, and monasteries ("Battered Wives: The Home as a Total

TABLE 4.1

Similarities Between the Battered Wife's Home and Total Institutions

Total Institution	Battered Woman
Rules are made by the staff who are in authority; recalcitrance is punished.	House rules are made by the husband—the sole authority in the family; recalcitrance is punished.
Confinement to the institution: all the daily activities are carried out within it.	Confinement to the home; most of her daily activities take place within it.
The inmates have only limited contact with the outside world; consequently staff feel superior and the inmates inferior.	Limited contact with her family and friends; consequently the husband feels superior to his wife.
Mortification of the inmate's self.	Mortification of self due to the husband's suspicion.
Constant exposure to the staff and to the other inmates.	Constant exposure to her husband's surveillance.
Outside interference can not protect the inmate from the threat to his physical existence.	The private nature of the home precludes interference and protection of outsiders.

Source: Noga Avni, "Battered Wives: The Home as a Total Institution," *Violence and Victims*, vol. 6, no. 2, 1991. Copyright © Springer Publishing Company, Inc., New York 10012. Used by permission.

Institution," *Violence and Victims*, vol. 6, no. 2, 1991). In institutions, the staff tends to feel superior and self-rightcous, while the inmates feel weak and inferior. The inmates are detached from the outside world, while the staff has access to and is in control of what outside information is made available to the inmates. Table 4.1 compares the total institution and the battered woman.

Characteristics of the Women

Avni interviewed 35 women who came to seek protection in a shelter. They ranged in age from 19 to 57 years old. Only two had completed high school; the rest had completed from four to eight years of elementary school. In half the families, neither spouse worked, and the family depended on welfare. In 25 percent of the cases, the wife was the sole provider (95 percent of them worked as cleaners). The final quarter were supported by an employed husband with an average income. In all the cases, the women had been severely abused during their marriages. For 87 percent of the women, the first violent incident took place within the first month of marriage. Only four of the women had been battered during courtship.

Avni believes that severely battered women go through a process in their marriages similar to that experienced by inmates in institutions. An inmate who resists is punished until he or she submits. The women who were battered in the first month of marriage were undergoing an obedience test, and when they failed to resist, they tacitly (in an unspoken manner) confirmed their husbands' role as "boss" of the house. The relationship is based on the inequality of the relationship — the husband is the master, and the wife is his property.

As master, the husband establishes the rules of the house. Women must fulfill the role of housekeeper, but the men are not obliged to be the providers. Women are not permitted to say what they think or to disagree with their spouses, while men are permitted to say whatever they please. Finally, women are not permitted to bring people into the house or to go where they please, although their husbands are free to do both. Avni compares these women to citizens in totalitarian regimes who are isolated from any outside influences or ideas.

The Husband's Control

All the women in this study married their husbands when they were very young (half were not yet 17 years old) and had never been independent or taken responsibility for themselves. This lack of experience led them to depend on their husbands for support. By restricting the woman's movements, the husband cut off her access to information, which helped him to control his jealousy and suspicion, emotions that frequently haunt highly abusive men.

Avni described the man's constant surveillance of his wife as psychological torture for her. These women reported they were frequently accused of merely looking at another man, which was justification for a beating; any suspicion of an actual relationship with another man would surely result in death. The women were constantly on guard and became so insecure that they further isolated themselves and became afraid to go out. Since the accusations were false, the woman's behavior could never be sufficiently modified to appease him. The women began to believe their husbands' accusations because they could not deal with the conflict between what they knew and what they were told — a process which Avni refers to as brainwashing.

For the battered woman, the home is the place of maximum exposure. Intimacy and constant contact allow endless opportunities for control. The other side of this is that the home is a place of privacy. The husband can do what he pleases behind closed doors, and the woman maintains the privacy because she is too ashamed to tell anyone what is truly happening.

Avni concluded that it is very difficult for a woman who is imprisoned in her home with no individual freedom to seek help because she has been physically and psychologically locked into her situation.

DIFFERENT PERCEPTIONS OF REALITY

Self-Blame

Researchers have found that women who return to abusers have higher levels of self-blame than women who have left abusive relationships. Self-blaming women believe that if they caused the abuse, they could or should be able to prevent it by changing their own behavior. In "The Relationship Between Violence, Social Support, and Self-Blame in Battered Women," Ola Barnett et al. found that battered women had higher levels of self-blame and female aggression and that they perceived lower levels of social support than non-battered women (*Journal of Interpersonal Violence*, vol. 11, no. 2, June 1996).

Escalating levels of violence in a relationship often lead to greater use of violence by the woman in self-defense and in retaliation. This can result in greater self-blame as the woman faults herself for the violence in the house. This can also deter her from seeking help and encourage her to think there is no help for her because she is the cause of the violence. Further, outside sources of help may well be less helpful if the woman presents the problem as her fault, and therefore, there is less social support for a self-blaming woman. This vicious cycle must be broken by outsiders, who can help the woman shift the blame to her abusive mate. In fact, some researchers suggest that, while women may blame themselves when the abuse begins, as the frequency and severity of the abuse increases over time, they do begin to place the blame on the perpetrators.

The Role of Alcohol

The association between alcohol and abusive relationships has been well documented (see Chapter III). Many batterers abuse alcohol and exhibit personality traits similar to alcoholics. One similarity is that both alcoholics and batterers tend to increase the severity and frequency of their destructive behavior over time, while minimizing the consequences of their behavior. When a woman excuses her partner's violent behavior because she attributes it to alcohol abuse, she may be less likely to leave the relationship.

In "Excuses, Excuses: Accounting for the Effects of Partner Violence on Marital Satisfaction and Stability," (*Violence and Victims*, vol. 10, no. 4, Winter 1995), Jennifer Katz et al. found that women who held a spouse responsible for his negative behavior were less satisfied with their marriages than women who attributed the behavior to something about their spouses that was not likely to change. Alcohol abuse was seen as a part of his personality, and the wife was, therefore, more tolerant of his negative behavior.

It's Not So Bad

Tracy Herbert et al. compared the perceptual differences of women who left abusive relationships and those who stayed ("Coping with an Abusive Relationship: How and Why Do Women Stay?" *Journal of*

Marriage and the Family, vol. 53, 1991). The authors theorized that all relationships are a mixture of good and bad elements, but as long as a person perceives that the good outweighs the bad, he or she will maintain the relationship.

The authors recruited 130 women to answer a questionnaire on how they viewed their relationships. They suspected that the women who stayed would stress the positive aspects of their marriages and minimize the negative because as long as they could maintain a positive image, they would remain. Studies have found that women are often finally convinced to go to a shelter when the husband's abuse suddenly becomes more severe or the balance of his kindness to the woman after the beating decreases, thereby forcing a change in the woman's perceived reality.

The women reported the frequency of abuse was, on average, once a month or less, and 78 percent reported verbal and physical abuse. Of these, 77 percent felt the verbal abuse was as difficult or more difficult to deal with than the physical abuse. The more frequently the woman was verbally abused, the less capable she was of seeing her relationship as positive. One woman wrote, "Bruises, cuts, etc., heal within a short time. When you listen to someone tell you how rotten you are and how nobody wants you day after day, you begin to believe it. Verbal abuse takes years to heal, but before that happens, it can ruin every part of your life."

The researchers did not find evidence that the women were trapped by low self-esteem or the length of the relationship. The three variables they found most closely linked to the women who stayed, compared to the women who left, were that those who stayed:

• Perceived more positive aspects to their relationships.

• Saw little or no change in the frequency or intensity of the battering or love that their husbands expressed.

• Felt their relationships were not as bad as they might be.

WHAT CAN A WOMAN DO?

Richard Gelles and Murray Straus found that only 13 percent of the severely abused women in their 1985 *National Family Violence Survey* felt that things were completely hopeless and out of their control. That leaves a large percentage of women who did seek help in different ways. In *Intimate Violence: The Definitive Study of the Causes and Consequences of*

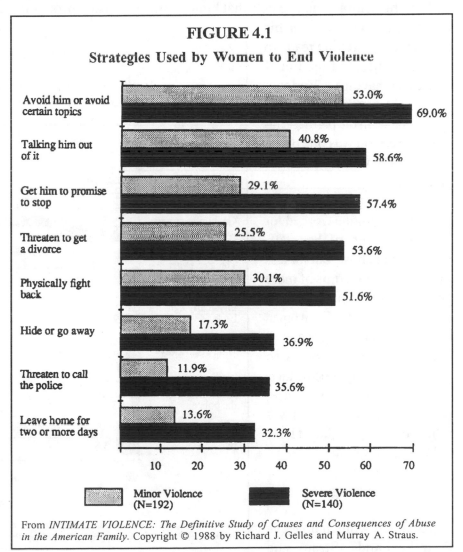

FIGURE 4.1

Strategies Used by Women to End Violence

Strategy	Minor Violence (N=192)	Severe Violence (N=140)
Avoid him or avoid certain topics	53.0%	69.0%
Talking him out of it	40.8%	58.6%
Get him to promise to stop	29.1%	57.4%
Threaten to get a divorce	25.5%	53.6%
Physically fight back	30.1%	51.6%
Hide or go away	17.3%	36.9%
Threaten to call the police	11.9%	35.6%
Leave home for two or more days	13.6%	32.3%

From *INTIMATE VIOLENCE: The Definitive Study of Causes and Consequences of Abuse in the American Family*. Copyright © 1988 by Richard J. Gelles and Murray A. Straus.

Abuse in the American Family (Simon and Schuster, New York City, 1988), Gelles and Straus found that women who experienced more severe violence and grew up in more violent homes were more likely to stay. Women who were less educated, had fewer job skills, and were more likely to be unemployed were more likely to stay. Women with young children were also more likely to put up with abuse.

Avoidance

Gelles and Straus interviewed 192 women who had suffered minor violence and 140 who had suffered severe violence and asked what long-range strategies they used to avoid violence. (See Figure 4.1.) Fifty-three percent of the minor violence victims and 69 percent of the severe violence victims learned to avoid issues they thought would anger their partners. "I have learned what gets him mad. I also know, just by looking at him, when he gets that kind of weird, screwed-up expression on his face, that he is getting ready to be mad.... Most of the time I figure I just have to walk on eggshells." (Many women reported that a change in the partner's facial expression was one of the first signs he was about to start abusing her.)

This technique worked for about 68 percent of those suffering minor abuse, but for less than a third of victims of more severe abuse. Avoidance is an exhausting strategy. The woman can never let down her guard, and the tension becomes so great that sometimes being hit is actually a relief. One woman reported, "When he hit me, I was relieved. At least I didn't have to be so tense anymore."

Leaving

Battered women do leave their husbands. Straus and

Gelles found that 70 percent had left their spouses in the year preceding the interview. Only about half of those who left, however, reported that this was a "very effective" method of ending the abuse. In fact, for 1 out of 8, it made things worse. Batterers put incredible pressure on their partners to return, and if they did, they often were abused more severely than before as revenge or because the man learned once again that he could get away with it. Women who returned also risked losing the aid of personal and public support systems because these agencies saw their help or advice was useless or ignored.

Just Say No

The most effective means of stopping violence is not to permit it from the start. Many believe that there is real truth to the statement that men abuse because they can. A wife who will not permit herself to be beaten from the very first act of minor abuse like a

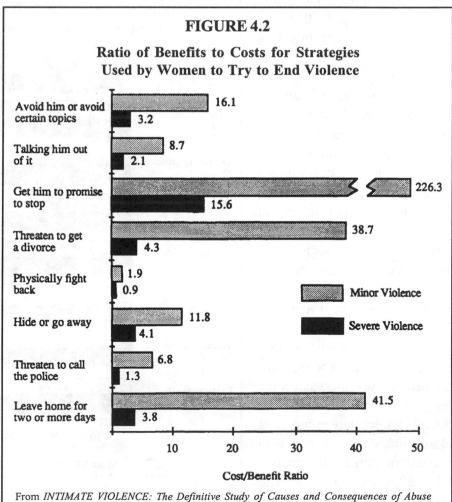

FIGURE 4.2

Ratio of Benefits to Costs for Strategies Used by Women to Try to End Violence

From *INTIMATE VIOLENCE: The Definitive Study of Causes and Consequences of Abuse in the American Family.* Copyright © 1988 by Richard J. Gelles and Murray A. Straus.

slap or a push is the most successful at stopping it. Gelles and Straus worked out a "cost-benefit" ratio by dividing the percent of women who said a strategy was effective by the percent who said it made things worse.

Figure 4.2 shows that "get him to promise to stop," as simplistic as it sounds, was, by far, the most effective strategy, especially in cases of minor violence, which is how most severe abuse starts. Threatening to divorce or leaving home worked in about 40 percent of the minor abuse cases, but in less than 5 percent of the severe abuse situations. Physically fighting back was the most unsuccessful method — it worked in 1.9 percent of the minor abuse cases and not even 1 percent of the severe abuse cases. One woman explained, "He hit me when I was nice and tried to reason. I shouldn't have been too surprised that he hit me when I hit him back."

Empowerment of Battered Women

According to Desmond Ellis and Lori Wight ("Estrangement, Interventions, and Male Violence Toward Female Partners," *Violence and Victims*, vol. 12, no. 1, Spring 1997), abused women want the violence to stop, and most, if not all, attempt to do something to stop it. They found evidence showing that empowerment of the abused female partner was related to a decrease in the likelihood of further violence. Interventions they recommend to promote gender equality include

- Social service agencies (counseling/shelters), which provide information and support.

- Mediation, which facilitates the women's control over the process.

- Prosecution with a drop-charge option, also facilitating control by female victims.

- Separation, which indicates the women's strength in decision-making.

Ellis and Wight found that separation/divorce is one of the most effective strategies for ending the abuse. Postseparation violence, according to these researchers, varies with the type of legal separation/divorce proceedings. Those who participated in mediation, prior to the separation, were less likely to be harmed, either physically or emotionally, than those whose separation was negotiated by lawyers. Restraining orders and protection orders were found to be relatively ineffective in protecting female partners.

CHAPTER V

RAPE AND SEXUAL HARASSMENT

AROUND THE WORLD

It went on for hours. I don't know how many policeman came through the room. It could have been fifty. I will never forget their laughter, their shouting. I cried, I prayed, I asked God why me, a respectable woman, a grandmother, who had never known any man's body except my husband's. — Ahmedi Begum, a Pakistani woman

These men cannot be punished. It will give a bad name to the police if they are. — A senior police official commenting on the Begum case

Historically, women have often been seen as the property of men. Sexual abuse of a woman was more a violation of a man's property than a violation of a woman's "bodily integrity." Therefore, until recently, rape laws were a means of protecting a man's, or family's, property. However, primarily through the efforts of women's advocacy groups around the world, rape is no longer seen as a violation of family honor but as an abuse and violation of women. In most countries, rape is now considered a crime.

According to the United Nations "Declaration of the Eradication of Violence Against Women" (UN Resolution 48/104, December 1993), violence against women includes "any act of gender-based violence that results in, or is likely to result in, physical, sexual, or psychological harm or suffering to women, including threats of such acts, coercion, or arbitrary deprivation of liberty, whether occurring in public or private life." The declaration specifically mentions marital rape, sexual abuse of female children, trafficking in women (selling her into slavery or into prostitution or both), forced prostitution, and other acts.

In many countries, only women of "good character" deserve protection from rape. In some Latin American countries, the law only recognizes rape of chaste women. These attitudes are generally based on the concept of rape as the defilement of a virgin. Traditionally, legal recourse required the offender to compensate the girl's father for her lost value in the marriage market.

Pakistan has perhaps the harshest attitudes towards rape in the world. Any sex outside of marriage (*zina*) is against the law, resulting in the arrest of the raped woman rather than the rapist. In a Karachi court, about 15 percent of rape trials result in the woman being charged and imprisoned. A staff nurse in a Karachi prison was raped by a patient and his two friends. Although she did not go to the police, the men reported her for *zina*. The judge found that if she were a "decent" woman, she would not work at night and sentenced her to five years in prison, five lashes, and a fine equivalent to a year's salary.

The Pakistani court uses a finger test to assess a woman's virtue — if two fingers can fit in the woman's vagina, sex must be habitual and her testimony is discounted. According to the Women's Action Forum, a women's rights organization, an estimated 75 percent of all women in Pakistani jails are there on charges of *zina*, many because they were raped. Once in police custody, about 72 percent are raped again, this time by the police. Human Rights Watch estimates that at least 1,500 Pakistani women are in prison on charges of *zina*.

The Purpose of Rape

Punitive rape is sometimes practiced in countries where men resent women taking initiative or power. In Latin America, feminists contend that women are raped as a way to force them back into their traditional sphere of home and children. In India, a leader of the Women's Development Programme (an organization to help women start businesses) was gang-raped in front of her husband by men who disapproved of her campaigning against child marriages.

In most wars throughout history, rape has been practiced as a tool of war or an inherent right of victorious forces. In 1993, for the first time, the United Nations passed a resolution identifying rape as a war crime. Recent cases of documented wartime rape have occurred in Liberia, Rwanda, El Salvador, Guatemala, Kuwait, the former Yugoslavia, and Bangladesh.

There is little information on the rate of rape, especially in developing countries. Just the problem of defining rape makes data collection nearly impossible. Mary Koss, Lori Heise, and Nancy Russo, in "The Global Health Burden of Rape" (*Psychology of Women Quarterly*, vol. 18, 1994), presented statistics on sexual assault and rape for different countries. At least 60 percent of the victims in each country reportedly knew their victimizers, and between one-third and nearly two-thirds were girls under 15 years old (Table 5.1). Koss et al. detailed the many ways rape can affect societies around the world, including suicide, murder, pregnancy, AIDS, disability, and healthy years of life lost.

MARITAL RAPE

When you're raped by a stranger, you have to live with a frightening nightmare.

When you're raped by your husband, you have to live with your rapist. — David Finkelhor

It was very clear to me. He raped me. He ripped off my pajamas, he beat me up. I mean, some scum bag down the street would do that to me. So to me it wasn't any different because I was married to him, it was rape — real clear what it was. It emotionally hurt worse. I mean you can compartmentalize it as stranger rape—you were at the wrong place at the wrong time. You can manage to get over it differently. But here you're at home with your husband, and you don't expect that. I was under constant terror even if he didn't do it. — A victim of marital rape

Rape, although it involves the genitals, has little to do with the sexual relations usually associated with love and marriage. Rape is an act of violence by one person against another; it is an act of power that aims to hurt at the most intimate level. Rape is a violation of a woman whether it occurs on the street at the hands of a stranger or within the home at the hands of an abusive husband.

TABLE 5.1
Statistics on sexual crimes, selected countries[a]

City or country	Percent of perpetrators known to victim	Percent of victims 15 years and under	Percent of victims 10 years and under
Lima, Peru	60	—	18[c]
Malaysia	68	58	18[b]
Mexico City	67	36	23
Panama City	63	40	—
Papua New Guinea	—	47	13[d]
Santiago, Chile[e]	72	58	32[c]
United States	78	62[f]	29

Note: Data are from the following sources: Malaysia data (Consumer's Association, 1988); Mexico City data (COVAC, 1990 & *Carpeta Basica*, 1991. Mexico City: Procurador de Justicia del Distrito Federal de Mexico); Panama City data (Perez, 1990); Peru data (Portugal, 1988); Papua New Guinea data (Riley, 1985, as cited in Bradley, 1990); Chile data (Avendano & Vergara, 1992); United States data (National Victims Center, 1992). These data have appeared previously in a report commissioned by the World Bank (1993).
[a]Studies include rape and sexual assaults such as attempted rape and molestation except for U.S. data which includes only completed rapes. [b]Percentage of survivors age 6 and younger. [c]Percentage of survivors age 9 and younger. [d]Percentage of survivors age 7 and younger. [e]Based on 5-year averages derived from crimes reported to the Legal Medical Service, 1987–1991; Anuario Estadistico del Servicio Medico Legal de Chile. [f]Percentage of survivors age 17 and younger.

Source: Mary P. Koss et al., "The Global Health Burden of Rape," *Psychology of Women Quarterly*, vol. 18, 1994

The National Violence Against Women Survey (NVAW, 1996), sponsored jointly by the National Institute of Justice and the Centers for Disease Control and Prevention, estimates that 1.5 million women and 834,700 men are raped and/or physically assaulted by an intimate partner each year. (See Table 5.2.) Of all surveyed women age 18 years and older, 1.5 percent said they were raped and/or physically assaulted by a current or former spouse, cohabiting partner, or date in the previous 12 months, compared to 0.9 percent of all surveyed men.

As previous reports have consistently shown, the NVAW survey confirms that violence against women is primarily partner violence. Figure 5.1 shows that 76 percent of the women who were raped and/or physically assaulted since the age of 18 were assaulted by a current or former husband, cohabiting partner, or date. Nine percent were assaulted by a relative other than a husband, and 17 percent were assaulted by an acquaintance, such as a friend, neighbor, or coworker. Rape or assault by a stranger accounted for 14 percent of incidents. By comparison, men were primarily raped and physically assaulted by strangers and acquaintances rather than intimate partners.

Some researchers estimate that close to 2 million incidents of marital rape occur each year and that this form of rape is more common than both stranger and acquaintance rape. The definition of rape used and the way the questions in the survey are presented affect the responses. The common factor in marital rape is that the sexual activity was coerced from a wife unwilling to perform it. An overview of the research on marital rape tends to indicate that 7 to 14 percent of women have been raped by a partner.

TABLE 5.2

Persons Raped or Physically Assaulted by an Intimate Partner in in Previous 12 Months by Sex of Victim

| | In Previous 12 Months[a] | | | |
| | Percentage | | Number[b] | |
Type of Violence	Women (n=8,000)	Men (n=8,000)	Women (100,697,000)	Men (92,748,000)
Rape	0.2	–[d]	201,394	–[d]
Physical assault[c]	1.3	0.9	1,309,061	834,732
Rape and/or physical assault[c]	1.5	0.9	1,510,455	834,732

a. Intimate partner includes current and former spouses, opposite-sex cohabiting partners, same-sex cohabiting partners, dates, and boyfriends/girlfriends.

b. Based on estimates of men and women in the United States aged 18 years and older, U.S. Bureau of the Census, Current Population Survey, 1995.

c. Differences between women and men are statistically significant: p-value ≤ .05.

d. The number of men rape victims was insufficient to reliably calculate prevalence estimates.

FIGURE 5.1

Distribution of Adult Rape and Physical Assault Victims by Victim-Perpetrator Relationship and Sex of Victim

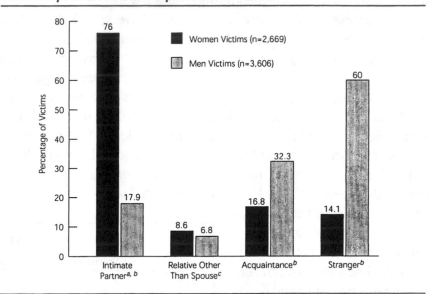

a. Intimate partner includes current and former spouses, same-sex cohabitating partners, opposite-sex cohabitating partners, dates, and boyfriends/girlfriends.

b. Differences between women and men are statistically significant: p-value ≤ .001.

c. Differences between women and men are statistically significant: p-value ≤ .01.

Note: Total percentages by sex of victim exceed 100 because some victims had multiple perpetrators.

Source of table and figure: *Prevalence, Incidence, and Consequences of Violence Against Women: Findings from the National Violence Against Women Survey*, National Institute of Justice and Centers for Disease Control and Prevention, Washington, DC, 1998

In *Rape in Marriage* (Indiana University Press, Bloomington, Indiana, 1990), D. Russell reported on the interviews of a randomly selected, representative community sample of 930 women in the San Francisco area. Of all the women who had ever been married, 14 percent had been raped by their spouses at least once. Of this number, one-third reported being raped once, one-third reported between two and 20 incidents, and one-third said they had been raped by their spouses more than 20 times.

According to Russell, the first incident of rape usually occurred in the first year of marriage. Although marital rape occurred more frequently in a spousal relationship where emotional and physical abuse was present, it could also happen in marriages where there was little other violence.

M. A. Whatley ("For Better or Worse: The Case of Marital Rape," *Violence and Victims*, vol. 8, no. 1, 1993) reviewed the research on marital rape and found that it was most likely in violent marriages and in those with an alcoholic husband. Couples who married because the wife was pregnant also had higher rates of marital rape, perhaps because the husband felt "trapped" and took his revenge by raping his wife. High levels of exposure to pornography have also been linked to increased sexual aggression in marriage. Women who have several children, were never employed before marriage, and have less education are more likely to be victims of marital rape.

State laws on marital rape vary. By 1993, marital rape had become a crime in all 50 states. In 33 states, however, there are exemptions from prosecution, for example, when the husband has not used force or if the woman is legally unable to consent because of a severe disability (temporary, permanent, physical, or mental). The tendency still exists to consider marital rape far less serious than either stranger or acquaintance rape.

Marital Rape Categories

Louis J. Shiro and Kersti Yllö, in the Maine State Bar Association *Bar Bulletin* (vol. 19, no. 5, September 1985), estimated that perhaps 10 to 14 percent of all married women have been raped by their husbands. Shiro and Yllö noted that "when talking about a problem of these dimensions, it is no more fair to say that marital rape is always a savage attack than it is to say that it is always a bedroom squabble. We are talking about a spectrum of which both of these are a part."

Shiro and Yllö interviewed 50 assault victims and, based on their findings, divided the rapes into three categories — battering rapes, force-only rapes, and obsessive rapes. About 45 percent of the women suffered battering rapes. In these rapes, the batterer used sexual assault as another brutal form of abuse against his wife. Because of the particularly demeaning and degrading nature of some of the acts, this violent behavior appears more brutal than the other violence the abuser may have heaped on his wife. The battering rapist is often angry and may have an alcohol or other drug problem.

Shiro and Yllö found non-battering, force-only rapes "substantially different." Non-battering rape generally occurred "in more middle class marriages where there was much less of a history of violence and abuse" and involved about 45 percent of the cases. The immediate reason for the rape was often a specifically sexual reason — for example, how often to have sex and what kinds of sex. The force used was much more restrained — enough to force intercourse, but not enough to cause severe injury. "These rapes," observed Shiro and Yllö, "seemed to be motivated less by anger than by a desire to assert power, establish control, teach a lesson, show who was boss."

The final category, obsessive marital rape, involved about 10 percent of those interviewed. In these instances, the husband had very unusual, often deviant, sexual demands (often involving other men or violence) that the wife was refusing to fulfill. This type of rapist may be heavily involved in pornography.

Raquel Kennedy Bergen (*Wife Rape*, Sage Publications, Thousand Oaks, California, 1996) extensively interviewed 40 victims of wife rape. Most (55 percent) had been raped 20 times or more during their marriages, while 17 percent had experienced this abuse only once.

Most of the women in this sample reported that their husbands felt a sense of ownership that gave them sexual rights to their wives' bodies. Because of their perceived entitlement, the men did not interpret their behavior as rape. Several women also believed that the abuse was an attempt to punish them and that the rape was an attempt to control and assert power.

ACQUAINTANCE RAPE

According to a number of highly publicized studies, young women are at high risk of being sexually assaulted by acquaintances or boyfriends. Studies have found rates ranging from a low of 15 percent for rape to 78 percent for unwanted sexual aggression. Experts surmise that acquaintance rape is especially underreported because the victimized woman believes nothing can or will be done, and she is unsure of how to define what has happened. (Was it my fault because I led him to believe I wanted it?)

Aggression Levels

David Riggs and K. Daniel O'Leary analyzed aggression questionnaires from 345 undergraduates and found that, overall, rates of aggression by men and women were quite similar ("Aggression Between Heterosexual Dating Partners," *Journal of Interpersonal Violence*, vol. 11, no. 4, December 1996). About one-third of both men and women reported engaging in physical aggression in their current relationships, and nearly all respondents had used at least one form of verbal aggression (Table 5.3).

Men were somewhat more likely to use serious forms of aggression (for example, 5 percent of men physically forced their partner to have sex, compared to 1.7 percent of women), while women were twice as likely to slap a partner and more than five times as likely to kick, hit, or bite. On the verbal scale, women were more likely to have engaged in nearly all forms of aggression. Riggs and O'Leary admitted that their research did not reveal how much of the high level of aggression shown by women was in self-defense.

TABLE 5.3
Rates of Overall Aggression and Specific Aggressive Acts

Aggressive Act	Men (%)	Women (%)
Physical aggression		
push, grab, or shove partner	25.0	28.1
slap partner	9.0	18.2
kick, bite or hit partner	2.5	13.2
choke partner	5.0	3.7
physically force partner to have sex	5.0	1.7
beat up partner	3.4	2.9
threatened partner with knife or gun	3.4	2.5
any physically aggressive act	30.0	33.6
Verbal agression		
insulted or swore at partner	60.5	71.9
refused to give partner sex or affection	42.0	65.8
sulked or refused to talk about a problem	79.0	82.6
stomped out of the room or house	56.3	63.2
done or said something to spite partner	64.7	67.8
threatened to break-up with partner	39.5	47.1
threatened to throw something at partner	19.3	22.3
thrown, hit or kicked some object	46.2	26.0
any verbally aggressive act	93.3	97.5

Source: David S. Riggs and K. Daniel O'Leary, "Aggression Between Heterosexual Dating Partners: An Examination of a Casual Model of Courtship Aggression," *Journal of Interpersonal Violence*, vol. 11, no. 4, December 1996

Sexual Coercion

Two recent studies have examined the frequencies of the use of sexual coercion in dating relationships (Lisa Waldner-Haugrud and Brian Magruder, "Male and Female Sexual Victimization in Dating Relationships: Gender Differences in Coercion Techniques and Outcomes," and Michèle Poitras and Francine Lavoie, "A Study of Prevalence of Sexual Coercion in Adolescent Heterosexual Dating Relationships in a Quebec Sample," both in *Violence and Victims*, vol. 10, nos. 3 and 4, 1995).

The first study found a "phenomenal" amount of sexual coercion reported by 422 college students. Only 17 percent of the females and 27 percent of the males reported never experiencing any of the coercion techniques. The most common techniques experienced by both sexes were persistent touching and the use of alcohol and drugs. Together these methods comprised more than half the reported incidents of coercion. Women were more likely to experience unwanted sexual behavior as a result of detainment, persistent touching, lies, and being held down. (See Table 5.4.)

The Quebec study by Poitras and Lavoie questioned 644 adolescents between 15 and 19 years of age. The most frequently occurring unwanted sexual experiences were kissing, petting, and fondling. Verbal coercion was the most frequently used technique. Two in 5 girls reported sexual contact through verbal coercion, and 1 in 5 reported intercourse through verbal coercion. Approximately 1 in 10 females reported intercourse through the use of force or alcohol or drugs. Boys rarely reported the use of force, although about 2.3 percent reported attempted penetration after giving their partners drugs or alcohol, and 2.9 percent reported intercourse as a result of verbal coercion. (See Table 5.5.) The authors noted that some of the large differences in the reported rates of girls sustaining (being the recipient of) coercion and boys inflicting it can be attributed to the fact that adolescent girls frequently date older men who may be more likely than boys to engage in coercive behaviors.

College Rape

According to *Preventing Alcohol-Related Problems on Campus: Acquaintance Rape* (Higher Education Center for Alcohol and Other Drug Prevention, Newton, Massachusetts, 1997), rape is the most common crime committed on college campuses. A 1985 survey of 6,159 students from 32 colleges found that 17 percent of the women had experienced rape or attempted rape in the past year. One out of every 15 male students admitted he had raped or attempted to rape a female student during the past year. These numbers may be low since students frequently do not report attempted or completed acquaintance rapes. In fact, many female students who have been raped drop out of school.

In "Acquaintance Rape and the College Social Scene" (Sally Ward et al., *Family Relations*, vol. 40, January 1991), the researchers surveyed 518 women

TABLE 5.4

Frequencies of Sexual Behaviors by Coercive Methods for Males and Females

Coercive Methods	Males f	Males (%)	Females f	Females (%)
Intoxication				
Not applicable	85	(42.9)	86	(39.3)
Kissing	23	(11.6)	21	(9.6)
Fondling	44	(22.1)	67	(30.6)
Intercourse	46	(23.2)	45	(20.5)
Coercion totals	113	(56.9)	156	(60.7)
Terminate				
Not applicable	172	(86.4)	189	(86.3)
Kissing	11	(5.5)	11	(5.0)
Fondling	7	(3.5)	5	(2.3)
Intercourse	9	(4.5)	14	(6.4)
Coercion totals	27	(13.5)	30	(13.7)
Blackmail				
Not applicable	182	(91.4)	210	(95.5)
Kissing	8	(4.0)	3	(1.4)
Fondling	6	(3.0)	1	(.5)
Intercourse	3	(1.5)	5	(2.3)
Coercion totals	17	(8.5)	9	(4.2)
Guilt				
Not applicable	154	(77.3)	151	(70.0)
Kissing	15	(7.5)	8	(3.7)
Fondling	13	(6.5)	25	(11.6)
Intercourse	17	(8.5)	32	(14.8)
Coercion totals	45	(22.5)	65	(30.1)
Detainment				
Not applicable	177	(88.9)	174	(79.8)
Kissing	15	(7.5)	23	(10.6)
Fondling	7	(3.5)	6	(2.8)
Intercourse	0	(0.0)	15	(6.9)
Coercion totals	22	(11.0)	44	(20.3)
Touching				
Not applicable	97	(48.7)	66	(30.1)
Kissing	36	(18.1)	54	(24.7)
Fondling	39	(19.6)	73	(33.4)
Intercourse	27	(13.6)	26	(11.9)
Coercion totals	102	(51.3)	153	(70.0)
Use of lies				
Not applicable	142	(71.4)	126	(58.0)
Kissing	13	(6.5)	15	(6.9)
Fondling	19	(9.5)	37	(17.0)
Intercourse	25	(12.6)	40	(18.3)
Coercion totals	57	(28.6)	92	(42.2)
False promises				
Not applicable	171	(86.0)	185	(85.0)
Kissing	9	(4.5)	7	(3.2)
Fondling	9	(4.5)	10	(4.6)
Intercourse	10	(5.0)	16	(7.3)
Coercion totals	28	(14.0)	33	(15.0)

(continued)

and 337 men at a large university. The female respondents reported that 34 percent had experienced unwanted sexual contact (attempted or actual kissing, fondling, or touching in a sexual or intimate way), 20 percent had experienced unwanted attempted sexual intercourse, and 10 percent had experienced completed unwanted intercourse. (Intercourse was defined as any form of sexual penetration including vaginal, anal, and oral.) The majority of incidents were party-related, and 75 percent of males and over half the females had used alcohol.

The majority of women reported that men who perpetrated sexual contact or attempted intercourse "just did it," as did 46 percent of the men who forced intercourse. The percentage of cases involving force by men ranged from 8 percent for sexual contact to 21 percent for completed intercourse. Most of the women verbally protested, although 20 percent of those who were raped reported being too frightened to protest. Victims most frequently chose a roommate or close friend to confide in; however, 41 percent of women who were raped told no one. Counselors were almost never told of any incidents. (See Table 5.6.)

The men reported a very different picture of unwanted sexual behavior on campus. Only 9 percent reported committing either unwanted sexual contact or attempted intercourse, and 3 percent admitted to incidents of unwanted sexual intercourse. The researchers proposed that the different results are because men and women read sexual cues and form sexual expectations differently. Studies have found that men are far more likely than women to interpret a woman's behavior as sexual and therefore an invitation to sexual intimacy.

Fraternities and Athletics

Fraternity members are frequently blamed for being perpetrators of college rapes. Martin Schwartz and Carol Nogrady ("Fraternity Membership, Rape Myths,

TABLE 5.4 (Continued)

Coercive Methods	Males		Females	
	f	(%)	f	(%)
Restraint				
Not applicable	182	(91.5)	180	(82.2)
Kissing	11	(5.5)	9	(4.1)
Fondling	4	(2.0)	7	(3.2)
Intercourse	2	(1.0)	23	(10.5)
Coercion totals	17	(8.5)	39	(17.8)
Threat of force				
Not applicable	187	(94.0)	204	(93.2)
Kissing	7	(3.5)	3	(1.4)
Fondling	4	(2.0)	5	(2.3)
Intercourse	1	(.5)	7	(3.2)
Coercion totals	12	(6.0)	15	(6.9)
Use of weapon				
Not applicable	190	(95.5)	216	(98.6)
Kissing	6	(3.0)	2	(.9)
Fondling	3	(1.0)	0	(0.0)
Intercourse	1	(.5)	1	(.5)
Coercion totals	10	(4.5)	3	(1.4)
Physical force				
Not applicable	191	(96.0)	207	(94.5)
Kissing	3	(1.0)	1	(.5)
Fondling	5	(2.5)	6	(2.7)
Intercourse	0	(0.0)	5	(2.3)
Coercion totals	8	(3.5)	12	(5.5)
Incident totals by sex	457		628	
Total incidents	1,085			

Source: Lisa K. Waldner-Haugrud and Brian Magruder, "Male and Female Sexual Victimization in Dating Relationship: Gender Differences in Coercion Techniques and Outcomes," *Violence and Victims*, vol. 10, no. 3, Fall 1995. Copyright © Springer Publishing Company, Inc., New York 10012. Used by permission.

and Sexual Aggression on a College Campus," *Violence Against Women*, vol. 2, no. 2, June 1996) think this characterization is false. They cite a study that alleged, "The men who are most likely to rape in college are fraternity pledges" (1993), while an often-cited article (1989) explained that fraternity members are more likely to have a narrow conception of masculinity, espouse group secrecy, and sexually objectify women. Instead, the authors claim, alcohol is the crucial variable. Because fraternity members are often heavy drinkers, researchers have made a false link between these men and sexual aggression (see "Alcohol," below).

Mary Koss (author of the often-cited study that produced the "one-in-four" statistic, see below), and Hobart Cleveland, in "Athletic Participation, Fraternity Membership, and Date Rape: The Question Remains — Self-Selection or Different Causal Processes?" (*Violence Against Women*, vol. 2, no. 2, June 1996), consider date rape and whether or not it is more likely perpetrated by athletes and fraternity members. They believe that the party situation brings acquaintances of the same social network together, while the fraternity controls the limited physical space with very little supervision. "[A] structure is created that not only provides the physical facilities for rape and lends legitimacy to the actions of members, but it also encourages drinking by potential victims and thereby suppresses the likelihood of reporting as well as perceived culpability and credibility of any women who do report." The researchers think there is very low reporting of fraternity rape.

A number of studies have found that peer support of violence and social ties with abusive peers are predictors of abuse against women. In addition, training for violent occupations such as athletics and the military can "slip over" into personal life. Athletics is sex-segregated, promotes hostile attitudes towards rivals, and rewards the athletes for physically dominating others. Todd Crosset et al., in "Male Student-Athletes and Violence Against Women" (*Violence Against Women*, vol. 2, no. 2, June 1996), gathered data from the judicial affairs offices of 10 Division I schools (the largest athletic programs). Based on information from 1991 to 1993, while male student-athletes made up 3 percent of the student population, they accounted for 35 percent of the perpetrators reported. Whether the data are skewed because women assaulted by athletes are more likely to report the attack to university authorities than women assaulted by other men is not known.

The authors, however, believe that the special society of athletics promotes violent, women-hating attitudes. In an interview in *Sports Illustrated* (Gerry Callahan et al., "Special Report: Domestic Violence," vol. 83, no. 5, July 31, 1995), Crosset explained, "Part of the male athlete's subworld is *not* to be a woman. Women are degraded. You don't want to be skirt-of-the-week. You don't want to be a wimp, a sissy. To be a man is *not* to be a woman. Women are not to be respected. Women are despised."

While batterers are rarely identified in other fields of endeavor (lawyers, politicians, corporate heads), most Americans can name more than one athlete who has been charged with abuse. Some of the better-known athletes charged with domestic violence include O. J. Simpson, Mike Tyson, Warren Moon, Lawrence Phillips, Darryl Strawberry, Jose Canseco, Jimmy Brown, and many others.

TABLE 5.5

**Percentage of Coercive Sexual Experiences
Sustained and Inflicted by Boys and Girls in an Adolescent Sample**

Experience	Sustained				Inflicted			
	Girls (n = 318)		Boys (n = 305)		Girls (n = 336)		Boys (n = 307)	
	n	%	n	%	n	%	n	%
1. Sexual contact or sex play through verbal coercion	130[a]	41.0	23	7.5	19	5.7	36	11.7
2. Sexual contact or sex play through misuse of authority	10	3.1	2	0.7	0	0	1	0.3
3. Sexual contact or sex play through threat or use of physical force	30	9.4	2	0.7	1	0.3	2	0.7
4. Attempt to obtain penetration through threat or use of physical force	36	11.3	2[b]	0.7	0	0	6	2.0
5. Attempt to obtain penetration through use of alcohol or drugs	29	9.1	8[b]	2.6	0	0	7	2.3
6. Intercourse through verbal coercion	61[a]	19.2	8	2.6	6	1.8	9	2.9
7. Intercourse through misuse of authority	4[a]	1.3	0	0	0	0	0	0
8. Intercourse through use of alcohol or drugs	16	5.0	3	1.0	0	0	1	0.3
9. Intercourse through threat or use of physical force	20	6.3	0	0	0	0	0	0
10. Oral or anal sex acts through threat or use of physical force	16	5.0	1[a]	0.3	0	0	4	1.3

Notes. Subjects with more than two missing data were discarded from analyses.
[a]One subject with missing data.   [b]Two subjects with missing data.

Source: Michèle Poitras and Francine Lavoie, "A Study of the Prevalence of Sexual Coercion in Adolescent Heterosexual Dating Relationships in a Quebec Sample," *Violence and Victims*, vol. 10, no. 4, Winter 1995. Copyright © Springer Publishing Company, Inc., New York 10012. Used by permission.

Alcohol

Alcohol use has been implicated in most sexual assault cases on campuses. According to the Center on Addiction and Substance Abuse ("Rethinking Rites of Passage: Substance Abuse on America's Campuses," Columbia University, New York City, 1994), 90 percent of all college rapes occurred when either the victim or the attacker was under the influence of alcohol. Other studies show estimates of the use of alcohol by one or both parties that range from one-third to three-quarters of all rape and sexual assaults.

Alcohol is reported to be involved in most campus crimes, not just assault. Jan Sherrill, assistant dean of students at George Washington University, thinks date rape is a subset of the larger problem of alcohol abuse. "I don't know of one case of sexual assault where students haven't been drinking." Antonia Abbey et al., in "Alcohol and Dating Risk Factors for Sexual Assault Among College Women" (*Psychology of Women Quarterly*, vol. 20, 1996), concluded that having one's sexual intentions misperceived was directly related to experiencing sexual assault and that women tended to be misperceived in situations where alcohol was consumed.

Researchers suggest that alcohol consumption increases the likelihood that sexual assault will occur. In men, it appears to promote the expression of traditional gender beliefs about sexual behavior and activates alcohol expectancies associated with male sexuality and aggression, providing justification for men to commit sexual assault. In addition, drinking increases the likelihood that men will misread women's friendly cues as signs of sexual interest.

Alcohol consumption, for women, limits their ability to correct misperceptions of sexual intent. Drinking also decreases the capacity to resist sexual assault and makes the victim feel responsible for sexual assault.

According to a forensic scientist, Mahmoud Elsohly, a study of urine samples taken from 578 rape victims who reportedly had been drugged showed alcohol to be the most common drug found. Alcohol was present in 208 cases (36 percent), marijuana in 93 (17 percent), tranquilizers in 49 (8 percent), and cocaine in 40 (7 percent). In 40 percent of the cases, no drugs were found. In this study, only 5 (less that .01 percent) showed the presence of the so-called date rape drug Rohypnol.

The "Date Rape Pill"

A hypnotic sedative 10 times as powerful as Valium, Rohypnol (known as "Roofies," "Roches," and "Ropies") has been used to obtain nonconsensual sex. Mixed in a drink, it causes memory impairment, confusion, and drowsiness. The woman is not aware of the sexual assault until she awakens the next morning. The only way to determine if a victim has been given Rohypnol is to test for drugs within two or three days of the episode, something hospital emergency rooms rarely do. Experts advise women not to accept drinks at parties but to get their own and not leave a drink sitting and return to it later.

Though Rohypnol is legally prescribed outside of the United States for the short-term treatment of severe sleep disorders, it is neither manufactured nor approved for sale in the United States. The importation of the drug has been banned since March 1996 when the U.S. Customs Service began seizing all quantities of Rohypnol at U.S. borders. The manufacturers recently reformulated the drug as green tablets that can be detected in clear fluids and are visible in the bottom of a cup.

In October 1996, President Clinton signed a bill into law (PL 104-305) amending the Controlled Substances Act to increase penalties for using drugs to disarm potential victims of violent crime. Anyone convicted of slipping a controlled substance, including Rohypnol, to an individual with intent to commit a violent crime faces a prison term of up to 20 years and a fine as high as $2 million. The law also increased penalties for manufacturing, distributing, or possessing with the intent to distribute Rohypnol.

Two other drugs have also been used as "date rape pills." GHP, known as liquid ecstasy, enhances the effects of alcohol, which releases inhibitions, in addition to causing a form of amnesia. Ketamine hydrochloride, also known as "Special K," is used to impair a person's natural resistance impulses. Ketamine is an animal tranquilizer.

The Political Conflict: "One in Four"

The actual frequency of date rape has become a highly controversial subject. The most widely publicized rate of date rape and the source of this controversy is the declaration of "one in four" that originated in a study by Mary Koss et al. ("The Scope of Rape: Incidence and Prevalence of Sexual Aggression and Victimization in a National Sample of Higher Education Students," *The Journal of Consulting and Clinical Psychology*, vol. 55, 1987).

Koss and her associates interviewed more than 3,000 college women nationwide. The women were asked 10 questions about sexual violations, the last three of which were counted as evidence of rape: Have you had sexual intercourse when you didn't want to because a man gave you alcohol or drugs? Have you had sexual intercourse when you didn't want to because a man threatened or used some degree of physical force to make you? Have you had sexual acts (anal or oral intercourse or penetration by objects other than the penis) when you didn't want to because a man threatened or used some degree of physical force to make you?"

Koss determined from the responses that 15.4 percent of the women had been raped and 12.1 percent had been victims of attempted rape, or a total of 27.5 percent of the women were victims of rape or attempted rape. The women, however, did not see their experiences the same way. Only 27 percent of the women Koss counted as raped labeled themselves as raped. Forty-nine percent said it was "miscommunication," 14 percent said it was a "crime but not rape," and 11 percent said they "don't feel victimized." Furthermore, Koss found that 42 percent of those she counted as raped had sex again on another occasion with their attackers.

Critics of Koss's study faulted her for counting as raped the women who said they had intercourse as a result of alcohol or drugs. If a woman has passed out and her partner has intercourse with her, she has been raped. Not everyone agrees, however, that she has been raped if she has had too much to drink, engages in sex because her judgment is impaired, and later regrets her actions. Katie Roiphe (author of *The Morn-*

TABLE 5.6

Characteristics of "Most Serious" Incidents

	Type of Experience		
	Contact (N = 176)	Attempted Intercourse (N = 102)	Intercourse (N = 50)
Location			
Dorm	32%	41%	50%
Fraternity	28	10	8
Apartment	29	43	36
Other	11	6	6
Occasion			
Date	9%	8%	14%
Party	68	65	57
Other	24	27	29
Alcohol Use			
Male use	80%	77%	76%
Female use	57%	54%	65%
Relationship			
Stranger	18%	9%	12%
Acquaintance/friend	66	57	47
Boyfriend	14	30	33
Other	2	5	8
Male Tactics			
Just did it	77%	62%	46%
Verbal	15	28	33
Force	8	10	21
Female Response[a]			
Too frightened	6%	6%	20%
Said no	76%	91%	70%
Cried	5%	9%	22%
Struggled/fought	17%	16%	28%
Other protests	17%	7%	12%
What Resulted[a]			
Physical Injury	0%	3%	10%
Psychological Injury	18%	30%	51%
Required counseling	2%	2%	8%
Who Was Told[a]			
No one	23%	30%	41%
Roommate	41%	38%	25%
Close friend	59%	54%	41%
Counselor	< 1%	< 1%	4%

[a]Percentages do not add to 100 because of multiple responses.

Source: Sally K. Ward, Kathy Chapman, Ellen Cohn, Susan White, and Kirk Williams, "Acquaintance Rape and the College Social Scene," *Family Relations* (Minneapolis: National Council on Family Relations, 1991). Copyrighted 1991 by the National Council on Family Relations, 3989 Central Avenue NE, Suite 550, Minneapolis, MN 55421. Reprinted by permission.

Source: Sally K. Ward, Kathy Chapman, Ellen Cohn, Susan White, and Kirk Williams, "Acquaintance Rape and the College Social Scene," *Family Relations* (Minneapolis: National Council on Family Relations, 1991). Copyrighted 1991 by the National Council on Family Relations, 3989 Central Avenue NE, Suite 550, Minneapolis, MN 55421. Reprinted by permission.

ing After: Sex, Fear, and Feminism, Back Bay Books, 1994) observed in an interview, "Date rape has become a synonym for bad sex, for sex that is pressured, drunk, or regretted the next day. If we call this rape, then I would guess that almost everybody has been 'raped' at one point or another."

If the women in Koss's study who had sex under the influence of drugs and alcohol and those women who did not identify their experience as rape are removed from the total, the rate of 1 in 4 for rape and attempted rape drops to between 1 in 22 and 1 in 33.

Koss defended her inclusion of these women, citing Ohio's law, "No person shall engage in sexual conduct with another person ... when ... for the purpose of preventing resistance the offender substantially impairs the other person's judgment or control by administering any drug or intoxicant to the other person." She now agrees, however, that her question was ambiguously worded because she omitted the portion of the statute that reads, "the situation where a person plies his intended partner with drink or drugs in hopes that lowered inhibition might lead to a liaison."

Critics charge that Koss's figures instill unnecessary fear in women and that the high rape figures have created an image of women as helpless victims. Rather than empowering women, this belittles them. Neil Gilbert, professor at the University of California, Berkeley ("Was It Rape?," *The American Enterprise*, September/October 1994), cited the study as an example of "advocacy research" that "demonizes men and defines the common experience in heterosexual relations as inherently violent and menacing."

Furthermore, critics claim the data have been used in universities nationwide to institute expensive and unnecessary programs to combat rape. In 1992, Congress authorized $10 million to the neediest colleges to fund rape education and prevention services. The most recent crime reports (1992) compiled by the *Chronicle of Higher Education* found 466 reported

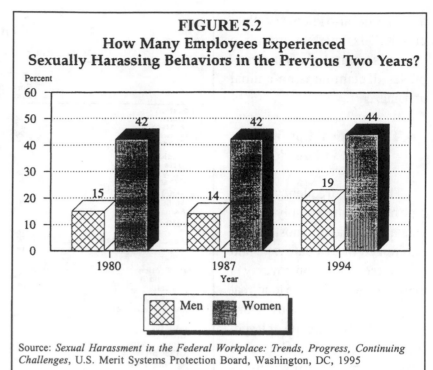

FIGURE 5.2
How Many Employees Experienced Sexually Harassing Behaviors in the Previous Two Years?

Source: *Sexual Harassment in the Federal Workplace: Trends, Progress, Continuing Challenges,* U.S. Merit Systems Protection Board, Washington, DC, 1995

rapes and 448 reported forcible sex offenses in 744 institutions. This works out to slightly more than one sex offense per college. Neil Gilbert pointed out that this fund would spend $10,000 for every reported campus rape. In contrast, federal legislation funds about $650 per reported rape in the community at large, "where most rape occurs."

SEXUAL HARASSMENT

Guys were encouraged to get as drunk as they could — and do whatever they could to the women. If they felt like grabbing a woman by the boob or the ass, that was O.K.

They would use their power and authority to make you think you didn't have a job if you didn't go along. — former sales representatives of a pharmaceutical company

Harassment is nothing new; in the early days of Hollywood, it was generally accepted that many starlets slept their way into films by acquiescing to directors' requests for sexual favors. The businessman chasing his secretary around the desk was commonly presented in cartoons and movies. Male remarks heavy with sexual innuendo were considered acceptable in the workplace. As women have become more prominent in the business world and in the military, however, what was in many instances generally accepted has become sexual harassment.

Definitions

Sexual harassment is a form of sexual discrimination prohibited by Title VII of the Civil Rights Act of 1964 (PL 88-352). According to the U.S. Department of Justice, "Sexual harassment has been defined as unwelcome sexual advances, requests for sexual favors, and other verbal or physical conduct that enters into employment decisions and/or conduct that unreasonably interferes with an individual's work performance or creates an intimidating, hostile, or offensive working environment." There are two forms of harassment: quid pro quo (something for something) and hostile work environment harassment.

Quid pro quo harassment occurs when an employee is pressured to choose between submitting to sexual advances or losing a job benefit (e.g., a promotion, a raise, or even the job itself). Hostile work environment harassment is unwelcome conduct that is so severe as to create an intimidating, hostile, or offensive work environment.

In 1986, the Supreme Court in the landmark case, *Meritor Savings Bank v. Vinson* (477 U.S. 57), established the legal standing of a hostile work environment. Initially, a lower court had ruled against Mechelle Vinson (who claimed her supervisor harassed her constantly and even raped her) because the court found that sexual favors had not been a condition of her employment (quid pro quo harassment). The Supreme Court reversed this decision, however, focusing on the "hostile environment clause of the law.... Title VII affords employees the right to work in an environment free from discriminatory intimidation, ridicule, and insult."

Cases

The Equal Employment Opportunity Commission (EEOC) is the federal agency responsible for handling charges of sexual harassment. In 1990, 6,127 cases were filed with the EEOC; by 1997, the number had risen to 15,889. In 1990, monetary awards for the year totaled $7.1 million, compared to $49.5 million in 1997. Changes in the 1991 Civil Rights Act gave women the right to jury trials and permission to sue for compensatory and punitive damages, opening the door to larger monetary awards.

Critics charge that the huge awards are way out of proportion to the offense, and they encourage women to file charges in questionable cases. A jury awarded a Wal-Mart shipping clerk more than $50 million in June 1995, but the judge reduced the award to $5 million. One of the woman's lawyers objected, pointing out that $5 million is nothing for a huge corporation like Wal-Mart, and that in order to set an example, the award must have an impact on the company.

Some experts had predicted that sexual harassment would fade away as women became more accepted in the workplace. Instead, 1998 brought four major cases to the Supreme Court, three of which were brought under Title VII of the Civil Rights Act of 1964. The three cases clarified employer liability for sexual harassment in the workplace. The first case involved Joseph Oncale, who was sexually assaulted by his co-workers and a supervisor on an oil rig off the coast of Louisiana. He filed a federal lawsuit alleging both types of sexual harassment, quid pro quo and hostile work environment. Oncale lost in the lower courts because he and his harassers were male. However, according to the unanimous ruling by the Supreme Court, in *Oncale v. Sundowner Offshore Services* (66 LW 4172), same-sex sexual harassment constitutes illegal discrimination.

In *Faragher v. City of Boca Raton* (66 LW 4643), Beth Faragher, who was employed for five years as a lifeguard for Boca Raton, Florida, alleged that she endured repeated incidences of touching, sexual gestures, and sexual comments from two male bosses. Because Faragher feared retaliation, she never reported it. After quitting her job, she filed a sexual harassment suit against the city of Boca Raton. The city responded that because they were never made aware of the events, they had no liability for the alleged actions of the supervisors. Although the city had adopted a sexual harassment policy, it had not distributed that policy to Faragher or her department. The Supreme Court made it clear that any large employer must establish, distribute, and enforce a sexual harassment policy.

In *Burlington Industries v. Ellerth* (66 LW 4634), the Court considered the case of Kimberly Ellerth, who claimed she was subjected to constant sexual harassment by a manager. Burlington Industries argued that Ellerth was not financially encumbered by the harassment and that, as a result, Burlington was not liable. The Supreme Court held that an employer could be liable when a supervisor causes a hostile work environment even when the employee suffers no tangible job consequences and the employer is unaware of the offensive conduct. The manager's numerous alleged threats were found to constitute severe or pervasive conduct.

In both the Faragher and Ellerth cases, the Court made clear that a worker who is being harassed has a duty to report it. Employers must have a sexual harassment policy that is in compliance with the law, ensure employees have effective avenues to file complaints, disseminate the policy so that all employees know about it and how to use it, respond promptly and effectively to complaints, and enforce the policy with appropriate action.

The fourth case, *Gebser v. Lago Vista Independent School District* (66 LW 4501), was brought under Title IX of the Education Amendments Act of 1972. It concerns a school district's liability for a teacher's sexual involvement with a 14-year-old student. Alida Gebser, a student in the Lago Vista school district, said that the relationship was consensual, but she also claimed that she was afraid to tell anyone about the relationship for fear she would be barred from the advanced level courses the teacher taught. The teacher pled guilty to charges of statutory rape, and Gebser filed a civil suit against the school district. The Supreme Court ruled that a school district could not be held liable because the student had not told a supervisor, stating that a student must prove a school district acted with "deliberate indifference" to a complaint.

Sexual Harassment in the Military

Sexual harassment in the military has captured headlines since at least 1991, when 83 female officers claimed to have been abused at a convention of naval and marine pilots — the so-called Tailhook scandal. In November 1996, four drill instructors and a captain at the Army's Aberdeen, Maryland, training center were charged with harassment and rape of female recruits. One month later, more than 50 women had filed charges of sexual assault or rape. The army's most senior enlisted man, Army Sergeant Major Gene McKinney was tried on charges of coercing sexual favors from six women. The women accused him of harassing or even assaulting them. After a month-long trial, a military jury acquitted him of all sex-related charges and found him guilty on a single count of obstructing justice. He was demoted to master sergeant.

Military regulations forbid intimate relations between officers and enlisted personnel and between superiors and their subordinates. The official Army policy on sexual harassment is "zero tolerance," and it is drilled into every soldier from his or her first day in the service. Nevertheless, violations continue throughout the armed services. Through the Department of Veterans Affairs, female veterans are counseled for sexual trauma. Caseloads are up sharply, from 2,090 in 1993 to 9,000 in 1997.

The situation in the military is aggravated by the almost absolute power a superior has over a subordinate, especially in basic and advanced training units. From the moment recruits enter basic training, they learn that they must always obey their drill sergeants. The drill sergeant has the power, or certainly appears to have the power, to make a purposely difficult situation even worse. On the other hand, as retired Commander Louis Prentiss explained, "The rules can't be any clearer.... The drill sergeants have to walk a straight, stiff line. He is the embodiment of power. It absolutely cannot be a confused relationship."

A 1995 Pentagon survey of 90,000 men and women on active duty in the military found that in the Army, 61 percent of respondents reported being harassed in the last year; the Navy reported 53 percent;

TABLE 5.7
Is It Sexual Harassment?[*]

Type of Uninvited Behavior by a Supervisor	Percentage of Women Who Consider It Harassment		
	1980	1987	1994
Pressure for sexual favors	91	99	99
Deliberate touching, cornering	91	95	98
Suggestive letters, calls, materials	93	90	94
Pressure for dates	77	87	91
Suggestive looks, gestures	72	81	91
Sexual teasing, jokes, remarks	62	72	83

	Percentage of Men Who Consider It Harassment		
	1980	1987	1994
Pressure for sexual favors	84	95	97
Deliberate touching, cornering	83	89	93
Suggestive letters, calls, materials	87	76	87
Pressure for dates	76	81	86
Suggestive looks, gestures	59	68	76
Sexual teasing, jokes, remarks	53	58	73

Type of Uninvited Behavior by a Coworker	Percentage of Women Who Consider It Harassment		
	1980	1987	1994
Pressure for sexual favors	81	98	98
Deliberate touching, cornering	84	92	96
Letters, calls, other materials	87	84	92
Pressure for dates	65	76	85
Suggestive looks, gestures	64	76	88
Sexual teasing, jokes, remarks	54	64	77

	Percentage of Men Who Consider It Harassment		
	1980	1987	1994
Pressure for sexual favors	65	90	93
Deliberate touching, cornering	69	82	89
Letters, calls, other materials	76	67	81
Pressure for dates	59	66	76
Suggestive looks, gestures	47	60	70
Sexual teasing, jokes, remarks	42	47	64

[*] *Based on the percentage of respondents who indicated that they "definitely" or "probably" would consider the identified behavior sexual harassment.*

Source: *Sexual Harassment in the Federal Workplace: Trends, Progress, Continuing Challenges*, U.S. Merit Systems Protection Board, Washington, DC, 1995

the Air Force, 49 percent; the Marine Corps, 64 percent; and the Coast Guard, 59 percent.

HARASSMENT IN THE FEDERAL WORKPLACE

The U.S. Merit Systems Protection Board (*Sexual Harassment in the Federal Workplace*, Washington, DC, 1995) polled federal workers about sexual harassment in 1980, 1987, and 1994. Rates of sexual harassment have remained fairly stable over the 14 years of surveys. In 1987, 14 percent of men and 42 percent of women reported harassment, compared to 19 percent of men and 44 percent of women in 1994 (Figure 5.2). These rates included behavior that ranged from actual rape to pressure for dates or sexual jokes.

TABLE 5.8	
How Did Victims React?	
Percentage of victims who said they took the indicated informal action in response to sexual harassment, 1994	
Ignored it/did nothing	44
Asked or told harasser to stop	35
Avoided the harasser	28
Made a joke of it	15
Reported it to a supervisor or other official	12
Threatened to tell/told others	10
Went along with the behavior	7

Note: Some respondents took more than one action.

TABLE 5.9	
What Should Targets of Sexual Harassment Do?	
Percentage of all 1994 respondents who believe the indicated action would be most effective in stopping sexual harassment	
Asking or telling the person to stop	88
Reporting the behavior	83
Filing a formal complaint	66
Threatening to tell or telling others	23
Avoiding the person	23
Ignoring the behavior	17

Note: Respondents could choose more than one action.

Source of both tables: *Sexual Harassment in the Federal Workplace: Trends, Progress, Continuing Challenges*, U.S. Merit Systems Protection Board, Washington, DC, 1995

In the 1980 survey, 91 percent of women and 84 percent of men thought it was harassment for a supervisor to pressure for sexual favors. When sexual favors were pressed by a co-worker, 81 percent of women and 65 percent of men thought it was harassment. In 1994, nearly all of the respondents thought pressure for sexual favors from a supervisor was harassment (99 and 97 percent of women and men), while 98 percent of women and 93 percent of men thought it was harassment when the behavior originated with a co-worker. (See Table 5.7.)

Different Perceptions

The survey revealed that men and women see harassment differently when it consists of sexual teasing, jokes, or remarks. In 1987, less than half the men (47 percent) thought this behavior was harassment from a co-worker, while 64 percent of women though it was. In 1994, these percentages had risen to 64 percent for men and 77 percent for women.

This difference in perception is the heart of a legal controversy on how to define sexual harassment. Normally, the court defines behavior as harassment if a "reasonable person" views the situation that way. Some advocates insist that harassment needs to be defined on a "reasonable woman" standard instead. The U.S. Court of Appeals (*Ellison v. Brady*, 924 F.2d 872, 1991) advocated a "reasonable woman" standard, arguing that what a man might find to be mild harassment, women found threatening and perhaps a prelude to more serious sexual assault. The Cato Institute (a Libertarian think tank of Washington, DC) disagrees, charging that this standard would have the effect of "gutting the concept of neutrality under the law."

Handling Harassment

The most frequent response to harassment is to ignore it (about 44 percent of victims). The reason for some of this inaction may be related to the perceived insignificance of the offense. For some, however, the harassing behavior is quite serious, and yet they do nothing. The next most common reactions to unwanted sexual attention are asking or telling the harasser to stop (35 percent) and avoiding the harasser (28 percent) (Table 5.8). The survey found that the most effective methods of dealing with harassment was to ask or tell the person to stop and to report the situation to a supervisor. While avoiding the harasser can be successful, it can also have a negative effect on a person's work performance if he or she spends a lot of time trying to avoid the harasser. (See Table 5.9.)

CHAPTER VI

TREATMENT FOR MALE BATTERERS

Why should men want to change when we got it all already? — A man in a battering program

Batterer intervention programs were originally established in the late 1970s when activists working with battered women realized that no real progress could be made in the reduction of domestic violence unless interventions were taken to change the behaviors of the offenders. As a result, criminal justice agencies have responded by referring an increasing number of batterers to such programs in an effort to deter further violence. Several hundred batterer programs now exist.

Studies of the treatment programs for male batterers have not reached a consensus on whether or not they are effective. Some follow-up reports done 4 to 24 months after completion of batterer intervention programs indicated nonviolence rates of between 53 percent and 85 percent. Other reports, however, have found no difference in outcomes between those attending batterer programs and control groups that did not. Many factors must be considered, such as which types of batterers are most likely to change their behavior and what treatment approach works best. Although researchers are beginning to identify different types of abusers, they have not yet found which treatment approach works best with which type of abuser.

STANDARDS FOR BATTERER INTERVENTION PROGRAMS

As of 1996, more than half the states and the District of Columbia had adopted standards or guidelines regulating male batterer intervention programs; 13 other states were developing them. State standards vary in terms of which programs they apply to, whether batterers must attend such programs, and how they will be punished if they do not. Some critics of state standards feel they result in inflexible programs that fail to take into account the research that points to the need for different approaches that consider the individual profiles of batterers.

In "Standards for Batterer Intervention Programs: In Whose Interest?" (*Violence Against Women,* vol. 5, no. 1, 1999), Larry Bennett and Marianne Piet address the question of legislating standards for batterer intervention programs. Some critics claim that the standards were written by feminists in the battered women's movement who view regulation as a necessary step to ensure that male batterers are held accountable for their actions against women. They believe such standards focus on domestic violence as a crime, requiring criminal sanctions. In contrast, mental health professionals view domestic abuse as evidence of a disorder or a dysfunction. Therefore, they believe treatment of batterers with mental disorders requires a mental health professional. These critics argue that professional associations in the mental health community were not consulted when the standards were formulated.

Others fear that standards may limit programs to a certain treatment approach, although research has not yet determined the effectiveness of any particular practice over another for deterring further domestic abuse. Some observers are concerned that judges and attorneys do what they want regardless of standards.

Bennett and Piet believe that much of the conflict over batterer program standards emerges from a misunderstanding of the purpose of standards. Rather than focusing on program content and thereby possibly stifling innovative practices, they feel that standards should be designed to "hold men accountable for their actions, hold providers accountable for their interventions, and increase the safety of the victims of domestic violence."

The Battered Women's Justice Project (*State Batterers Programs,* Minneapolis, Minnesota, 1995) compared standards in 11 states. The review found near-consensus in areas such as treatment choices (group treatment is specified in 80 percent of the standards), treatment providers' legal duty to warn victims of impending violence, insistence on victims' safety, and mandatory substance abuse assessments. Little consensus, however, was found in such areas as provision of affordable services, use of mental status examinations, professional credentials, and evaluation of outcomes.

A NATIONAL INSTITUTE OF JUSTICE STUDY

In *Batterer Intervention: Program Approaches and Criminal Justice Strategies* (National Institute of Justice, Washington, DC, 1998), Kerry Healey and Christine Smith reported on their study of batterer intervention programs. This study was designed to help criminal justice personnel better understand the issues surrounding batterer intervention. Based on this knowledge, they would then be able to make appropriate referrals to programs and to communicate effectively with program providers. Healey and Smith studied both "mainstream" programs and innovative approaches in programs operating across the country. While programs were found to be structurally similar, they were diverse in theoretical approaches to domestic violence.

The Feminist Model

Most of the early intervention programs use the feminist model, which attributes the domestic abuse problem to societal values that legitimize male control. In this view, violence is one means of maintaining male dominance in the family. Feminist programs attempt to raise consciousness about sex role conditioning and how it influences men's emotions and behavior. These programs use education and skill building to resocialize batterers, helping them learn to build relationships based on trust instead of fear. In addition, most feminist approaches support confronting men about their power and control tactics.

Critics claim that the feminist perspective overemphasizes sociocultural factors to the exclusion of individual factors, such as growing up abused. Some observers argue that the feminist approach is too confrontational, alienating the batterer and increasing his hostility.

The Family Systems Model

The family systems model is based on the belief that violent behavior stems from dysfunctional family interactions. It focuses on building communication and conflict resolution skills within the family. According to this model, both partners may contribute to the escalation of conflict, with each attempting to dominate the other. Either partner may resort to violence, although the violence of the male will likely have greater consequences. From this perspective, interactions produce violence; therefore, no one is considered to be the perpetrator or victim.

Critics of the family systems model do not think that partner abuse involves shared responsibility. They believe that batterers bear full responsibility for the violence; victims do not cause the violence. Even if one spouse does irritate the other, this is no justification for violence. Many also fear that couple counseling can put the victim at risk after the session if the woman expresses complaints. In fact, couple counseling is expressly prohibited in 20 state standards.

Psychological Approaches

The psychological perspective views abuse as a symptom of underlying emotional problems. This approach, based on the belief that domestic violence is related to the batterer's psychological problems, emphasizes therapy and counseling to uncover the batterer's subconscious problems and resolve them consciously. Proponents of this approach believe that other interventions are superficial and only suppress violence temporarily. Critics argue that giving psychiatric labels to batterers gives them an excuse for their behavior.

Another psychological approach is cognitive-behavioral group therapy. This therapy is intended to help individuals function better by changing how they think and act in current situations. According to this theory, behaviors are learned as a result of positive and negative reinforcements, and interventions should focus on "cognitive restructuring" (changing thought patterns) and skill building. Feminist proponents criticize the approach for failing to explain why batterers are not violent in other relationships and why some men continue to abuse women even when the behavior is not rewarded.

Batterer Intervention Program Content

Among the programs studied by Healy and Smith, most combine elements of different theoretical models. Of the three mainstream programs studied by Healey and Smith, the Duluth Curriculum uses a classroom format to focus on issues of power and control. The development of critical thinking skills is emphasized to help batterers understand and change their behavior. In contrast, the other two mainstream models — EMERGE and AMEND — include more in-depth counseling and are of longer duration.

The Duluth Curriculum

The Duluth model was developed in the early 1980s by the Domestic Abuse Intervention Project of Duluth, Minnesota. The classroom curriculum focuses on the development of critical thinking skills around the themes of nonviolence, nonthreatening behavior, respect, support and trust, honesty and accountability, sexual respect, partnership, and negotiation and fairness. Two or three sessions are spent on each theme, beginning with a video demonstration of the specific controlling behavior being highlighted. Discussion on the actions used by the batterer in the video follows, and, during subsequent sessions, each group

member describes his own use of the controlling behavior. The group then explores alternative behaviors that can build a healthier, more equal relationship.

EMERGE

EMERGE, a 48-week batterer program in Cambridge, Massachusetts, begins with eight weeks of orientation consisting of educational and skills-building sessions. Program members who complete this phase and admit to domestic violence may then progress to an ongoing group that blends cognitive-behavioral techniques with group therapy centered on personal accountability. This program is more flexible that the Duluth model, which uses a preset curriculum.

In the group, new members introduce themselves, describe the incident that brought them to the program, and admit their violence. Responding to questions by group members, the new member shares details about his acts of violence. Short check-in statements for regular group members follow, focusing on their actions of the previous week. There may then be discussion of particular incidents disclosed by a group member.

EMERGE focuses not only on the abusive behavior but on the broader relationship between the batterer and the victim. Each member formulates goals related to his control tactics, and the group helps him develop ways to address these concerns.

AMEND

The designers of AMEND, a program in Denver, Colorado, share the same commitment to longer-term treatment as the founders of EMERGE. The purpose of AMEND is to establish client accountability, increase awareness of the social context of battering, and build new skills. AMEND group leaders serve as "moral guides" who take a firm position against violence and confront the client's behavior as unacceptable and illegal.

The program's long-term approach has four stages. The first two stages consist of several months of education and confrontation to break through the batterer's denial. Several months of advanced group therapy follow, during which the batterer begins to recognize his own rationalizations for his abusive behavior and to admit the truth. This stage includes ongoing contact with the partner, who can reveal relapses or more subtle forms of abuse. During this stage, the client develops a plan that includes a support network to avoid future violence. The fourth, and optional, stage consists of involvement in community service and political action to stop domestic violence.

Other Approaches

Most observers have concluded that a "one-size-fits-all" intervention cannot accommodate the diversity of batterers. Contrary to the mainstream programs, innovative approaches focus on the individual profile of the batterers. Some base their interventions on the various typologies, or categories, of batterers. For instance, the criminal justice system categorizes offenders based on the danger they pose, substance abuse data, their psychological problems, and the risk of dropout and rearrest. Interventions focus on the specific type of batterer and an approach that may be the most successful for that type of batterer, such as linking substance abuse treatment with a batterer intervention program. Other specialized approaches focus on program retention of specific populations based on sociocultural characteristics, such as poverty, race, ethnicity, and age.

Program Procedures

Regardless of an intervention program's philosophy or methods, program directors and criminal justice professionals generally closely monitor the offenders' behaviors. The following procedures are used by all mainstream programs: intake and assessment, victim contact, orientation, group treatment, leaving the program, and completion.

The batterer's first contact with the intervention program occurs at the intake interview, likely occurring at the courthouse. The intake assessment may last up to eight weeks. During this period, the client agrees to the terms of the intervention, begins the behavior assessment, and is screened for other problems. If the batterer is found to have other problems, such as substance abuse or mental illness, he may be referred to a program that addresses these issues. Not all batterers are accepted at intake. Some programs consider batterers inappropriate for treatment if they deny having committed violence.

Several states require that the victims be notified at various points in the intervention, and programs with a strong advocacy policy make victim contact every two or three months. Victims may be asked for additional information about the relationship, are given information about program goals and methods, and are helped with safety planning. In addition, the batterer's counselor will inform the victim if further abuse appears imminent.

During the orientation, the assessment process continues and the reeducation process begins. Batterers learn the program goals and rules for participating in the group. Orientation sessions tend to be in lecture format while group treatment is more informal and therapeutic.

Batterers leave the program either because of successful completion or because they are asked to leave. Reasons for termination include noncooperation, nonpayment of fees, or revocation of parole or probation. The most common reasons for the threat of termination are failure to attend group sessions regularly or violation of program rules (for example, being disruptive or aggressive).

In defining a successful completion of the program, most programs distinguish between simply attending sessions and the accomplishment of intervention goals. With court-mandated clients, the final report to probation indicates whether the client has worked successfully in the program. Completion rates, however, tend to be low.

The Criminal Justice Response

To be effective, batterer intervention programs must be supported by the criminal justice system in a coordinated response that includes all branches of the system, from police to pretrial screeners, prosecutors, judges, victim advocates, and probation officers. Healey and Smith (*Batterer Intervention,* see above) suggest the following actions to reinforce the message that battering is a crime and to support the efforts of batterer programs:

- Expedite domestic violence cases (trial dates, sentencing, probation contact, and batterer program intake).

- Use specialized domestic violence prosecution and probation units and centralized dockets, where all aspects of domestic violence interventions can be handled in one location (to improve services to victims and better coordinate batterer prosecution, sentencing, and supervision).

- Gather broad-based offender information quickly (including previous arrests and convictions, substance abuse, child welfare contacts, and victim information).

- Take advantage of culturally competent or specialized interventions (seek appropriate interventions for batterers who are indigent, high-risk, mentally ill).

- Coordinate batterer intervention with substance abuse treatment (mandate treatment when appropriate and monitor intensively).

- Be alert to the risks to children in domestically abusive households (coordinate with child protective services to ensure that batterers' children are safe and are receiving appropriate services).

- Create a continuum of supports and protection for victims (use victim advocates to assist victims with the criminal justice system and to monitor their safety when their batterers are sentenced to a batterer program).

- Encourage interagency cooperation (organize formal coordinating committees of probation officers, prosecutors, battered women's advocates, child protection workers, and batterer intervention providers to discuss referral and monitoring policies).

ABUSER SEES WIFE AS OBJECT

David Adams, president and co-founder of EMERGE, gives a broad definition of battering. To Adams, battering is "any act that causes the victim to do something she does not want to do, prevents her from doing something she wants to do, or causes her to be afraid." Violence does not always mean physical violence. It also includes psychological violence, which EMERGE defines as "behavior that directly undermines ... self-determination or self-esteem."

Violence is not a series of isolated blow-ups. It is a process of deliberate intimidation intended to coerce the victim to do the victimizer's will. According to David Adams, the abuser's level of control is shown in how he is able to be agreeable (or conciliatory) with police, bosses, neighbors, and others with whom it is in his best interests to appear reasonable.

Even when abusive men are supposed to be working on their relationships, EMERGE counselors have observed that the men devalue and denigrate their partners rather than trying to understand them. Ellen Pence of Duluth noticed that men rarely call the women they abuse by their names because they refuse to see them as people in their own right. In one group session, she counted 97 references to women, many of them obscene, before someone used his partner's name. When Pence insisted they use their partners' names, she reported they could hardly speak.

PTSD AND SHAME

Donald G. Dutton, a psychology professor and author of *The Batterer: A Psychological Profile* (Basic Books, New York City, 1995), found among his clients many of the same symptoms that define post-traumatic stress disorder (PTSD), a psychological response to extreme trauma. PTSD symptoms include depression, anxiety, sleep disturbance, and dissociation (flashbacks, out-of-body experiences). Dutton's batterers had psychological profiles surprisingly similar to Vietnam veterans who had been diagnosed with PTSD. Abusers are rarely seen as being victims themselves, yet their psychological profiles revealed them to be trauma victims. Dutton felt that the batterers' chronic anger and abusiveness pointed to a common source of early childhood trauma.

Dutton's research into his clients' childhoods revealed that the crucial factor in abusive behavior is shame the men suffered as children. "Shame is an emotional response to an attack on the global sense of self. When we are shamed, our very sense of who we are is threatened." The wife beaters had experienced childhoods characterized by "attacks on their selfhood, humiliation, embarrassment, and shame." Through his research with abusive men, Dutton found that the factor of physical abuse alone did not predict abusive behavior, but that the combination of shaming and being abused as a child was a dangerous combination.

According to Dutton, shame teaches the child that he is worthless and attacks his entire identity. Punishing a child at random is also a serious attack to his identity. Because the punishment does not relate to a particular behavior, it tells the child that his very being is wrong and unlovable, not that his behavior is wrong. The child's rage and shame have no means of expression until he enters an intimate relationship. Then his mask of being a "tough guy" risks being uncovered by his girlfriend or wife, and he responds with rage. The shame of his rage is too great to bear, so he blames the woman, and a pattern is established.

Dutton listed what he found to be the greatest childhood contributors to wife assault in order of importance: feeling rejected by one's father, feeling a lack of warmth from one's father, being physically abused by one's father, being verbally abused by one's father, and feeling rejected by one's mother.

DIFFERENT ABUSE TYPES

I always felt unattractive. I thought, "I'm not cute enough for her. She'll find a nicer-looking guy with a better car." But she wasn't looking for that. She was just looking for a little compassion and honesty. I didn't give her any of that. — A man in group therapy for battery

Daniel G. Saunders ("A Typology of Men Who Batter: Three Types Derived from Cluster Analysis," *American Journal of Orthopsychiatry*, vol. 62, no. 2, 1992) surveyed 165 abusive men on psychological measures including childhood victimization, severity of violence, psychological abuse, domestic decision making, level of conflict, anger, jealousy, depression, impression management (the man's ability to present a good impression of his behavior), and alcohol use. He also defined three types of batterers:

• Type I men are characterized as "family-only" aggressors. These men reported low levels of anger, depression, and jealousy. They were the least likely to have been severely abused as children. They claimed the most satisfaction in their relationship and the least marital conflict, and they were the least psychologically abusive. Their violence was associated with alcohol about half the time. Members of this group suppressed their anger until alcohol or a stressor triggered its release.

• Type II men are "generally violent" and were the most likely to be violent inside and outside the home. The majority had been severely abused as children, yet they reported low levels of depression and anger. Their lower anger may reflect an attitude of "I don't get mad, I get even." Their violence was usually associated with alcohol, and they reported the most frequent severe violence. Their attitudes about sex roles were more rigid than Type I men.

• Type III men reported the highest levels of anger, depression, and jealousy. They were characterized as "emotionally volatile" aggressors. They were most likely to fear losing their partners and to be suicidal and angry. These men were not as physically aggressive as Type II men, but they were the most psychologically abusive and the least satisfied with their relationships. They also had the most rigid sex role attitudes. About half of these men had previously received counseling and were thought to be the most likely to complete treatment.

Based on the three categories of batterers, Saunders proposed different types of counseling that would be most effective for each type of aggressor. The generally violent man (Type II) may need help dealing with the psychic wounds of his childhood, stopping his abuse of alcohol, and learning how to express his feelings rather than exploding. He needs to see that his rigid sex role notions are harmful. This abuser will probably need more than the standard three- to six-month treatment program.

The emotionally volatile man (Type III) needs to learn to express his feelings in non-aggressive ways and accept his "weaker" feelings of jealousy and depression rather than express them through anger. He also needs to understand the damage caused by his psychological abuse and rigid sex role beliefs.

The family-only aggressor (Type I) might gain the most from an emphasis on the communication aspects of assertiveness training. He needs to learn how to express anger and understand his rights. He may be helped by couples' counseling if his past violence level is low enough and if he remains nonviolent and committed to the relationship.

Anti-Social Men

Drs. J. Gottman and N. Jacobson et al. ("The Relationship Between Heart Rate Reactivity, Emotionally Aggressive Behavior, and General Violence in Batterers," *Journal of Family Psychology*, vol. 9, 1995) completed the first laboratory study to observe couples where wife-battery is common. The authors found that many of the most vicious husbands became physiologically calmer while they argued with their wives. As their anger mounted, their heart rates dropped and their attention sharpened, making their violence an act of calculated terrorism designed to control their wives through fear. These "anti-social" men were about 15 times more likely than other abusive husbands to be violent outside their marriages.

The authors defined two types of violent husbands:

Type I

- Heart rate goes down as the argument proceeds, making the violence more deliberate.

- In arguments, they are highly belligerent, insulting, and threatening to the wife.

- They use a general strategy of controlling the wife by instilling fear.

- Forty-four percent are violent toward other family members and others.

- Fifty-six percent had fathers who abused their mothers.

- None were divorced.

Type II

- Heart rate climbs as they become more angry, making their violence more impulsive.

- In arguments, they are less emotionally abusive.

- They fear abandonment or rejection, or feel jealous.

- Only 3 percent are violent outside marriage.

- Thirteen percent had fathers who abused their mothers.

- Twenty-eight percent were divorced or separated.

During the course of the two-year study, none of the wives of these most abusive men left their husbands. Gottman and Jacobson theorized that some of the women married to Type I men were genuinely afraid to leave them. Type I men may be successful in inhibiting their wives' anger, which would give the wives the impetus to leave. (The wives of Type I men showed remarkably low levels of anger during arguments.)

On the other hand, a significant proportion of women married to Type I men are themselves anti-social and may be more habituated to a violent relationship than other women would be. The researchers did not think that any form of marital therapy or counseling could help these couples.

PROGRAM DROPOUT RATES

Dropout rates are high even though most clients have been court-ordered to batterer intervention programs. A number of studies indicate that between 20 percent and 30 percent of men who begin short-term (3 months) treatment do not complete it. A 1990 survey of 30 programs of differing lengths found a wide range in completion rates. Half of the programs reported completion rates of 50 percent or less. If dropout rates are based upon attendance at the intake session, rather than the first treatment session, noncompletion rates are even higher. A recent study that documented the dropout rate after the initial assessment found that 59 percent of those who completed the initial assessment never attended a single session and that 75 percent dropped out before the 10-week program was over.

High dropout rates in batterer intervention programs make it difficult to evaluate program success. Evaluations based on men who complete batterer programs focus on a very select group who likely do not reflect the composition of the group when it began. Since follow-up is not done with program dropouts, those probably the most likely to continue their violence, studies generally fail to accurately indicate the success or failure of a program.

Certain characteristics are generally related to dropout rates. Unemployment is the one characteristic most consistently related to dropping out of treatment. Other factors include youth, not being legally married, having low income and little education, unstable work histories, criminal histories, and excessive drinking. Voluntary clients, especially those with college educations, stay in treatment longer. Some researchers have found better attendance among college-educated men regardless of whether they were court-ordered or voluntary.

Dropout rates are high, in part, because the courts rarely impose penalties for nonattendance. One researcher reported that 45 percent of surveyed programs indicated that the court's failure to penalize those who did not attend batterer intervention programs was a problem. In addition, many court-ordered participants resisted the counseling and dropped out because they saw it as a form of punishment.

Batterer intervention programs must better address the issue of dropouts. Reducing or eliminating intake

sessions and getting batterers immediately involved in useful interventions may help. Counselors should provide more information about the purpose of the program in preprogram orientation sessions. Other suggested retention measures include courtroom assistance, mentors, and stiffer and quicker penalties for dropping out. One study found that home visits after a batterer missed a meeting also helped decrease dropout rates.

RECIDIVISM RATES

In "Patterns of Reassault in Batterer Programs" (*Violence and Victims,* vol. 12, no. 4, 1997), Edward Gondolf reported on his evaluation of four "well-established" batterer programs to assess the pattern of reassault, or a return to battering. The research sites, all of which had been in operation for five years or more and had at least 40 to 50 referrals per month, were Pittsburgh, Pennsylvania; Dallas, Texas; Houston, Texas; and Denver, Colorado. The programs represented a range of duration (from three months to nine months) and services.

TABLE 6.1		
Assault and Abuse Reported by Women During 15-month Follow-up (*n* = 662)		
Item	Number	Percent
Reassaults		
any reassault	210	32
more than once	123	19
during more than follow-up	68	10
Severest Tactics		
any "severe" tactic	133	20
beat up	49	7
knife or gun used	24	4
Injury		
bruised or injured	128	19
medical help sought	26	4
Other Abuse		
verbal abuse	460	70
controlling behaviors	299	45
threats	282	43
stalked	103	16
Quality of Life		
feel "better off"	436	66
feel "worse off"	79	12
feel "very safe"	480	73

Source: E.W. Gondolf, "Patterns of Reassault in Batterer Programs," *Violence and Victims*, vol. 12, no. 4, 1997. Copyright © Springer Publishing Company, Inc., New York 10012. Used by permission.

Eight hundred and forty batterers (210 per site) were recruited and tested during program intake at each site. Of the 840 batterers, 82 percent were referred to the programs by the court; 18 percent entered the programs voluntarily. Both batterers and their partners were interviewed by phone every three months for 15 months after intake. A female partner was interviewed for 79 percent of the batterers at least once during the 15-month follow-up.

In follow-up reports (662 total), 32 percent of the female partners interviewed reported at least one reassault during the 15 months. Of the 210 reassault cases, over half (61 percent) resulted in bruises or injuries, and 12 percent required medical attention. (See Table 6.1.) Not surprisingly, the reassault rate was significantly higher for program dropouts than for those who completed the program. Voluntary participants were also more likely to reassault their partners.

While the proportion of women who were reassaulted was relatively low, the proportion of women subjected to verbal abuse (70 percent), controlling behaviors (45 percent), and threats (43 percent) was high. Nonetheless, most women considered their "quality of life" to have improved (66 percent) and reported feeling "very safe" (73 percent) during the follow-up periods. (See Table 6.1.)

Fourteen percent of first-time reassaults occurred in the first three-month period, and 8 percent more occurred within six months (Figure 6.1). Early reassault appeared to be a high risk marker for continued abuse. Men who reassaulted their partners within three months (67 percent) were much more likely to repeat their attacks than were men who reassaulted for the first time after three months (8 percent). The repeaters were also highly likely to use severe tactics and to inflict injuries. Gondolf speculated that this group of men "may be resistant to, or unaffected by, the intervention because of previous contact with the criminal justice system or severe psychological disorders."

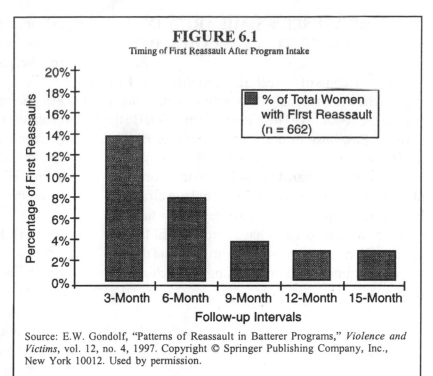

FIGURE 6.1
Timing of First Reassault After Program Intake

Source: E.W. Gondolf, "Patterns of Reassault in Batterer Programs," *Violence and Victims*, vol. 12, no. 4, 1997. Copyright © Springer Publishing Company, Inc., New York 10012. Used by permission.

Gondolf felt the rate of those who stopped their violence following participation in batterer programs was noteworthy, considering "the history of abuse, previous criminality, substance abuse, and psychological problems of the men referred to these programs." He concluded that "well-established" programs seem to contribute to the cessation of assault, at least in the short term. For the "resistant batterers," he encourages more extensive monitoring and intervention.

Other Studies

Daniel G. Saunders, in "Husbands Who Assault: Multiple Profiles Requiring Multiple Responses" (published as Chapter II in *Legal Responses to Wife Assault*, by Zoe Hilton, ed., Sage Publications, Newbury Park, California, 1993), reviewed the available information on male batterers and found that the recurrence of violence six months or more after treatment averaged about 35 percent across a number of studies. For men not completing treatment, the average was 52 percent. The men most likely to return to violence were, on average, younger, reported alcohol problems, scored higher for narcissism (self-love) on psychological tests, and had longer histories of pretreatment violence.

THE ABUSER'S SIMILARITY IN TREATMENT TO AN ALCOHOLIC'S

David Adams of EMERGE (see above) noted that the men he treats typically deny their violence ("Identifying the Assaultive Husband in Court: You Be the Judge," *Response to the Victimization of Women and Children*, vol. 13, no. 1, 1990). Like drug abusers, batterers compare themselves to the worst case abuser, the man who is severely abusive on a daily basis, and conclude that because they are not that bad, they therefore do not really have a problem. EMERGE has also found that men will lie outright about the violence or minimize it, calling choking or punching self-defense.

Adams finds similarities between the alcoholic and the abuser:

• Perhaps the most common manipulation pattern of the abusive man is to project blame for his violence onto his wife. In treatment programs for abusers, statements like "she drove me to it," "she provoked me," and "she really knows how to push my buttons" are common. Statements like these reveal the abuser's attempts to divert attention away from his own behavior and choices. In the early stages of treatment, abusers resist self-criticism by projecting responsibility for their violence onto others. This is similar to the alcoholic's tendency to blame other people, things, and circumstances for his drinking. The abusive husband, like the alcoholic, presents himself in treatment as a victim.

• Fifty percent of EMERGE's clients drop out of treatment within the first month, a figure similar to other programs. "The typical battering man, like the alcoholic, brings a 'quick fix' mentality to counseling. His desire to restore the status quo [the way things were] outweighs his desire to change."

THE FAILURE OF RESEARCH

Hamberger and Hastings, in "Court-Mandated Treatment of Men Who Assault Their Partner" (*Legal Responses to Wife Assault*, Sage Publications, Newbury Park, California, 1993), were dismayed by how little is really known about the short- and long-term effectiveness of treatment. In a review of 28 studies, they found recidivism (returning to violence) rates ranging from 4 and 5 percent to 50 percent. In addition, they charged that researchers are unprepared to provide even partial answers to which treatment types are most effective for which types of client and under what circumstances. Some of the research shortcomings included small sample size, lack of control groups, inconsistency of variables across studies, and infrequent use of psychological tests to determine changes in the subjects.

CHAPTER VII

ABUSE AND THE JUDICIAL SYSTEM

At one time, turning to the judicial system for help was unlikely to result in assistance or justice for the victim of spousal abuse. The judicial system tended to view wife abuse as a matter to be resolved within the family. After all, "a man's home is his castle," and the United States government has traditionally been reluctant to violate the sanctity of the home. Furthermore, many legal authorities believed the wife was, to some degree, responsible for her own beating by somehow inciting the husband to lose his temper.

Alcohol, and later illegal drug abuse, was sometimes considered the root of the problem. The authorities urged the treatment of alcoholism on the assumption that curing the drinking or drug problem would bring an end to the abuse. Finally, some traditional values implied that it was the wife's duty to put up with the abuse because that was her fate.

While appealing to the judicial system for help will not solve all the problems facing an abused victim, the reception an abused wife can expect from the system has improved markedly over the past decade. The Violence Against Women Act (VAWA, PL 103-322), signed into law by President Bill Clinton in September 1994, strengthened prevention and prosecution of violent crimes against women. This law provides tools for both criminal and civil prosecution of people who batter their intimate partners. Although the system is still far from perfect, legal authorities are far more likely to handle abuse complaints as serious than would have been the case only a dozen years ago.

CONTACTING THE POLICE

The police are often the initial contact the victim has with the judicial system, making the police response particularly important. The manner in which the police handle a domestic violence incident will likely color the way the victim looks at the judicial system — whether the system takes her complaint seriously and whether it is a place of support. Not surprisingly, when police project the blame for domestic violence on the wife, and she perceives this attitude, she will be reluctant to report further abuse to the police.

Family disturbance calls (often spousal disputes) are labeled by the police as the "common cold" of police work. These calls constitute a large category of calls received by police departments. In the mid-1960s, Detroit police dispatchers were instructed to screen out family disturbance calls unless they suspected "excessive" violence. A 1975 police guide, *The Function of the Police in Crisis Intervention and Conflict Management*, taught officers to avoid arrest at all costs and to discourage the victim from pressing charges, emphasizing the consequences of testifying in court, potential loss of income, etc.

Arrest policies have changed significantly in the past 20 years. Most states now authorize probable cause warrantless arrests in domestic violence cases (see below). Police departments have adopted pro-arrest or mandatory arrest policies. Pro-arrest strategies include everything from a warning to mandated treatment to prison time.

Who Calls the Police?

Most women do not report incidents of wife abuse to the police. Several studies have estimated the rate of reported incidents to be about 1 in 10. The *Second National Family Violence Survey* (NFVS), conducted in 1985 by Richard Gelles and Murray Straus, found that only 6.7 percent of all husband-to-wife assaults were reported to police. (The following NFVS information was published as Chapter 26, "Response of Victims and the Police to Assaults on Wives" by Glenda Kaufman Kantor and Murray Straus, in *Physical Violence in American Families: Risk Factors and Adaption to Violence in 8,145 Families*, Gelles and Straus, eds., Transaction Publishers, New Brunswick, New Jersey, 1990.)

When the assaults were categorized by severity,* only 3.2 percent of minor violence cases and 14.4 percent of severe violence cases were reported to the police. That four times as many cases of severe violence as minor violence were reported contradicts the claim by some police that "domestic" calls are social work that should be handled by other agencies.

Based on crime data from 17 states ("Violence Against Women: A Week in the Life of America," Senate Judiciary Committee, 1992), experts estimated that 1.37 million domestic violence offenses were reported to the police in 1991. Women were the victims in 1.13 million cases, or 83 percent of the total.

National Crime Victimization Survey

A Bureau of Justice Statistics report (Lawrence A. Greenfeld, et al., *Violence by Intimates*, Washington, DC, 1998), based on the *National Crime Victimization Survey* (NCVS), studied how often women called the police. The NCVS is an ongoing nationwide survey that gathers data on criminal victimization from a national sample of household respondents, ages 12 or older. The survey provides an annual estimate of crimes experienced by the public, whether or not a law enforcement agency was contacted about the crime.

According to the NCVS, about half the women who were victims of intimate violence reported an incident to the police. The percentage changed very little from 1993 (48 percent) to 1996 (56 percent). (See Figure 7.1.) The survey also found that Black female victims (68 percent) were more likely to report intimate violence to the police than women of other races (White, 49 percent; other, 44 percent).

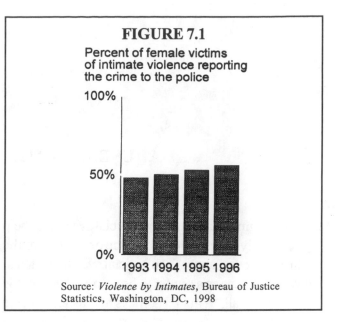

FIGURE 7.1

Percent of female victims of intimate violence reporting the crime to the police

Source: *Violence by Intimates*, Bureau of Justice Statistics, Washington, DC, 1998

The reasons given for not calling police about intimate violence are shown in Table 7.1. One-third of the women who did not report incidents (or 15 percent of all female victims of intimate violence) said they felt this was a private or personal matter. Other common reasons given included the fear of retaliation (7.3 percent) and the belief that the police would not do anything (4.4 percent).

Kaufman Kantor and Straus point out that "respondents participating in the NCVS are informed that they are part of the National *Crime* Survey and asked if they have been victimized by *crime* in the previous six months." Many women do not report spouse abuse to the NCVS because they interpret it as a family problem, not a crime.

Should a Woman
Call the Police?

The Bureau of Justice Statistics, in a study of violence against women (Patrick A. Langan and Christopher A. Innes, *Preventing Domestic Violence Against Women*, Washington, DC, 1986), found that during the average six-month period following the

---

* The research from the NFVS uses a "Conflict Tactics Scale" to measure the level of violence. See Chapter II.

women's initial victimization, about 180,000 of the 1.1 million victims who called (16 percent) were victimized again, compared to about 165,000 of the 700,000 (23 percent) who had not called.

In addition, the study found no evidence that later crimes became more serious (in terms of bodily injury) as a result of the victim having called the police. An estimated 2.9 percent of women who called the police had a later violent incident more serious than the initial one, compared to 4.4 percent of women who had not called the police. (Because of the low numbers involved, these differences are not considered statistically significant.)

Langan and Innes further reported that when the abuser in the initial incident was the woman's spouse or ex-spouse, the risk of later domestic violence was 18.1 percent among women who called the police, compared to 30.9 percent among women who did not call. In the case of married women (as opposed to the combination of married, divorced, and separated women), the effect of calling the police was even more noticeable. The risk of later violence by a married woman's spouse was 15.4 percent when she called the police versus 41 percent when she did not call. The study concluded that calling the police was associated with lower rates of repeat violence, and those who called the police were no more likely to suffer later violence than those who did not call.

THE POLICE RESPONSE

According to the *National Crime Victimization Survey* (see above), the police responded to about 90 percent of intimate violence calls. In about 20 percent of the incidents, the offender was arrested at the scene. See Table 7.2 for actions taken by the police. Most victims (60 percent) reported that police responded to their calls within 10 minutes (Figure 7.2).

Determining Police Response

In a study of four precincts of the Detroit Police Department, Eve Buzawa and Thomas Austin, in "Determining Police Response to Domestic Violence Victims" (*American Behavioral Scientist*, May 1993),

---

TABLE 7.1

Female victims of intimate violence, 1992-96

Violent crime against an intimate reported to the police 52.1%	Violent crime against an intimate not reported to the police 47.8%

Most important reasons given for not reporting

Private or personal matter	15.4%
Afraid of offender retaliation	7.3
Police would do nothing	4.4
Incident was not important enough	3.5
No one reason most important	1.7
Reported to another official	1.1
Don't know	.7*
Other	13.6

*Fewer than 10 cases.

Source: *Violence by Intimates*, Bureau of Justice Statistics, Washington, DC, 1998

---

discovered several factors that affected police decisions to arrest offenders:

- The presence of bystanders or children during the abuse.

- The presence of guns and sharp objects as weapons.

- An injury resulting from the assault.

- The offender and victim sharing the same residence, married or not.

- The victim's desire to have the offender arrested. (Of those who expressed such a desire, arrests were made in 44 percent of the cases. When the victim did not want the offender arrested, arrests were made in only 21 percent of the cases.)

In interviews with 110 victims, Buzawa and Austin found that 85 percent of victims were satisfied with the police response. Not surprisingly, they were particularly satisfied when the police responded to their preferences for arresting or not arresting the offender. Though most women victims interviewed were satisfied with the police response, not one male victim was.

Lynette Feder, in "Police Handling of Domestic and Nondomestic Assault Calls: Is There a Case for Discrimination?" (*Crime and Delinquency*, vol. 44, no. 2, April 1998), found that domestic assault calls were nearly twice as likely to result in arrests than were nondomestic assault calls. However, overall rates of arrest were fairly low — 23 percent of domestic assault calls and 13 percent of nondomestic assault calls. Feder's study also indicated four variables as significant in the probability of arrest: the presence of the offender when the police arrived, the victim's desire for the arrest of the offender, the extent of the victim's injuries, and a disrespectful demeanor toward police.

Victims' Dissatisfaction

Raquel Kennedy Bergen studied 40 women who, in addition to physical abuse, had been raped by their husbands (*Wife Rape: Understanding the Response of Survivors and Service Providers*, Sage Publications, Thousand Oaks, California, 1996). Only 37 percent of these women (15 out of 40) reported calling the police for help on at least one occasion. (Three women in the study felt it was impossible to call the police because their spouses were members of the police department.) About 80 percent of those who did call were not satisfied with the police response. Of the total group, eight spouses were eventually charged with rape by the criminal justice system.

One woman reported that when the police interviewed her (several times), they made a point to ask embarrassing questions and ask repeatedly for intimate details. "Could you say that again, miss? Speak up, miss," and "What kind of underwear were you wearing, miss? Were you wearing fancy negligees?" Most found their police experiences so unsatisfactory they stopped calling the police for help.

Another woman who found the police unresponsive lied to get them to come. She called to report that "some guy was beating up some lady in front of the house with a gun. They first asked me if the guy was married to the woman.... I said no, and they showed up in 15 minutes."

A Source of Frustration

There can be little doubt that "domestic quarrels" are a cause of great frustration to the police. According to the *FBI Law Enforcement Bulletin* (October 1997), domestic violence calls "are repetitious as often officers respond to the same homes over and over,

TABLE 7.2

Female victims of intimate violence, 1992-96

Violent crime against an intimate reported to the police 51%		Violent crime against an intimate not reported to the police 49%
Police responded or victim went to the police 88%	Police did not respond 11%	

Actions taken by the police

Took an official report	70%
Questioned witness/suspect	29
Arrested the offender	20
Searched for/collected evidence	6
Promised surveillance/investigation	4

Ultimately, about 1 in 3 offenders identified by the victim were eventually arrested or charged for the victimization between the time of the incident and the interview with the victim.

Source: *Violence by Intimates*, Bureau of Justice Statistics, Washington, DC, 1998

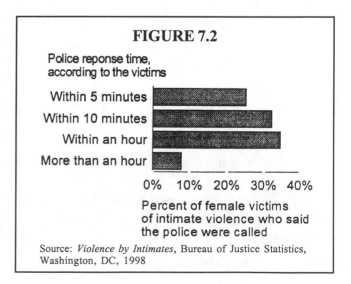

FIGURE 7.2

Police reponse time, according to the victims

Within 5 minutes
Within 10 minutes
Within an hour
More than an hour

0% 10% 20% 30% 40%

Percent of female victims of intimate violence who said the police were called

Source: *Violence by Intimates*, Bureau of Justice Statistics, Washington, DC, 1998

take up valuable time that could be spent on other investigative matters, and frequently produce no legal action against offenders." Police claim 90 percent of domestic violence calls are repeat calls, and the police typically know by the location and address who is calling. Although battered women think the police are sometimes insensitive, the police become exasperated after answering numerous calls from the same women. Some officers may think, "If that's the way she wants to live, what can I do about it?"

Research has found that few women will file complaints against their batterers. In spite of significant legislative changes, police officers still meet victim resistance to arresting the abusive partner. In addition, arrests have not decreased repeat offenses as hoped.

Kathleen Ferraro and Lucille Pope, in "Battered Women, Police, and the Law," (*Legal Responses to Wife Assault*, N. Zoe Hilton, ed., Sage Publications, Thousand Oaks, California, 1993), examined the cultural context of law enforcement's attitude to arrest. Based on 440 hours of field observation of the Phoenix police, the authors concluded that among the most influential factors in police attitudes were the officers' background beliefs about race and class. Women from low-income, minority communities were more likely to be seen as "enmeshed in a culture of violence." A specific violent event was likely to be viewed as part of a larger pattern of culture and, therefore, beyond the scope of police intervention.

Ferraro has found in past research that, while the police express frustration that women refuse to press charges, the proportion of cases dropped because of victim reluctance (13 percent) was not much larger than the proportion dropped because of the inadequacy of police reports documenting the evidence (10 percent).

Police blame not only the women for refusing to file charges, but also the courts for undermining the seriousness of the crime by not following through with jail sentences or probation. A review of court cases (cited in Ferraro and Pope) reported that only 1 out of 250 cases of wife assault actually ended up with a report to police, a court conviction, and a serious sentence.

Ferraro and Pope's police observation revealed that some officers resented the time it took to process an arrest. They viewed domestic violence calls as time spent that could be better used on other police work. One officer complained that she had been unable to respond to an armed robbery call because she was transporting a woman to a shelter. Police officers are not often rewarded or promoted for their efforts to prevent spouse abuse, but they do receive recognition for their work on high-profile crimes such as drug busts or armed robberies.

Traditional Attitudes Prevail

George Rigakos, in "Constructing the Symbolic Complainant: Police Subculture and the Nonenforcement of Protection Orders from Battered Women" (*Violence and Victims*, vol. 10, no. 3, 1995), studied how police officers' attitudes influenced the treatment women received in a suburb of Vancouver, British Columbia. He found that a traditional masculine culture contributed to "negative stereotypes of women as liars, manipulators, and unreliable witnesses."

According to Rigakos, interviews with police officers and justice officials revealed four major themes. First, justice officials and police felt that they were doing all they could for women, but other institutions impeded their work. Police officers blamed the legal system, charging the courts with liberally issuing unenforceable restraining and protective orders (see below). "[Y]ou're looking for your judge to guarantee or back the civil restraining order. Which typically doesn't seem to be done. It's done by some judge who mass produces them.... It's like a big legal bureaucracy, from what I've seen, which doesn't help the people." In addition, according to the police, judges issue them incorrectly.

You need both parties there who both agree with the legal restraining order. This is the facts and if both people agree to the facts then we can stand by and keep the peace but that's it. But usually that's not the case. Both parties aren't there, only one party is there so we're reluctant to enforce [restraining orders].

For their part, the justices blame the police for lack of enforcement. They believe the police misunderstand the law and fail to respond adequately.

Second, the police in this study held conservative attitudes toward marriage that resulted in their excusing men's behavior. Officers expressed preferences for women who adhered to traditional behaviors, such as mothering and housekeeping.

You have some real [deleted] who keep the house like a pig-sty. Then the guy gets angry ... and she's drunk and slaps him. If he fights back, she calls the police. Most of these things are started by the women anyways; it's just that they're smaller and end up losing the fight.

Third, traditional beliefs turned the police's attention to the women, making the women's behavior appear "unreliable." According to a policeman, "Women are using these [restraining] orders to manipulate their husbands. Like for custody battles and divorces.... Women aren't stupid, they know we have to arrest, we have no bloody choice, so they're using it against their husbands." The officer continued, "Women are good at arguing, but when men respond the only way they know how they get arrested. It's not fair, is it?" Even some female officers blamed the women: "If this woman was yapping in my face.... She didn't ask to be assaulted, but...."

Distorted Perceptions

Finally, according to Rigakos, the officers made generalizations that were supported by their beliefs about women but were not upheld by official court records. The police perception was that, after the police had spent tremendous effort and time to prepare a case, women frequently did not pursue the charges. A fairly representative statement from the police was, "I've been doing this for some 26 years, and I've had thousands and thousands. The ones where there is actual violence on an ongoing basis, you charge, you go to court, and the women don't show. And after a while it's like 'don't cry wolf if you're not prepared to go through with it.' " These negative perceptions of women have led to a "selective memory" that magni-

fies every event of a battered woman failing to appear to testify against a partner and diminishes those in which she does.

A survey of the court records for 1993 found that out of 49 cases, five women were "uncooperative," one refused to testify, three were no-shows, and one stated she had lied. Rigakos concluded that

The police officers' selected memories of trial experiences gone sour revolve around feelings of betrayal when a survivor became a reluctant witness. These images over-shadow the hundreds of cases that have resulted in guilty pleas or successful prosecutions throughout their careers. They become amplified because of their profound personal effect on the witnessing officer and ease with which these incidents can be accounted for when viewed within prevailing patriarchal constructions of women.

Innovations in Police Departments

In recent years, a number of police departments have developed programs and "General Orders" to make their handling of spousal abuse calls more effective and consistent. These include recognizing that a crime has been committed, arresting the abuser, and providing some form of protection for the victim. See Figure 7.3 for an example of the Duluth directive.

Duluth has been a pioneer in initiating strong anti-abuse policies. More than 15 years since this directive, Duluth's program is still being driven by its original goal — to make every agent of the justice system (police, prosecutors, probation officers, and judges) deliver the same message: domestic violence is a crime that the community will not tolerate. Police are instructed to arrest batterers. Representatives from battered women's shelters and batterers' treatment programs are sent to talk with the parties immediately after the arrest. Typically, a first-time offender is sentenced to 30 days in jail and probation until completion of a 26-week batterers' program. If he misses classes, he is usually sent to jail. Aspects of their program have been imitated throughout the country.

FIGURE 7.3

DULUTH POLICE DEPARTMENT
Duluth, Minnesota

GENERAL ORDER #83-9
November 29, 1983

REVISION OF GENERAL ORDER #82-3

TO: All Members of the Department

SUBJECT: Revision of General Order 82-3 regarding Domestic Violence

Effective Thursday, December 1, 1983, the following policy will replace the existing policy regarding domestic violence under section 506.92 of the Department manual. Language previously contained in that section will be disregarded.

These language changes are intended to reflect recent legislative changes to the probable cause arrest statute and to increase the department's effectiveness in responding to domestic assault cases. In a continuing effort to cooperate with the St. Louis County Court system and other Duluth agencies to provide a more uniform and consistent response to domestic assault cases, the following guidelines shall be enacted.

1. An officer shall arrest and take into custody a person whom the officer has probable cause to believe has violated an order for protection restraining the person or excluding the person from the residence if the existence of the order can be verified by the officer.

   (Note: Because state law requires an arrest regardless of whether or not the person was invited back into the home, county court judges have agreed when issuing this order to inform the excluded party that the court must formally change the order in order for him/her to return to the residence.)

2. An officer shall arrest and take into custody an adult whom the officer has probable cause to believe assaulted another adult with whom he/she is residing with or has formerly resided with if:

   a) There are visible signs of injury or physical impairment

   or

   b) There was a threat with a dangerous weapon.

   The arrest must take place within four hours of the alleged assault and the officer must believe that the injuries were the result of an assault by the alleged assailant.

   (Note: Probable cause is defined as follows: Based on the officers' observations and statements made by the parties involved and witness (if any) the officer using reasonable judgement believes an assault did occur and the person to be arrested committed the assault.)

3. An officer may arrest when responding to a call involving persons (of any age) residing together or who have resided together in the past if the officer has probable cause to believe that the alleged assailant has within the past four hours placed the alleged victim in immediate fear of bodily harm.

4. Whenever an officer investigates an allegation that an incident described above occurred, whether or not an arrest is made, the officer shall make a written report of the alleged incident and submit that report to the Inspector of the Patrol Division. In addition, the officer shall advise victims of the availability of the Women's Coalition and the Domestic Abuse Intervention Project and give victims legal rights and services cards.

5. Following a domestic related arrest, the officer shall advise the victim that an advocate will contact her/him within the next several hours to explain the legal and service options available. The officer shall request that the jailer contact the Women's Coalition at 728-3679 immediately following the booking procedure and inform them that an arrest has been made. Advocates will be sent to talk to the

---

Note: Section 1, 3 and 4 of this order are required of an officer as department policy and Minnesota state law. Minnesota statute 1982, Sec. 629.341 provides immunity from civil and criminal liability to officers making good faith arrests under this law.

By Order:

[signature]

Eugene Sisto
Deputy Chief of Police

Minnesota Probable Cause Arrest Law

§ 629.341

PREVENTION OF CRIME

629.341. Probable cause arrests; domestic violence; immunity from liability

Subdivision 1. Arrest. Notwithstanding the provisions of section 629.34 or any other law or rule to the contrary, a peace officer may arrest without a warrant a person anywhere, including at his place of residence if the peace officer has probable cause to believe the person within the preceding four hours has assaulted, threatened with a dangerous weapon, or placed in fear of immediate bodily harm his spouse, former spouse, or other person with whom he resides or has formerly resided, although the assault did not take place in the presence of the peace officer.

Subd. 2. Immunity. Any peace officer acting in good faith and exercising due care in the making of an arrest pursuant to subdivision 1 shall have immunity from civil liability that otherwise might result by reason of his action.

Subd. 3. Notice of rights. The peace officer shall advise the victim of the availability of a shelter or other services in the community and give the victim immediate notice of the legal rights and remedies available. The notice shall include furnishing the victim a copy of the following statement:

"IF YOU ARE THE VICTIM OF DOMESTIC VIOLENCE, you can ask the city or county attorney to file a criminal complaint. You also have the right to go to court and file a petition requesting an order for protection from domestic abuse which could include the following: (a) an order restraining the abuser from further acts of abuse; (b) an order directing the abuser to leave your household; (c) an order preventing the abuser from entering your residence, school, business, or place of employment; (d) an order awarding you or the other parent custody of or visitation with your minor child or children; (e) an order directing the abuser to pay support to you and the minor children if the abuser has a legal obligation to do so."

The notice shall include the resource listing, including telephone number, for the area battered women's shelter, to be designated by the department of corrections.

Subd. 4. Report required. Whenever a peace officer investigates an allegation that an incident described in subdivision 1 has occurred, whether or not an arrest is made, the officer shall make a written police report of the alleged incident. The officer must submit the report to his supervisor or other person to whom the employer's rules or policies require reports of similar allegations of criminal activity to be made.

Subd. 5. Training. The board of peace officer standards and training shall provide a copy of this section to every law enforcement agency in this state on or before June 30, 1983.

Upon request of the board of peace officer standards and training to the bureau of criminal apprehension, the subject matter of at least one training course must include instruction in the subject matter of domestic abuse. Every basis skills course required in order to obtain initial licensure as a peace officer must, after January 1, 1985, include at least three hours of training in handling domestic violence cases.

Amended by Laws 1983, c. 226, § 1; Laws 1984, c. 655, art. 1, § 79.

1983 Amendment. Revised this section. For former text see the main volume.

1984 Amendment. Laws 1984, c. 655 was a revisor's bill, which by its title purported to correct erroneous references, eliminate redundant and superseded provisions, reenact certain laws and correct 1984 session legislation. The

Act inserted "or" preceding "other person with whom he resides" in subd. 1.

Law Review Commentaries

Duluth domestic abuse intervention. Ellen Pence. 1983 Hamline L.Rev. 247.

New family laws. Cathy E. Gorlin. July-Aug. 1983, 52 Hennepin Lawyer 12.

DOES ARREST HELP?

The Bureau of Justice Statistics, in *Preventing Domestic Violence Against Women* (above), supported arrest, stating that it could

- Prevent further criminal behavior.

- Prevent further injury to the victim.

- Demonstrate to the offender that he will face legal consequences.

- Demonstrate to the victim, the offender, and the community that domestic violence is criminal behavior.

- Increase the number of offenders subject to prosecution, court supervision, treatment, and other community intervention.

Arrest became a much more popular tactic after the publication of the influential National Institute of Justice study, "The Specific Deterrent Effects of Arrest for Domestic Assault" (Lawrence Sherman and Richard Berk, *American Sociological Review*, April 1984). Over an 18-month period, Berk and Sherman examined the effectiveness of various police actions in domestic violence cases in Minneapolis.

The police randomly selected three different approaches: arrest, advice or mediation, and ordering the offender to leave the house for an eight-hour period. They found that offenders not arrested had almost twice the repeat violence during a six-month follow-up period. Almost all offenders were released shortly after their arrest, so this difference was not because they were in jail and could not commit violence. In addition, only 3 of the 136 arrested offenders were actually punished by fine or imprisonment, so it appeared that it was not punishment, but the actual arrest that contributed to the decline.

Sherman and Berk pointed out the weaknesses of their study. It was a small study dealing with a single police department, and several changes had to be made with the format because few police officers properly followed the test procedure. Consequently, the conclusions should be used with care. Nonetheless, the researchers concluded that, in instances of domestic violence,

> An arrest should be made unless there are good, clear reasons why an arrest would be counterproductive. We do not, however, favor requiring arrest in all misdemeanor domestic assault cases.... We feel it is best to leave police a loophole to capitalize [on the individual situation] ... it is widely recognized that discretion is inherent in police work. Simply to impose a requirement of arrest, irrespective of the features of the immediate situation, is to invite circumvention.

Arrest Is Not More Effective

Rarely has a single research experiment played such a major role in changing a police policy (or any other policy, for that matter). Ellen G. Cohn and Lawrence W. Sherman, in "Police Policy on Domestic Violence, 1986: A National Survey" (*Crime Control Reports*, no. 5, 1987), found more than a fourfold increase in the number of police departments reporting arrest as their preferred policy in domestic violence disputes.

In an effort to further validate the results of the Minneapolis study, the National Institute of Justice funded experiments in six other cities. J. David Hirschel et al. reported on the results of the Charlotte, North Carolina, study in "The Failure to Deter Spouse Abuse" (*Journal of Research in Crime and Delinquency*, vol. 29, no. 1, 1992). In Charlotte, three police procedures were measured: advising and possibly separating the couple; issuing a citation requiring the offender to appear in court to answer charges; and arresting the offender. The experiment involved the entire police force and was in effect 24 hours a day. Cases that met all the criteria for the study (686) were followed up six months after the original intervention through interviews and police records.

Table 7.3 shows the rates of rearrest during the six months following the original three types of intervention. In about 18 percent of the cases in which the officers had arrested the offender, the offender was rearrested for abuse. The rate for those who had been issued a citation was 19 percent, while those who had received advice or had been separated reoffended at a rate of nearly 12 percent. Through interviews with the victims, the researchers found that 59 percent of the victims reported being abused since the original arrest, 31 percent of whom were abused five times or more. Rates were comparable for the other two interventions — 65 percent of the citation offenders and 60 percent of the advise/separate offenders had repeated their violence in the six-month period (Table 7.4).

The study concluded that arrest was no more effective than any other measure used by the police. Furthermore, police data had implied that repeat offenses were the exception, while interview data with victims showed the contrary — that reoffending is the rule and not the exception. The researchers proposed a number of reasons why their data did not support the findings of the Minneapolis study:

- The majority (69.4 percent) of the offenders in the sample had previous criminal records, so arrest was not an unusual occurrence for them.

- For many of the couples in the study, abuse is a common occurrence, and it is unrealistic to expect one arrest to deter chronic behavior.

- Arrest alone may not be a strong enough deterrent. Time spent in jail is often minimal. The median amount of time between the incident and release from jail was 9.4 hours, with over a quarter of the men spending less than 4 hours in jail.

- Although not officially part of the project, the researchers found that in only 35.5 percent of the cases in which the offender was either arrested or issued a citation was he prosecuted, and in less than 1 percent of the cases did the offender spend any time in jail beyond the initial arrest.

- As jails become more and more overcrowded, it is not difficult for offenders to realize that premium jail space will not be devoted to misdemeanor spouse abusers.

This study shows only that arrest is not a deterrent in misdemeanor spouse abuse cases. It does not address the issues of whether arrest would be effective in cases of felony assault or in cases of lower levels of abuse that are not considered misdemeanors.

TABLE 7.3
Prevalence and Incidence of Arrest Recidivism, by Treatment[a]

| Arrest Recidivism | Treatment Assigned | | | |
	Arrest	Citation	Advise/ Separate	Total
Number of subsequent arrests				
0	175	181	187	543
1	36	33	24	93
2	2	7	1	10
3	1	1	0	2
4	0	2	0	2
Total failures	39	43	25	107
Total cases	214	224	212	650
Prevalence[b]	18.2	19.2	11.8	16.5
Incidence[c]	.201	.259	.123	.195

a. As measured 6 months subsequent to presenting incident.
b. $\chi^2 = 5.063$; $df = 2$; $p = .080$.
c. F ratio = 4.211; $df(1) = 2$; $df(2) = 647$; $p = .015$.

TABLE 7.4
Victim-Reported Recidivism, by Treatment[a]

| Victim-Reported Recidivism | Treatment Assigned | | | |
	Arrest	Citation	Advise/ Separate	Total
Number of incidents				
0	46	43	41	130
1	14	18	10	42
2	2	12	8	22
3	12	6	13	31
4	3	9	3	15
5 or more	35	36	27	98
Total failures	66	81	61	208
Total N interviewed	112	124	102	338
Prevalence[b]	58.9	65.3	59.8	61.5
Incidence[c]	2.152	2.226	2.078	2.157

a. Based on initial and 6-month interviews combined.
b. $\chi^2 = 1.202$, $df = 2$, $p = .548$
c. F ratio = .132; $df(1) = 2$; $df(2) = 335$; $p = .875$

Source of both tables: J. David Hirschel et al., "Failure to Deter Spouse Abuse," *Journal of Research in Crime and Delinquency*, vol. 29, no. 1, 1992

Arrest Does Deter Some Men

Sherman et al. looked at the rates of recidivism (a relapse into criminal behavior) in a police study in Milwaukee ("Crime, Punishment and Stake in Conformity: Legal and Extralegal Control of Domestic Violence," *American Sociological Review*, vol. 57, 1992). Sherman found that arrest deters men who have strong attachments to their local communities, perhaps through a job, friends, or family. Those who have little "stake in conformity," such as those who are unemployed and unmarried, may actually be more violent in response to arrest. The study did not consider, however, other factors that may have influenced the results. For example, employed offenders may have had less violent histories or less stressful home lives or may have been older, all factors that might have affected their rate of recidivism.

Peter G. Jaffe et al., in "The Impact of Police Laying Charges," (*Legal Responses to Wife Assault — Current Trends and Evaluation*, Sage Publications, Newbury Park, California, 1993), studied the effect of police intervention in London, Ontario. The participants were 90 female victims of assault, 52 of whom had called for police intervention and filed criminal charges; 14 had police intervention, but no charges were filed; and 24 had neither police help, nor had they filed charges.

Table 7.5 shows that while there was no change in the level of violence when the police intervened but no charges were filed, there was a sharp drop between the 12 months before the violent event and the 12 months after filing charges. The bottom portion of the table combined those respondents who had no police intervention and those who had intervention but no charges filed, compared with women for whom

charges were filed. Although arrest alone did not decrease the violence in this study, it was a significant deterrent when charges were filed. The authors urge that police support be integrated into a community response that would include all aspects of support for battered women.

Probable Cause Warrantless Arrests

In the early 1970s, it was legal for the police to make probable cause warrantless arrests for felonies, but only 14 states permitted it for misdemeanors. Because the crime of simple assault and battery is a misdemeanor in most states, family violence victims were forced to initiate their own criminal charges against the batterer. Today, only West Virginia does not authorize warrantless probable cause misdemeanor arrests in domestic violence cases; however, more than half the

---

TABLE 7.5

Severity of Violence Used by Males Against Female Partner
During 12-Month Periods Before and After Target Incident

	Mean Violence Severity Score (range 0 = never occurred, to 1 = occurred 1 or more times)					
a.	No Police		Police/No Charges		Police/Charges	
	Before	After	Before	After	Before	After
Insulted/swore at	0.6	0.7	0.7	0.5	0.7	0.4*
Slapped	0.58	0.47	0.3	0.3	0.64	0.19*
Kicked, bit, or hit with fist	0.5	0.4	0.3	0.4	0.5	0.17*

b.	No Charges		Charges	
	Before	After	Before	After
Threatened to hit or throw something	0.63	0.63	0.71	0.38*
Pushed, grabbed, or shoved	0.83	0.70	0.80	0.37*
Slapped	0.48	0.41	0.64	0.19*
Kicked, bit, or hit with fist	0.43	0.40	0.50	0.17*

*$p < .05$.

Source: Peter G. Jaffe et al., "The Impact of Police Laying Charges," *Legal Responses to Wife Assault — Current Trends and Evaluation*, N. Zoe Hilton, Ed., p. 83, copyright © 1993 by Sage Publications. Reprinted by permission of Sage Publications, Inc.

states have added qualifiers such as visible signs of injury or report of the violence within eight hours of the incident. Most state codes authorizing warrantless arrests require police to inform victims of their rights, which include the acquisition of protection orders, emergency and shelter facilities, and transportation.

Mandatory Arrests

By 1992, 15 states, the District of Columbia, and dozens of municipalities had instituted a mandatory arrest policy whenever the police are called in to a domestic violence situation. Some battered women's advocates do not support mandatory arrest. They fear that poor, minority families are treated more harshly than middle-class families and that, if the police arrive and both spouses are bloodied by the fight, both will be arrested, forcing the children into foster care. In Connecticut, where a strict arrest policy is mandatory, the dual arrest rate is 14 percent.

Recent data suggest that mandatory arrests may actually increase violence, especially if the batterer is unemployed or has a criminal record. Some observers have suggested that mandatory arrest be replaced with mandatory action, such as providing transportation to a shelter or granting the victim the option to arrest the offender or not. Mandatory action would allow the police officer to make decisions appropriate to each individual case.

Some police departments have adopted a presumptive (also called preferred) arrest policy. This policy means that an arrest should be made unless clear and compelling reasons exist not to arrest. Presumptive arrest provisions forbid officers from basing the decision whether to arrest on the victim's consent or request, or on a perception of the victim's willingness to testify or participate in the proceeding. Proponents point out that arresting an offender gives the victim a respite from fear and an opportunity to look for help. In addition, they claim it reduces bias in arrests.

Evan Stark, in "Mandatory Arrest of Batterers: A Reply to Its Critics" (*Do Arrests and Restraining Orders Work?*, Buzawa and Buzawa, eds., Sage Publications, Newbury Park, California, 1996), gives reasons for a mandatory arrest policy other than deterrence:

- Provides a standard against which to judge variation in police response.

- Provides immediate protection from current violence and gives victims time to consider their options.

- Reduces the overall incidence of domestic violence both directly (because arrest might deter recidivism) and by sending a clear message that battering is unacceptable.

- Provides victims access to services and protection that would not be available outside the criminal justice system.

PRO AND CON FOR ARREST

Richard Berk, in "On the Average, We Can Do No Better Than Arrest," (*Current Controversies on Family Violence*, Gelles and Loseke, eds., Sage Publications, Newbury Park, California, 1993), supports the use of arrest in certain circumstances. Follow-up studies to the Minneapolis study found that arrest was no more effective in preventing subsequent violence than any other approach. Berk points out, however, that this can also be interpreted as "one can do no better than by arresting the offender." On the other hand, the Milwaukee study found that arrest was beneficial in the case of offenders who had strong attachments to their communities (for example, men who were married and employed). If arrest is effective for some offenders, then it cannot be said that arrest does not work; the answer is that "it depends."

Eve and Carl Buzawa, in "The Scientific Evidence Is Not Conclusive" (*Current Controversies*; see above), disagree with Berk on the effectiveness of arrest. They contend that the arrest studies show increased violence after arrest, especially if the offender is released soon after. They cite Sherman (author of the Milwaukee study), who theorized that the anger engendered by arrest may overpower any deterrent effect of the arrest, especially in those who have little to lose.

The authors gave several reasons why they do not support arrest. They charge that the focus on arrest has diverted limited funds away from shelters, mistakenly based on "the 'fact' that arrests deter the violence prior to the need for shelter." Furthermore, mandatory arrest ignores the wishes of the victim and is patronizing towards battered women.

The actual cost of arrest is high, while the indirect costs in damage to community relations also could be damaging. Mandatory arrest undermines efforts to build trust between the police and the poor and minority groups who are likely to have experienced confrontations with the police. Some minority women fear that if they call the police, their partners will be beaten by the arresting officers.

Instead, the Buzawas would prefer to see the federal government fund services for victims and offenders. They believe that well-planned and properly funded rehabilitation programs (including substance abuse treatment) might dramatically decrease the need for arrests. The Buzawas believe that "long-term counseling and other rehabilitation measures may ultimately prove more effective than arrest in deterring future violence."

DOMESTIC VIOLENCE GUN BAN

The Omnibus Consolidated Appropriations Act of 1997 (PL 104-208) includes a domestic violence gun ban. The law prohibits batterers who have been convicted of domestic violence misdemeanor crimes or who have domestic violence protection orders filed against them from owning or carrying guns. During 1997, background checks of potential handgun buyers prevented an estimated 69,000 purchases. Most of those rejected (62 percent) had been convicted of a felony or were under felony indictment. Domestic violence misdemeanor convictions represented over 9 percent of the rejections, while domestic violence restraining orders accounted for 2 percent. (See Table 7.6.)

TABLE 7.6

Reasons for rejection of handgun purchase applications, national estimates, 1997

Reason for rejection	All States	Original Brady States	Brady States during 1997
Total	100.0%	100.0%	100.0%
Felony (indictment/ conviction/no disposition)	61.7	69.9	50.3
Fugitive	5.9	7.5	12.8
Domestic violence			
Misdemeanor conviction	9.1	9.6	14.6
Restraining order	2.1	2.2	0.4
State law prohibition	6.1	3.0	5.7
Mental illness or disability	0.9	0.1	0.2
Drug addiction	1.6	2.2	5.2
Local law prohibition	0.9	0.1	0.1
Other*	11.7	5.4	10.7

*Includes illegal aliens, juveniles, persons discharged from the armed services dishonorably, persons who have renounced their U.S. citizenship, and other unspecified persons. At the end of 1997, 23 of the 32 original Brady States were still under the Brady Act.

Source: *Presale Handgun Checks, 1997*, Bureau of Justice Statistics, Washington, DC, 1998

The passage of the domestic violence gun ban was a victory for the battered women's movement but resulted in an outcry by the law enforcement community. Because the ban applies retroactively, anyone (including police officers) who was convicted of domestic violence before the passage of the law on September 30, 1996, loses the right to possess and carry firearms.

The law has led to considerable debate. Some people feel that law enforcement officers and military personnel who use firearms in their professional duties should be exempt from the prohibition. Others want to apply the prohibition only to those convicted of domestic violence offenses after September 30, 1996, when the gun ban was enacted. Still others maintain that all persons convicted of such offenses should be prohibited from carrying firearms.

Response to the Ban

Amendments to eliminate the retroactive application of the gun ban have been proposed in both the House and the Senate. The House proposal reads "to amend title 18, U.S. Code, to provide that the firearms prohibitions applicable by reason of a domestic violence misdemeanor conviction do not apply if the conviction occurred before the prohibitions became law." Neither has passed at the time of this writing.

After the domestic violence gun ban was passed, John W. Magaw, of the Bureau of Alcohol, Tobacco, and Firearms (ATF), advised police officers to turn over their firearms to a third party if they had ever been convicted of a domestic violence misdemeanor ("Clarifying the Domestic Violence Provision of the Omnibus Consolidated Appropriations Act," *Police Chief*, February 1997). Most police groups claim that the law unfairly punishes officers who committed domestic violence offenses in the past, offenses that may have been minor incidents. They say that exceptions should be made for police officers who would be unable to conduct enforcement duties without firearms.

In 1998, at the request of the U.S. Department of Justice, the International Association of Chiefs of Police (IACP) drafted a *Model Policy on Police Officer Involved Domestic Violence*. In an attempt to address the domestic violence problem before it costs an officer his or her job, the policy takes a "continuum" approach, including:

- Prevention, education, and training.

- Early warning and intervention.

- Incident response protocols.

- Victim safety and protection.

- Post-incident administrative and prosecutorial actions.

Though the policy focuses on early prevention and intervention strategies, it also states that officers convicted of domestic violence are to be "removed from their enforcement position, and either reassigned or terminated." It calls on police departments to screen recruits for any indications of violent or abusive tendencies and to conduct background checks for histories of domestic violence or abuse. According to Nancy Turner, the IACP project coordinator, once the policy

is issued in its final form, the Justice Department is expected to provide funding for a number of pilot sites to test its effectiveness.

FILING CHARGES

In the past, the burden of filing charges in domestic violence cases was typically placed on victims. The victims were generally given little support or protection by prosecutors or the courts. The decisions to charge offenders in cases of domestic violence are notable for having less to do with legal criteria than with an evaluation of the victims' and offenders' personal attributes. Prosecutors are more likely to charge in cases where victims suffer serious injuries and defendants have a record of previous arrests.

Negative characteristics in the offender (alcohol or drug use, failure to comply with the police or courts, etc.) make it more likely that charges will be pressed, while these same attributes in the abused call into question her status as an innocent "victim." The Buzawas (above) claim that more than a third of misdemeanor domestic violence cases would have been felony offenses of rape, robbery, or aggravated assault if they had been committed by a stranger.

Who should file the charges: the state, through the prosecutor, or the victim? In *Confronting Domestic Violence: A Guide for Criminal Justice Agencies* (above), those advocating that the state bring the charge indicated that this policy would:

- Clearly establish spouse abuse as a crime.

- Force prosecutors to take domestic violence cases seriously, and eliminate prosecutor reluctance to handle these cases because of their view that victims tend to seek dismissals or refuse to testify.

- Protect the community as a whole. Innocent bystanders could be injured as a result of future violence.

- Give the criminal justice system more control over prosecution and increase the number of batterers convicted and held accountable for their actions (either through incarceration or court-ordered intervention).

- Reduce the likelihood that batterers will intimidate and harass victims because they hold the victims responsible for the fact that they are being prosecuted.

Those recommending that the abused wife bring the complaint claimed,

- Battered women have the right and the ability to decide whether or not they want criminal justice intervention, when given full information. For example, a battered woman might choose not to prosecute because she prefers civil remedies, faces life-threatening danger, fears race-biased sentencing, or would lose critical financial support.

- Civil remedies may be appropriate in some cases. If batterer counseling is viewed as a critical intervention, it can be mandated through properly monitored and enforced civil protection orders, as well as through criminal action.

- There are other ways to address the potential for victim intimidation and harassment, including statutes that make intimidation of a witness a substantive crime and the use of protection orders a condition of release.

- Policies that eliminate victim discretion can serve to alienate battered women and discourage them from calling police or seeking other legal intervention in the future, thereby placing them in jeopardy of extreme injury or death.

Should a Woman Be Forced to File?

Those who favor the victim's making the filing decision agree that when the lives of others are clearly endangered, battered women must be expected to cooperate with the prosecution. To pressure women to testify, some prosecutors have charged them with filing false police reports and perjury (lying), in rare instances even jailing them. Some prosecutors see this as a further abuse of an already demoralized woman, while others claim that allowing the woman to drop charges is sending her the message that the courts do not take her problems seriously.

In San Diego, if the victim will not testify, prosecutors use photos, tapes from 911 calls, and testimony from neighbors and police to press charges. In response to those who claim this takes the power away from the woman and further abuses her, attorney Casey Guinn counters that the policy protects women who fear the rage of their batterers if they testify. "When you give the victim control over the criminal prosecution, in reality you're giving control to the batterer, because the batterer controls the victim."

Some claim that if the courts helped the women file charges and supported them, many more women would follow through. The Brockton, Massachusetts, court found that 71 percent of women who got restraining orders did not appear at a hearing 10 days later. In comparison, in the Quincy, Massachusetts, court that has a separate office for restraining orders and support groups for the women, only 2.8 percent of the women failed to show at their court hearing. Abused women need supportive encouragement that will only come about when prosecutors and judges decide to pursue wife beating as a serious act of assault that warrants serious judicial interest and eventual punishment.

THE COURTS

An appeal to the American judicial system is supposed to be an effective method of obtaining justice. For battered women, however, this has not always been the case. Spouse abuse cases are often plagued with problems of evidence because domestic violence usually takes place behind closed doors. The complicated emotions and motivations influencing the behavior of both the abuser and the victim do not fit neatly into a legal case. Finally, society's changing attitudes towards abuse influence the responses of those in the judicial system.

Keeping the Family Together

Traditionally, the family in America has been the basis of our society. While the value of an intact family cannot be underestimated, the traditional family is one of the fastest-changing aspects of our culture. Staying together to preserve a marriage or "for the children's sake" is much less common than it was two generations ago. In many cases of abuse, however, there are still many women, police, lawyers, judges, etc., who feel that abuse is preferable to breaking up the family.

In the past, maintaining the family unit, although a lofty goal, has meant that many judges backed away from their responsibility to punish batterers under the pretense of protecting the family. *Confronting Domestic Violence: A Guide for Criminal Justice Agencies* (see above), prepared by the National Institute of Justice, cited a judge who claimed,

> Even if the woman shows up in my court with visible injuries, I don't really have any way of knowing who's responsible or who [sic] I should kick out of the house. Yes, he may have beaten her, but nagging and a sharp tongue can be just as bad. Maybe she used her sharp tongue so often ... she provoked him to hit her.

Confronting Domestic Violence noted that attitudes have been changing and cited several judges' statements from the bench. "I don't care if she's your wife or not," declared one judge. "A marriage license is not a hitting license. If you think that the courts can't punish you for assaulting your wife, you are sadly mistaken." When another defendant claimed his girlfriend had provoked a beating, the judge warned, "This is *your* problem, not your girlfriend's. You will damage your next relationship in the same way if you don't get help." Another judge took the pressure off the wife who was testifying against her abusive husband. "It's not your wife's fault that she's here to testify. She has no choice. I could have arrested her to make her come. She's not prosecuting you; the city is. She's required to tell the truth — it's perjury if she doesn't."

Victims Not Testifying

A victim's fear and mixed feelings about testifying and the importance of her behavior as a witness have undoubtedly discouraged many prosecutors from taking action. A victim's reluctance might stem from the batterer's threats of further retaliation for taking legal action. Although these abused women have already had the courage to initiate legal proceedings against their batterers, some are later reluctant to cooperate with the prosecution because of their emotional attachment to their abusers, mistrust or lack of information about the criminal justice system, or fear of the demands of court appearances.

On the other hand, a victim might choose not to move forward with prosecution because the violence ceases temporarily following arrest while the batterer is in custody. Most women do not want their husbands to go to jail with the attendant loss of income and community standing — they want their husbands to stop beating them.

Religious convictions, economic dependency, and family influence to drop the charges put great pressure on the women. Consequently, many prosecutors, some of whom might believe abuse is a personal social problem and others who believe winning the case is unlikely, test the victim's resolve to make sure she will not back out. This, in itself, forces many women to drop the charges because, after being controlled by their husbands, they feel that the judicial system is repeating the pattern by abusing its power. Hence, the prosecutors' not unjustifiable fears contribute to the problem, creating a self-perpetuating cycle.

Naturally, not all prosecutors and judges hold forgiving attitudes toward abusers. In California, the *Santa Barbara County District Attorney Family Violence Prosecution Manual* advises prosecuting attorneys,

> Remember that "my spouse made me angry" is not an excuse for violence. The offender will minimize and deny responsibility for the violence by shifting it to the victim. Prosecutors and judges should be able to abide by this simple credo: Violence as a response to the stresses of life is not legally acceptable. Commitment to the prosecution of family violence cases must come from individual as well as policy-making prosecutors.

Mandatory Prosecution

The number of jurisdictions adopting mandatory prosecution policies has been increasing. This policy requires government attorneys to file criminal charges against domestic violence offenders. Though mandatory prosecution removes the burden of decision from the victim, it also removes the victim's control over that decision, especially when a no-drop policy is also in effect. With a no-drop option, no consideration is given to a victim's preference to drop the charges against the batterer.

In "The Preventive Impacts of Policies for Prosecuting Wife Batterers" (Buzawa and Buzawa, *Domestic Violence: the Changing Criminal Justice Response,* Auburn House, Westport, Connecticut, 1992), David Ford and Mary Jean Regoli reported that no-drop policies may be effective in an unintended direction. Battered women who were given the option to drop charges were at lower risk for subsequent violence than women who were not allowed to drop charges. Just being able to make that decision, in addition to the alliance with the authorities, empowered the women.

In "Prosecution Response to Domestic Violence: Results of a Survey of Large Jurisdictions" (*Do Arrests and Restraining Orders Work?*; see above), Donald J. Rebovich reported that most prosecutors' offices proceeded with prosecution despite the non-cooperation of the victim. Two-thirds of the offices had no-drop policies, although there was usually some flexibility in these policies.

LEGAL RESPONSE TO NONSTRANGER CRIME

Research has shown that the victim-offender relationship is an important factor in determining how the offender is treated by the criminal justice system. In general, strangers are treated more harshly because stranger offenses are seen as the true targets of the justice system; against them, the criminal law is to be strictly enforced. Furthermore, the justice system tends to perceive nonstranger offenses as using the system inappropriately to cope with strained interpersonal problems.

Leonore Simon, in "Legal Treatment of the Victim-Offender Relationship in Crimes of Violence" (*Journal of Interpersonal Violence*, vol. 11, no. 1, 1996), examined the sentencing and incarceration of 273 male violent offenders. About half the offenders had victimized total strangers or strangers known only by sight. The nonstranger victims included casual and work acquaintances, close friends, family members, spouses, and girlfriends. While nonstrangers were charged with and convicted of more serious offenses, stranger offenders received longer sentences. It must be remembered that many nonstranger crimes never go to sentencing (victims drop charges or settle out of court) so that those that do proceed through the system are more likely to be the more serious crimes.

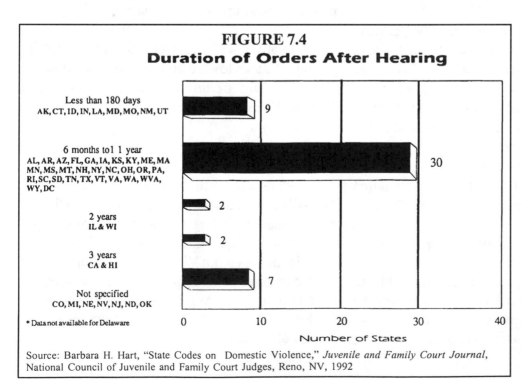

FIGURE 7.4
Duration of Orders After Hearing

Less than 180 days
AK, CT, ID, IN, LA, MD, MO, NM, UT — 9

6 months to 1 1 year
AL, AR, AZ, FL, GA, IA, KS, KY, ME, MA MN, MS, MT, NH, NY, NC, OH, OR, PA, RI, SC, SD, TN, TX, VT, VA, WA, WVA, WY, DC — 30

2 years
IL & WI — 2

3 years
CA & HI — 2

Not specified
CO, MI, NE, NV, NJ, ND, OK — 7

* Data not available for Delaware

Number of States

Source: Barbara H. Hart, "State Codes on Domestic Violence," *Juvenile and Family Court Journal*, National Council of Juvenile and Family Court Judges, Reno, NV, 1992

PROTECTION ORDERS

A victim in any state in the nation may go to court to get a protection order forbidding the abuser from harming her. Civil orders of protection are legally binding court orders that prohibit an individual who has committed an act of domestic violence from further abusing the victim. These orders generally prohibit harassment, contact, communication, or physical proximity. They are common and easily attainable though not always effective.

All states and the District of Columbia have passed laws that allow an abused adult to petition the court for an order of protection. States also have laws that permit people in other relationships with the abuser to file for protection orders. Relatives of the victim, children of either partner, couples in dating relationships, homosexual couples, and ex-spouses are among those who can file for a protection order in a majority of the states, the District of Columbia, and Puerto Rico. In Hawaii and Illinois, those who harbor an abused person can obtain a protection order against the abuser.

In addition to physical abuse, petitioners can file for protection orders in a number of circumstances, including sexual assault and marital rape, harassment, emotional abuse, and stalking. Protection orders are valid for different lengths of time depending on the state. In 30 states, the orders are in force for six months to a year; in Illinois and Wisconsin, two years; and in California and Hawaii, three years (Figure 7.4).

Effects of Protection Orders

In a National Center for State Courts study (*Civil Protection Orders: The Benefits and Limitations for Victims of Domestic Violence*, National Institute of Justice, Washington, DC, 1997), Susan Keilitz et al. reported that most women who petitioned for a civil protection order had suffered physical abuse for some time. One-fourth of the women interviewed had endured the abuse for more than five years before getting a protection order.

The researchers also found that temporary protection orders can be useful even when the victim does not follow through to obtain a permanent order. When victims were asked why they did not return for a permanent protection order, most said that their abusers had stopped bothering them.

Though respondents often violate their protection orders in some way, the orders generally deter repeated incidents of physical and psychological abuse. Keilitz et al. found that the majority of abuse victims felt that civil protection orders protected them against repeated incidents of abuse and helped them regain a sense of well-being. In initial interviews with women who had obtained protection orders, 72.3 percent of the participants reported that their lives had improved. In the six-month follow-up interviews, that proportion increased to 85.3 percent. More than 90 percent reported feeling better about themselves, and 80.5 percent felt safer. (See Table 7.7.)

About 72 percent of participants in the initial interviews reported no continuing problems following the petition for protection orders, compared to 65.3 percent six months later. In some areas, however, the percentage who reported problems rose between the two interviews — being stalked, (4.1 percent in the initial interview and 7.2 percent in the follow-up interview), repeated physical abuse (2.6 percent and 8.4 percent), and repeated psychological abuse (4.4 per-

---

TABLE 7.7

Perceived Effectiveness Measured by Quality of Life

	Initial Interview (n=285)	Follow-up Interview (n=177)
Life Improved	%	%
All Sites	72.3	85.3
Delaware	82.2	87.5
Denver	74.4	89.7
District of Columbia	61.9	79.4
Feel Better		
All Sites	72.3	92.7
Delaware	82.2	92.9
Denver	74.4	93.1
District of Columbia	61.9	92.1
Feel Safer		
All Sites	73.7	80.5
Delaware	77.8	83.7
Denver	83.3	82.9
District of Columbia	61.9	71.4

Source: *Domestic Violence and Stalking: The Second Annual Report to Congress Under the Violence Against Women Act*, Violence Against Women Grants Office, U.S. Department of Justice, Washington, DC, 1997

cent and 12.6 percent). (See Table 7.8.) Respondents with a criminal history of violent offenses were more likely to violate protection orders, leading the researchers to note that criminal prosecution may be required to stop abusive behavior in this group of perpetrators.

Adele Harrell and Barbara Smith, in "Effects of Restraining Orders on Domestic Violence Victims" (*Do Arrests and Restraining Orders Work?*; see above), found restraining orders less effective. Many of the victims interviewed in this study thought the restraining order was helpful in documenting that the abuse had occurred, but less than half thought the abuser believed he had to obey the order. Most women (60 percent) with temporary restraining orders reported that the orders were violated in the year after they were issued. Three out of ten (29 percent) reported that the violations were severe. Subsequent physical violence occurred as often for women with permanent orders as for women with temporary orders. Permanent orders, however, did significantly reduce psychological abuse.

The Strength of a Protective Order

Protection orders give victims an option other than filing a criminal complaint. They can be issued immediately, usually within 24 hours, and provide safety for the victim by barring or evicting the abuser from the household. However, this judicial protection has little meaning if the police do not maintain records and then arrest the abuser if he violates the order. Statutes in most states make violations of protection orders a matter of criminal contempt, a misdemeanor, or even a felony.

The Violence Against Women Act (VAWA, PL 103-322) mandates that a protection order issued by one state for a domestic violence incident must be enforced in all states. The VAWA also makes it a crime to cross state lines to commit domestic violence or to violate a protection order.

Courts and law enforcement agencies in most states have access to electronic registries of protection orders issued, both to verify the existence of an order

TABLE 7.8

Perceived Effectiveness Measured by Problems with Orders: All Sites

	Initial Interview (n=268)		Follow-up Interview (n=167)	
	No.	%	No.	%
No problems experienced	194	72.4	109	65.3
Respondent called home/work	43	16.1	29	17.4
Respondent came to home	24	9.0	14	8.4
Respondent stalked victim	11	4.1	12	7.2
Respondent physically re-abused victim	7	2.6	14	8.4
Respondent psychologically re-abused victim	12	4.4	21	12.6
Respondent caused other problems	3	1.1	1	0.6

Source: *Domestic Violence and Stalking: The Second Annual Report to Congress Under the Violence Against Women Act*, Violence Against Women Grants Office, U.S. Department of Justice, Washington, DC, 1997

and to assess whether violations have occurred. As of December 1996, 22 states and the District of Columbia had established protection order registries, and another 11 states were in the process of establishing them (Figure 7.5). However, Nancy Loving, Program Director of the Police Research Forum, notes,

[P]rotection orders alone cannot adequately prevent domestic violence or protect its victims. Protection orders must be part of a comprehensive program to combat violence, which includes shelters, police training, programs for batterers, and enforcement of legislation designed to protect victims. — "Federal Legislation for Abuse Victims," *Response to Violence in the Family & Sexual Assault*, March/April 1984

Lenore Walker, author of *Terrifying Love: Why Battered Women Kill and How Society Responds* (Harper and Row, New York City, 1989), agrees with Nancy Loving. She sees advantages to getting a protection order that affect the whole spectrum of the abuse situation:

... most batterers seem to comply with restraining [protection] orders, even though they are only "pieces of paper".... [F]or some women, just obtaining a restraining order ... makes her

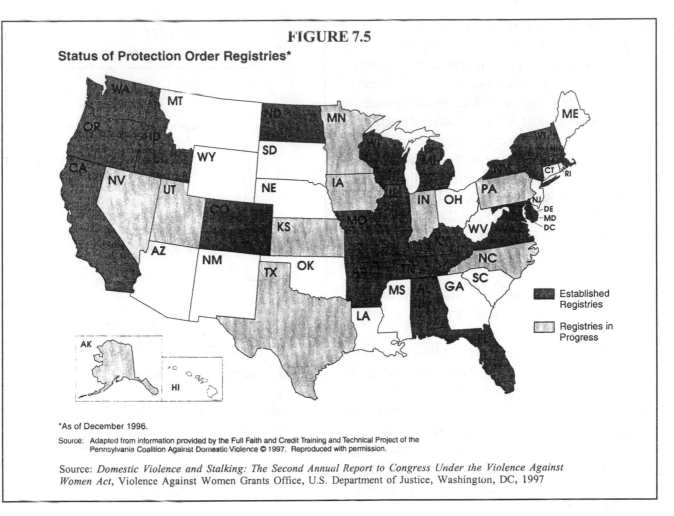

FIGURE 7.5

Status of Protection Order Registries*

Established Registries

Registries in Progress

*As of December 1996.

Source: Adapted from information provided by the Full Faith and Credit Training and Technical Project of the Pennsylvania Coalition Against Domestic Violence © 1997. Reproduced with permission.

Source: *Domestic Violence and Stalking: The Second Annual Report to Congress Under the Violence Against Women Act*, Violence Against Women Grants Office, U.S. Department of Justice, Washington, DC, 1997

feel more powerful, more in control. And police tend to respond more supportively towards women who get them; perhaps because it signifies to them that these women "mean business." Although spouse abuse is either a misdemeanor or a felony crime in all states, judges tend to issue greater sanctions when a batterer violates a restraining order than they do for the assaultive act itself. Furthermore, battered women who have previously obtained a restraining order and later kill their batterers in self-defense are more likely to be believed than those women who had never taken any self-protective legal actions.

STALKING

Many abused women who leave their partners feel threatened and are in physical danger of being attacked by them. This threatening behavior is known as stalking, generally referred to as "a course of conduct di-

rected at a specific person that involves repeated visual or physical proximity, nonconsensual communication, or verbal, written or implied threats, or a combination thereof, that would cause a reasonable person fear." Stalking is a series of actions, usually escalating from legal but annoying acts, such as following or repeatedly phoning the victim, to violent or even fatal acts.

Not all stalking incidents involve abusive couples. A stalker may fixate on an acquaintance or a stranger as the object of his (most stalkers are male, although not all) obsession. Celebrity stalking cases have been highly publicized, but they account for a very small percentage of stalking incidents. Stalking most often involves intimates or former intimates and either starts or continues after a victim leaves the relationship.

In recent years, a number of "cyberstalking" incidents have been reported. Repeated online harassment and threats are generally considered stalking.

However, appropriate interventions and recourse are unclear because often the stalker and his victim have never been in physical proximity to each other. In addition, the identity of the stalker may be difficult to find. In Dallas, a judge issued a temporary restraining order to stop an alleged offender from stalking his victim over the Internet. Because the alleged stalker's address was unknown, the restraining order was served through e-mail and posted on the Internet. (Laurie Wilson, "Restraining Order Issued in Online-Stalking; Ruling for Internet Firm Owners May Be the First in State," *The Dallas Morning News*, October 15, 1996)

The National Violence Against Women (NVAW) Survey

The National Violence Against Women survey, conducted between November 1995 and May 1996, provides the first national data on stalking in the United States. The survey found stalking to be more prevalent than previously thought. An estimated one million women and 370,990 men were stalked annually. Eight percent of all women (1 out of every 12) and 2 percent of all men have been stalked at some time in their lives. In *Stalking in America: Findings from the National Violence Against Women Survey* (National Institute of Justice and Center for Disease Control and Prevention, April 1998), Patricia Tjaden and Nancy Thoennes reported the following survey results:

- Seventy-eight percent of stalking victims are female, and 87 percent of stalking perpetrators are male.

- Four of 5 women who were stalked by an intimate were also physically assaulted by the stalker; 31 percent were sexually assaulted by the stalker.

- Adults between the ages of 18 and 29 comprise 52 percent of all stalking victims (Figure 7.6).

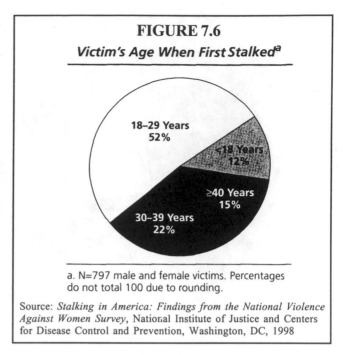

FIGURE 7.6

Victim's Age When First Stalked[a]

a. N=797 male and female victims. Percentages do not total 100 due to rounding.

Source: *Stalking in America: Findings from the National Violence Against Women Survey*, National Institute of Justice and Centers for Disease Control and Prevention, Washington, DC, 1998

- The average stalking case lasts 1.8 years.

- Women tend to be stalked by intimate partners. Thirty-eight percent were stalked by current or former husbands, 10 percent by current or former cohabiting partners, and 14 percent by current or former dates or boyfriends. (See Figure 7.7.)

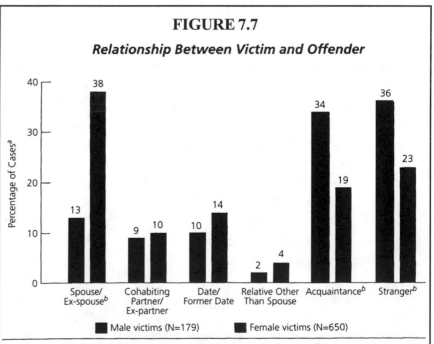

FIGURE 7.7

Relationship Between Victim and Offender

a. Percentages exceed 100% because some victims had more than one stalker.
b. Differences between males and females are significant at ≤.05.

Source: *Stalking in America: Findings from the National Violence Against Women Survey*, National Institute of Justice and Centers for Disease Control and Prevention, Washington, DC, 1998

Most men are stalked by strangers or acquaintances, 90 percent of whom are male.

Stalking appears to be a control issue. According to the victims, most of the stalking is motivated by the stalkers' desire to control or instill fear in their victims. (See Figure 7.8.) Only 7 percent of the victims reported that their stalkers were mentally ill or abusing drugs or alcohol.

Legal Response to Stalking

About half of the victims reported the stalking to the police. In most cases, the victim made the report. In the cases reported, the police responded most often by taking a report. Police were significantly more likely to arrest or detain a suspect stalking a female victim than one stalking a male victim. Other responses included referrals to prosecutor or court or to victim services and advice on self-protective measures. In 18.9 percent of the cases reported, police did nothing. (See Table 7.9.)

According to the survey, female victims (28 percent) were significantly more likely than male victims (9.7 percent) to obtain a protective or restraining order. Because women are more likely to be stalked by intimate partners with a history of violence toward them, this finding was expected. Of those who obtained protective orders, 68.7 percent of the women and 81.3 percent of the men said their stalker violated the order. (See Table 7.10.)

About 12 percent of all stalking cases resulted in criminal prosecutions. Of those cases reported to police, 13.1 percent of stalkers of female victims and 9 percent of stalkers of male victims were prosecuted. About half the stalkers (54

percent) who were prosecuted were then convicted. Of those convicted, 63 percent were sentenced to jail or prison. Perhaps of interest, although a larger percentage of persons stalking female victims were pros-

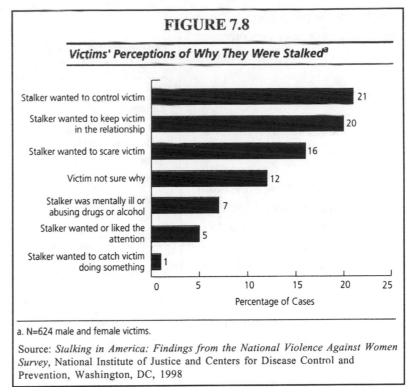

FIGURE 7.8

Victims' Perceptions of Why They Were Stalked[a]

Percentage of Cases

- Stalker wanted to control victim — 21
- Stalker wanted to keep victim in the relationship — 20
- Stalker wanted to scare victim — 16
- Victim not sure why — 12
- Stalker was mentally ill or abusing drugs or alcohol — 7
- Stalker wanted or liked the attention — 5
- Stalker wanted to catch victim doing something — 1

a. N=624 male and female victims.

Source: *Stalking in America: Findings from the National Violence Against Women Survey*, National Institute of Justice and Centers for Disease Control and Prevention, Washington, DC, 1998

TABLE 7.9

Percentage and Characteristics of Stalking Cases Reported to the Police, by Sex of Victim

Reported to Police/Response	Stalking Victims (%)		
	Male	Female	Total
Was case reported to the police?	(N=178)	(N=641)	(N=819)
Yes	47.7	54.6	53.1
No	52.3	45.4	46.9
Who reported the case?[a]	(N=84)	(N=350)	(N=434)
Victim	75.0	84.0	82.3
Other	25.0	16.0	17.7
Police Response[a,b]	(N=84)	(N=350)	(N=434)
Took report	66.7	68.6	68.0
Arrested or detained perpetrator[c]	16.7	25.1	23.5
Referred to prosecutor or court	19.0	24.3	23.3
Referred to victim services[c]	8.3	15.1	13.8
Gave advice on self-protective measures	29.8	34.0	33.2
Did nothing	16.7	19.4	18.9

a. Based on responses from victims whose stalking was reported to the police.
b. Percentages exceed 100 percent because of multiple responses.
c. Differences between males and females are significant at ≤ .05.

Source: *Stalking in America: Findings from the National Violence Against Women Survey*, National Institute of Justice and Centers for Disease Control and Prevention, Washington, DC, 1998

ecuted, a higher proportion of those stalking male victims were convicted and sentenced. (See Table 7.11.)

Antistalking Legislation

All states and the District of Columbia have laws making stalking a crime. In 1996, the Interstate Stalking Punishment and Prevention Act, part of the National Defense Authorization Act for 1997 (PL 104-201), was passed, making interstate stalking a felony offense. This federal statute addresses cases in which the interstate nature of the offense may make it difficult for the states to take action.

<table>
<tr><td colspan="4">TABLE 7.10
Percentage and Outcomes of Protective Orders in Stalking Cases, by Sex of Victim</td></tr>
<tr><td rowspan="2">Outcome</td><td colspan="3">Stalking Victims (%)</td></tr>
<tr><td>Male</td><td>Female</td><td>Total</td></tr>
<tr><td>Did victim obtain a protective or restraining order?^a</td><td>(N=175)</td><td>(N=597)</td><td>(N=772)</td></tr>
<tr><td>Yes</td><td>9.7</td><td>28.0</td><td>23.8</td></tr>
<tr><td>No</td><td>90.3</td><td>72.0</td><td>76.2</td></tr>
<tr><td>Was the order violated?^{a,b}</td><td>(N=16)</td><td>(N=166)</td><td>(N=182)</td></tr>
<tr><td>Yes</td><td>81.3</td><td>68.7</td><td>69.8</td></tr>
<tr><td>No</td><td>18.7</td><td>31.3</td><td>30.2</td></tr>
</table>

a. Differences between males and females are significant at ≤ .05.
b. Based on responses from victims who obtained a restraining order.

Source: *Stalking in America: Findings from the National Violence Against Women Survey*, National Institute of Justice and Centers for Disease Control and Prevention, Washington, DC, 1998

Recently, several state legislatures have amended their antistalking laws after constitutional challenges or judicial interpretations of the law made it difficult to prosecute alleged stalkers. For example, in 1996 the Texas Court of Criminal Appeals (*Long v. Texas*, 931 S.W.2d 285) ruled that the 1993 Texas antistalking law was unconstitutionally overbroad since it addressed conduct protected by the First Amendment. Legislators amended the statute in January 1997, clarifying the elements of stalking. The amendment states that, to be in violation of the statute, an alleged offender must knowingly engage in conduct that the offender "knows or reasonably believes the other person will regard as threatening."

Stalking Interventions

Criminal justice officials and victim service providers continue to develop programs, strategies, and protocols to address stalking, with the focus on victim safety. According to *Domestic Violence and Stalking: The Second Annual Report to Congress under the Violence Against Women Act* (U.S. Department of Justice, Washington, DC, 1997), intervention strategies must strike a balance between stopping the stalking and protecting the victim.

"Suspect intervention" and "victim intervention" are important aspects of the method used by the Los An-

geles Police Department Threat Management Unit to handle stalking cases. The primary goal of suspect intervention is to gain insight into the potential danger of the stalker. It also includes arrests, protection orders, confiscation of weapons, and face-to-face meetings with stalking suspects. Victim intervention includes educating the victims about stalking, instructing victims in protecting themselves and in assisting police in building the case, and recommending therapeutic interventions, such as support groups or self-defense training, to help the victim regain control over her life.

As police departments and victim services agencies implement new and modified strategies, those that prove to be effective deterrents to stalking will serve as models. The Department of Justice has committed to support basic research to better understand domestic violence and stalking. Evaluation of its efforts will better inform public policy decision making and guide the development of effective programs.

JUDICIAL RESPONSIBILITY TO PROTECT AN ABUSED WIFE

Sandra Baker was estranged from her husband. In 1955, the local Domestic Relations Court issued a protective order directing her husband, who had a history of serious mental illness, "not to strike, molest, threaten, or annoy" his wife. Sandra Baker called the police when her husband created a disturbance at the family home. She showed the police officer the court order, and he told her it was "no good" and "only a piece of paper" and refused to do anything.

Sandra Baker went to the Domestic Relations Court and told her story to a probation officer of that court. Later, she went to see the same officer. While making a phone call in the hall, she saw her husband in the corridor. She went to the probation officer and told him her husband was in the hall. She asked if she could wait in his office because she was "afraid to stand in the room with him." The probation officer told her to leave and wait in the waiting room. A few minutes later, her husband shot and wounded her.

Sandra Baker sued the City of New York, claiming the city owed her more protection than she was given. The New York State Supreme Court, Appellate Division, in *Baker v. the City of New York* (25 A.D.2d 770, 1966), agreed that the City of New York had not fulfilled its obligation to Sandra Baker. The Court found that Mrs. Baker was "a person recognized by order of protection as one to whom a special duty was owed ... and peace officers had a duty to supply protection to her." Neither the police officer nor the probation officer had fulfilled his duty, and they were therefore guilty of negligence. Since they were representatives of the City of New York, Sandra Baker had the right to sue the city.

Equal Protection

Another option that desperate women have used in response to unchecked abuse is to sue the police for failing to offer protection, alleging that the police violated their constitutional rights to liberty and equal protection under the law.

The "Equal Protection Clause" of the Fourteenth Amendment provides that no state shall "deny to any person within its jurisdiction the equal protection of the laws." This clause prohibits states from classifying by group membership unless they have a very good reason. If a woman can prove that a police department has a gender-based policy of refusing to arrest men who abuse their wives, she can claim that the policy is based on gender stereotypes and, therefore, violates the equal protection laws.

Thurman v. City of Torrington

Between October 1982 and June 1983, Tracey Thurman continually called the police of Torrington, Connecticut, to tell them that her estranged husband was repeatedly threatening her and her child's life. The police ignored her requests for help no matter how often she called or how bad the situation was. She tried to file complaints against her husband, but city officials ignored her.

Even when her husband was finally arrested, after attacking her in full view of a policeman, and the judge issued an order forbidding him to go to his wife's home, the police continued to ignore her pleas for help. Her husband violated the order and came to her house and threatened her. When she asked the police to arrest her husband for violating his probation and for threatening her life, they ignored her. She got a restraining order against her husband, which he violated, but again, the police ignored her.

TABLE 7.11

Percentage and Outcomes of Criminal Prosecutions in Stalking Cases, by Sex of Victim

Outcome	Stalking Victims (%)		
	Male	Female	Total
Was perpetrator prosecuted?	(N=178)	(N=645)	(N=823)
Yes	9.0	13.1	12.1
No	91.0	86.9	87.9
Was perpetrator convicted?[a]	(N=15)	(N=72)	(N=87)
Yes	60.0	52.8	54.0
No	40.0	47.2	46.0
Was perpetrator sentenced to jail or prison?[b]	(N=9)	(N=37)	(N=46)
Yes	77.8	59.5	63.0
No	22.2[c]	40.5	37.0

a. Based on responses from victims whose perpetrator was prosecuted.
b. Based on responses from victims whose perpetrator was convicted.
c. Based on five or fewer sample cases.

Source: *Stalking in America: Findings from the National Violence Against Women Survey*, National Institute of Justice and Centers for Disease Control and Prevention, Washington, DC, 1998

On June 10, 1983, Tracey Thurman's husband came to the house. She called the police. He then stabbed her repeatedly around the chest, neck, and throat. A police officer arrived 25 minutes later but did not arrest her husband, despite his repeated attacks. Three more policemen arrived. Mr. Thurman went into the house and brought out their child and threw him down on his bleeding mother. They still did not arrest Mr. Thurman, but allowed him to walk around free. While Ms. Thurman was on the stretcher, waiting to be put in the ambulance, her husband came at her again. At this point, the police finally arrested Mr. Thurman and took him into custody. Tracey Thurman sued the City of Torrington, claiming she was denied equal protection under law.

In *Thurman v. City of Torrington* (595 F.Supp. 1521, 1984), the U.S. District Court for Downstate Connecticut agreed.

City officials and police officers are under an affirmative duty to preserve law and order, and to protect the personal safety of persons in the community. This duty applies equally to women whose personal safety is threatened by individuals with whom they have or have had a domestic relationship as well as to all other persons whose personal safety is threatened, including women not involved in domestic relationships. If officials have notice of the possibility of attacks on women in domestic relationships or other persons, they are under an affirmative duty to take reasonable measures to protect the personal safety of such persons in the community.

... [A] police officer may not knowingly refrain from interference in such violence, and may not automatically decline to make an arrest simply because the assaulter and his victim are married to each other. Such inaction on the part of the officer is a denial of the equal protection of the laws.

For the Federal District Court, there could be little question that "such inaction on the part of the officers is a denial of the equal protection of the laws." The

police could not claim that they were promoting domestic harmony by refraining from interference in a marital dispute because research has shown that police inaction supports the continuance of violence. There could be no question, concluded the Court, that the City of Torrington, through its police department, had "condoned a pattern or practice of affording inadequate protection, or no protection at all, to women who have complained of having been abused by their husbands or others with whom they have had close relations." They had, therefore, failed in their duty to protect Ms. Thurman and deserved to be sued.

The federal court jury awarded Tracy Thurman $2.3 million in compensatory damages. Almost immediately the state of Connecticut changed the law, calling for the arrest of assaultive spouses. In the 12 months following the new law, the number of arrests for domestic assault almost doubled, from 12,400 to 23,830.

Due Process

The Due Process Clause of the Fourteenth Amendment provides that "no State shall deprive any person of life, liberty, or property, without due process of law," protecting against state actions that are extremely unfair or arbitrary. It does not, however, obligate the state to protect the public from harm or provide services that would protect them. A state may, however, create special conditions in which that state has constitutional obligations to particular citizens because of a "special relationship between the state and the individual" (*Escamilla v. Santa Anna*, 796 F.2d 266, 269, 1986). Abused women have used this argument to claim that being under a protection order put them in a "special relationship."

DeShaney v. Winnebago County Department of Social Services

The "special relationship" and the gains for women achieved in *Thurman* lost their power with the Supreme Court case of *DeShaney v. Winnebago County Department of Social Services* (489 U.S. 189, 1989). A young boy was repeatedly abused by his father. Despite repeated hospitalizations, the Department of Social Services (DSS) insisted that there was insufficient evidence to remove the child. Finally, the father beat the boy into a coma, causing permanent brain damage. The mother (who had not had custody) sued the DSS for not intervening. The Supreme Court ruled that the due process clause does not grant citizens any general right to government aid and that a "special relationship" is a custodial (i.e., incarcerated) relationship. The court's decision noted, "The facts of this case are undeniably tragic," but

the affirmative duty to protect arises not from the State's knowledge of the individual's predicament or from its expressions of intent to help him, but from the limitations that it has imposed on his freedom to act on his own behalf, through imprisonment, institutionalization, or other similar restraint of personal liberty.

The court concluded,

It is well to remember once again that the harm was inflicted not by the State of Wisconsin, but by Joshua's father. The most that can be said of the state functionaries in this case is that they stood by and did nothing when suspicious circumstances dictated a more active role for them. The people of Wisconsin may well prefer a system of liability that would place upon the State and its officials the responsibility for failure to act in situations such as the present one.... But they should not have it thrust upon them by this Court's expansion of the Due Process Clause of the Fourteenth Amendment.

Although this case was about a child, it also applies to abused women. Following *De Shaney*, women have been unable to win a case on the basis of due process or equal protection. Jena Balistreri's case (below) against the police department of Pacifica, California, began before *De Shaney*, but unfortunately for her, it was not finally decided until after the *De Shaney* precedent was set.

Balistreri v. Pacifica Police Department

Jena Balistreri first called the police in February 1982 when she was beaten by her husband. The police refused to arrest him; one of the officers stated that Mrs. Balistreri deserved the beating. In November 1982, Mrs. Balistreri obtained a restraining order forbidding her husband from "harassing, annoying, or having contact with her." Despite repeated vandalism (crashing his car into her garage, throwing a fire bomb into the home), the police refused to take Mrs. Balistreri seriously. Mrs. Balistreri turned to the courts in an effort to force the police to restrain her husband.

Two out of three of the judges of the Ninth Circuit Court of Appeals (both women) found that Jena Balistreri's case might convince a jury that the police were guilty either of "intentional harassment" or "reckless indifference to her safety." Their conduct "strongly suggest[s] an intention to treat domestic abuse cases less seriously than other assaults, as well as an animus against abused women," and their behavior may "violate equal protection."

Regarding the due process claim, Jena Balistreri argued that she had a special relationship with the state because the police knew she was being terrorized and had a protection order. Two judges ruled she might have a claim to a "special relationship" and the state might, after all, have "a duty to take reasonable measures to protect Balistreri from her estranged husband."

The third judge dissented, stating the restraining order "heightens the state's awareness" of her "risk of harm," but "the mere existence of the order" creates no "special relationship" to the state and imposes no constitutional duty to protect her. The case was initially returned to the lower courts for further proceedings; however, after *De Shaney*, the court reversed its decision and threw out Balistreri's due process claim. (*Balistreri v. Pacifica Police Department*, 855 F.2d 1421, 1988; as amended Feb. 27, 1990 and May 11, 1990.)

CHAPTER VIII

WHEN WOMEN KILL

Women do not kill nearly as often as men. In 1997, the Federal Bureau of Investigation reported that, of known murder offenders, only 10 percent were female (*Crime in the United States*, Washington, DC, 1998). When a woman kills, the victim is often her spouse. The Bureau of Justice Statistics (BJS), in *Murder in Families* (John Dawson and Patrick Langan, Washington, DC, 1994), found that spousal murders made up 41 percent of all family murders. Women represented 40.7 percent of spousal murderers and 59.8 percent of spousal victims (Table 8.1). According to BJS, in *Violence by Intimates* (1998), of the 20,311 men who were intimate murder victims in the years between 1976 and 1996, 62 percent were killed by wives. Of the 31,260 female intimate murder victims in those same years, 64 percent were killed by husbands.

In *Women in Prison* (Tracy Snell, Washington, DC, 1994), the BJS researchers found that, in 1991, nearly 12 percent of women inmates (about 4,500 women) had been sentenced for murder. Of those, 31.9 percent (or 1,400 women) had murdered an intimate, defined as a husband, ex-husband, or boyfriend (Table 8.2).

Between 1976 and 1996, there was a steady decline in intimate partner murders, falling from near 3,000 in 1976 to just over 1,800 in 1996. The largest portion of this decline was in the killing of men, especially Black men, by their female partners. One reason given for the fewer killings by spouses is that there are fewer young people with spouses. In 1970, 55 percent of men ages 20 to 24 had never been married; by 1992, the proportion had increased to 80

TABLE 8.1

Sex, race, and age, by the family relationship of murder victims and defendants, 1988

Relationship of victim to assailant	All	Sex		Race			Age				
		Male	Female	White	Black	Other	Under 12	12-19	20-29	30-59	60 or over
Victims											
All	100%	77.8%	22.2%	43.5%	54.2%	2.3%	4.8%	10.9%	35.6%	41.8%	7.0%
Nonfamily	100	82.2	17.8	44.4	53.3	2.3	2.1	12.2	38.5	41.1	6.1
Family	100	55.5	44.5	39.0	58.6	2.4	18.8	3.9	20.3	45.3	11.6
Spouse	100	40.2	59.8	41.2	56.4	2.4	0	0	27.9	65.0	7.1
Offspring	100	55.8	44.2	32.6	65.6	1.8	78.5	10.9	7.7	3.0	0
Parent	100	57.2	42.8	54.8	45.2	0	0	0	.9	56.7	42.4
Sibling	100	73.0	27.0	33.5	64.5	2.0	8.7	2.0	43.3	42.6	3.3
Other	100	74.9	25.1	34.1	61.0	4.9	4.6	8.2	19.1	47.5	20.6
Defendants											
All	100%	89.5%	10.5%	36.2%	61.9%	1.8%	.1%	21.8%	42.5%	31.4%	4.2%
Nonfamily	100	93.2	6.8	35.7	62.6	1.8	.1	23.1	44.5	28.4	3.8
Family	100	65.5	34.5	39.7	58.0	2.3	0	13.0	29.7	50.5	6.8
Spouse	100	59.3	40.7	41.8	56.1	2.2	0	.9	21.9	66.1	11.1
Offspring	100	45.4	54.6	34.5	64.5	1.0	0	17.2	36.4	40.3	6.0
Parent	100	81.6	18.4	49.8	50.2	0	0	38.2	30.7	29.4	1.7
Sibling	100	84.9	15.1	32.2	65.8	2.0	0	16.9	36.7	46.4	0
Other	100	83.5	16.5	38.1	56.1	5.9	0	18.0	35.9	41.3	4.9

Source: John M. Dawson and Patrick A. Langan, *Murder in Families*, Bureau of Justice Statistics, Washington, DC, 1994

TABLE 8.2

Women in Prison for Homicide

Relationship of victim to offender	Percent of females serving a sentence for homicide*
Intimate	31.9%
Relative	17.0
Well known	14.3
Acquaintance	12.8
Known by sight only	2.7
Stranger	21.3

*Homicide includes murder, negligent manslaughter, and nonnegligent manslaughter.

Source: Tracy Snell, *Women in Prison*, Bureau of Justice Statistics, Washington, DC, 1994

percent. In addition, experts say that women now have more opportunities to escape bad relationships. They are more financially independent, and the number of organizations devoted to helping women in abusive relationships, such as counseling centers and shelters, have increased dramatically after first emerging in the early 1970s. Still, an estimated 750 to 1,000 women kill alleged abusers every year in the United States.

Spouse Murder Defendants

The Bureau of Justice Statistics, in *Spouse Murder Defendants in Large Urban Counties* (Patrick Langan and John Dawson, Washington, DC, 1995), examined 540 spouse murders in the nation's 75 largest counties. They found that more husbands had killed wives (59 percent of the murders) than wives had killed husbands. More wives used a knife or a gun (95 percent) than husbands (69 percent), although overall firearm use was similar (58 percent compared to 50 percent). (See Table 8.3.) Husbands were far more likely to strangle or beat their spouses to death.

Proportionally, twice as many husbands (20 percent) as wives (10 percent) killed in a fit of jealousy. In addition, hus-

bands were more likely to be substance abusers. One-third (31 percent) of the husbands had a history of drug abuse, compared to 9 percent of the wives. More than one-fifth (22 percent) of the husbands had been using drugs at the time of the crime, and two-thirds (66 percent) had been drinking alcohol, compared to 3 percent and 37 percent of women, respectively. (See Table 8.4.)

Wives (31 percent) were far more likely to be acquitted by judges and juries than husbands (6 percent). Juries acquitted 27 percent of the wives, but none of the husbands, while judges acquitted 37 percent of the women and 17 percent of the men. Convicted men (94 percent) were somewhat more likely than women (81 percent) to receive a prison sentence. Wives received, on average, considerably shorter sentences (6 years versus 16.5 years). Eight percent of wives received life sentences, compared to 15 percent of husbands (Table 8.5). Among wives sentenced to prison, 15 percent received a sentence of 20 years or more; among husbands, 43 percent did.

Women were more likely to claim self-defense, which may explain their lower conviction rates. Many more wife defendants claimed that they had been assaulted by their victims (the husbands) at the time of the murder (44 percent) or in the past (58 percent) than husband defendants (10 percent). See Figure 8.1 for selected case summaries in which wife defendants were acquitted, convicted, or given probation (no jail or prison time).

TABLE 8.3

Spouse murder defendants: Weapons used, 1988

Murder defendant	Total number	Percent of spouse murder defendants						
		Total	Firearms				Knife	Other*
			All types	Handgun	Shotgun	Rifle		
All	540	100%	53%	45%	4%	4%	26%	21%
Husband	318	100	50	41	6	3	19	31
Wife	222	100	58	51	2	5	37	5

*Hands, feet etc.

Source: Patrick A. Langan and John M. Dawson, *Spouse Murder Defendants in Large Urban Counties*, Bureau of Justice Statistics, Washington, DC, 1995

TABLE 8.4

Spouse murder defendants: Substance abuse by defendants, 1988

Murder defendant	Percent of spouse murder defendants		
	Drug use		Alcohol use at time of murder
	At time of murder	In past	
All	14%	22%	55%
Husband	22	31	66
Wife	3	9	37

Note: Of the 540 cases, drug use at the time of murder was known in 255; in past, 540; alcohol use, 335.

Source: Patrick A. Langan and John M. Dawson, *Spouse Murder Defendants in Large Urban Counties,* Bureau of Justice Statistics, Washington, DC, 1995

EARLY WARNINGS

Angela Browne of the Family Research Laboratory at the University of New Hampshire compared 42 women charged with murdering or seriously injuring their spouses with 205 abused women who had not killed their husbands (*When Battered Women Kill*, The Free Press, New York City, 1987). She looked at why some women are unable to see that the men they are involved with are dangerously violent. Ironically, some of the factors that lead to severe abuse make these men especially attractive at the beginning of the relationship. The man appears to be intensely romantic, always wanting to know where his partner has been, which makes some women feel loved and cared for. Only later, when she cannot make a move without her partner's supervision and mistrust, does the woman realize that she is a virtual prisoner of her mate. (See also Chapter IV.)

The intensity of involvement of the early relationship develops into isolation for the woman. She is denied contact with her family and friends to the point where a casual conversation with a neighbor can be a cause for a beating.

The man, who was originally seen as "protective," now is extremely jealous and possessive. The woman belongs exclusively to him, a possession he can use as he pleases. A common thread in the cases reported to Angela Browne was the husbands' belief that the women were sexually promiscuous, driving them to extreme sexual abuse.

Browne's findings indicate a possible link between a high frequency of marital rape and homicide potential. Over 75 percent of the women in Browne's homicide group claimed they had been forced to have sexual intercourse with their husbands, compared to 59 percent in the nonhomicide group. Some 39 percent of the former group had been raped often (more than 20 times), compared to 13 percent of the nonhomicide group. Browne quoted one woman, "It was as though he wanted to annihilate me ... as though he wanted to tear me apart from the inside out and simply leave nothing there." When sexual abuse leads to extreme forms of sodomy, a woman sometimes considers this the last straw before she finally kills her husband.

MURDER AND SUICIDE THREATS

Spouse-murdered men had often threatened to kill their partners. In Browne's study, 83 percent of the men in the homicide group had threatened to kill someone, compared to 59 percent of the men in the nonhomicide group. The homicide group used their guns to frighten their wives and then were sometimes killed with their own weapons. Sixty-one percent of

TABLE 8.5

Defendants convicted of killing their spouse: Type of sentence imposed, by conviction offense, 1988

Murder defendant	Number convicted	Total sentences	Percent of spouse murder defendants convicted and sentenced to —				Straight probation	Mean prison term*
			Prison			Jail		
			Total prison	Life	Death			
All	431	100%	89%	12%	1%	1%	10%	13 yrs
Husband	275	100	94	15	2	1	5	16.5
Wife	156	100	81	8	0	1	18	6

*Excludes life and death sentences.

Source: Patrick A. Langan and John M. Dawson, *Spouse Murder Defendants in Large Urban Counties,* Bureau of Justice Statistics, Washington, DC, 1995

FIGURE 8.1

Spouse murder defendants who stood trial: Trial acquittals

Notes taken on prosecutors' records

Miami case #84 The couple has an on-again, off-again relationship for 20 years. Several weeks prior to the murder, she sees her common-law husband (the victim) leave a motel with another woman. Subsequently, the couple has several violent confrontations until one day she shoots him. Outcome: *The jury acquitted her of all charges.*

Chicago case #15 The couple is arguing when the 25-year-old wife finds a love letter to her 25-year-old husband (the victim, a fast-food restaurant employee) from a co-worker. The wife gets a kitchen knife and stabs him. She claims she was a victim of battered wife syndrome and was only defending herself. Outcome: *At a bench trial the judge acquitted her.*

Detroit case #98 The two are out drinking. They return home and begin arguing. According to the wife, age 30, her 25-year-old husband (the victim) attacked her. She grabs a knife and stabs him. She claims he has beaten her before. No witnesses are present at the time of the murder. Outcome: *She was acquitted of second-degree murder at a bench trial.*

Manhattan case #72 She, a 29-year-old artist, has lived with her 47-year-old common-law husband (the victim), a musician, for a few years. He frequently beats, starves, and tortures her. He repeatedly tells her he is going to kill her. For some time leading up to the murder, he has not let her eat or shower. On the day of the murder they are going to a bar when she asks him to let her go home because she is tired. He says "no" and begins hitting her and calling her names. The beating ends when she stabs him. He has numerous past arrests and convictions. Outcome: *The jury acquitted her.*

Spouse murder defendants who pleaded guilty

Notes taken on prosecutors' records

New Haven case #2 She, a 28-year old secretary, suffers years of physical and sexual abuse at the hands of her 30-year-old husband (the victim). Several times he tries to kill her. She stays with him at first because she thinks he will stop; then because she fears he will find her wherever she goes; and then because she fears losing her kids. At some point she buys a gun to defend herself. On the night of the murder she thinks he is possibly going to kill her. In the middle of a beating she grabs the gun from under the mattress and shoots him. Outcome: *She pleaded guilty to negligent manslaughter and was sentenced to straight probation (no confinement in prison or jail).*

Pittsburgh case #15 The husband (the victim) has a history of beating his wife. On the night of the murder, the husband comes home and begins ordering her around, as he frequently does. The wife leaves the room. When she returns she notices him looking through the closet for his gun. The wife earlier hid it under the bed. While he is searching, the wife retrieves the gun and shoots him repeatedly. She claims she was tired of the abuse. Outcome: *She pleaded guilty to nonnegligent manslaughter and was sentenced to straight probation (no confinement in prison or jail).*

Source: Patrick A. Langan and John M. Dawson, *Spouse Murder Defendants in Large Urban Counties,* Bureau of Justice Statistics, Washington, DC, 1995

Spouse murder defendants who stood trial: Trial convictions

Notes taken on prosecutors' records

Oklahoma City case #24 The 59-year old husband (the victim) comes home intoxicated and continues drinking. His 52-year old wife claims he became violent and began to beat her. She says she shot him in self-defense. The prosecution counters that there are no bruises or other signs of a beating. The prosecution contends she shot him while he lay in bed sleeping. Outcome: *The jury convicted her of first-degree murder. She was sentenced to life imprisonment.*

Rochester (NY) case #26 Throughout their turbulent 4-year marriage, the husband (the victim) verbally and physically abuses his wife. She never once leaves him, though. Prior to the night of the murder, the husband buys a gun and puts it in his dresser. The night of the murder, the husband is slapping the wife around, telling her to get out of the house. He calls the police to have her removed from the premises. While he is on the phone, telling police "she's a whore," the wife grabs his gun and shoots him four times. Outcome: *The jury convicted her of second-degree murder. She was sentenced to 15 years in prison.*

---

this group threatened to kill themselves. Many of the threats were made when a woman tried to leave the relationship or when the man was depressed. Browne questioned whether the threats were all genuine expressions of a will to die or whether they were used to manipulate the woman to increase her guilt and prevent her leaving.

On the other hand, almost half the women (48 percent) in the homicide group had threatened to commit suicide (compared to 31 percent of the nonhomicide group), and many had tried it. Among 350 battered women studied by M. Pagelow, almost half had contemplated suicide, and 23 percent had attempted it (*Woman Battering: Victims and Their*

Experience, 1981). Death appeared to be the only exit for these women. Their batterers could and would follow them anywhere; the only escape was to die. One woman in Browne's group decided not to get help after a severe beating because she thought, "It [death] might not be so bad; like passing out, only you never got beaten again."

About 60 percent of the maritally raped women in Raquel Kennedy Bergen's *Wife Rape* (Sage Publications, Thousand Oaks, California, 1996) reported that their husbands had threatened to kill them. Three of the women in Bergen's sample reported that they were finally able to break free of their abusive relationships when they realized that they would kill their husbands if they did not leave. About half the sample confessed to thinking about killing their partners, but did not believe they could actually go through with it. (See also Chapter V.)

Drug Use and Physical Abuse

Browne, in her comparison of abused women who had murdered a spouse and those who had not, found that in the homicide group, 29 percent of the men had used street drugs daily or almost daily, versus only 7.5 percent of the men in the nonhomicide group. She found even sharper differences in alcohol use. Eighty percent of the men in the homicide group reportedly got drunk every day, compared to 40 percent in the nonhomicide group. Lenore Walker, who is often hired as an expert witness in homicide cases, has been involved in cases where women killed a husband when he had passed out from extreme intoxication. Convinced the beating would resume when he awoke, the woman took this opportunity to kill him. The men, when autopsied, were found to have blood alcohol levels up to three times greater than what is normally defined as intoxicated.

Furthermore, while 77 percent of the men in the nonhomicide group had been arrested for anything from drunk driving to murder, 92 percent of the men in the homicide group had been arrested. A common feature of the homicide marriages was that the wife did not know anything about her husband's past, including his arrest record.

BATTERED WOMEN WHO KILL AND THE COURTS

In legal cases involving battered women who kill their abusers, the defendant most often admits to the killing and reveals a history of physical abuse against her by the victim. The charge is usually first- or second-degree murder, which is murder with malicious intent either with or without premeditation. The outcome of their trials depends on three main issues: self-defense, equal force, and imminent versus immediate danger. Expert witnesses are crucial in an abused woman's trial to explain how these issues are different for battered women than for other homicides.

Self-Defense

I've ruined everything. My husband is dead, and I'm as good as dead. I'm forty-six years old and my life is over.... I'm a convicted murderer. A person can cry self-defense all they want, but no one will accept my story. They will see me as crazy, a maniac, a murderer.... Hate the man, hit the man. But why'd you go and kill the man? Because he had it coming! He had it coming. A man would have done the same thing, they do it all the time. You hear them talk revenge, but a woman can't do it. A wife can't do it. And sure as hell a mother *can't do it!* — A mother of four sentenced to 15 to 20 years for murdering her abusive husband

Women often plead that they killed in self-defense, a plea that requires proof that the woman used such force as was necessary to avoid imminent bodily harm. "Self-defense" was originally intended to cover unexpected attacks by a stranger and did not take into account a past history of abuse or a woman's fear of renewed violence. Traditionally applied, a self-defense plea does not cover a woman who kills in a lull in the violence (perhaps when the drunken abuser passes out).

Many observers feel that self-defense law is "problematic, inadequate, and/or inappropriate" for use in self-defense cases of battered women (Diane

Follingstad et al., "The Impact of Elements of Self-Defense and Objective Versus Subjective Instructions on Jurors' Verdicts for Battered Women Defendants," *Journal of Interpersonal Violence*, vol. 12, no. 5, 1997). Traditionally, self-defense permits a person to use physical force when he or she reasonably believes it is necessary to prevent imminent or immediate danger of serious bodily harm. Furthermore, a person must use only a reasonable amount of force to defend himself or herself, and the defendant cannot be the one who provoked the encounter or initiated the violence. Most jurisdictions require that the defendant must reasonably believe that the attacker is using or is about to use deadly force to justify the use of reciprocal deadly force. Some jurisdictions further require that before resorting to deadly force, the defendant must make an effort to retreat, although this is not required in most courts if the attack took place in the defendant's own home.

What Is "Reasonable": Subjective versus Objective

Advocates of battered women have succeeded in getting many courts to accept a subjective standard to determine whether a battered woman who kills her husband was protecting her own life or has committed murder. That is, they will judge the circumstances of the crime in relation to the special needs of a battered woman and not as a strict definition of "self-defense" as it has been traditionally applied. This is especially important for women who have killed during a lull in the violence because, for them, "imminent danger" in its traditional meaning ("the defendant must reasonably fear serious injury or death at the *particular instant* that the defendant acted with force" [*People v. White*, 90 Ill. App. 3d 1067, 1980] — what is now referred to as immediate) is impossible to justify.

A subjective standard asks a jury to understand what is reasonable for a battered woman. Susannah Marie Bennett, in "Ending the Continuous Reign of Terror: Sleeping Husbands, Battered Wives, and the Right of Self-Defense" (*Wake Forest Law Review*, 1989), explained the critical difference. "The appearance of danger is viewed subjectively, from the perspective of one who saw what the defendant saw and

knew what the defendant knew. An objective standard still governs whether a reasonable person, in similar circumstances and with the same perceptions, also would have acted in self-defense." This is a "hybrid" (mixed together) definition of self-defense that supporters of battered women encourage the courts to adopt.

In order for this hybrid definition to work, the court must first be subjective in understanding the woman's circumstances and then must be objective in deciding if, given this situation, she truly did act in a reasonable manner. The court has already accepted the notion that self-defense does not require correctness in a situation, only reasonableness. Justice Oliver Wendell Holmes, in *Brown v. United States* (256 U.S. 332, 1921), said, "Detached reflection cannot be demanded in the presence of an uplifted knife." Now battered women are asking the courts to revise their definitions of imminent danger and proportionate force.

Equal Force

Self-defense permits the use of equal force — the least amount of force necessary to prevent imminent bodily harm or death. Women, however, who are generally physically weaker than men and who know the kind of physical damage their batterers are capable of, may justifiably feel that they are protecting their lives in shooting an unarmed man. In *State v. Wanrow* (559 P 2d 548, 1977), the Washington Supreme Court ruled that it was permissible to give the jury instruction that the objective standard of self-defense cannot always apply.

Yvonne Wanrow was sitting up at night, fearful that a male neighbor, whom she thought had molested the child in her charge, was going to make good on his threats to break into the house where she was staying. When the 6-foot-2-inch, intoxicated man did enter, Wanrow, who was incapacitated with a broken leg, shot him. The court ruled,

The respondent was entitled to have the jury consider her actions in the light of her own perception of the situation, including those perceptions that were the product of our nation's long and unfortunate history of sex discrimination.... Until such time as the effects of that history are eradicated, care must be taken to assure that our self-defense instructions afford women the right to have their conduct judged in light of the individual physical handicaps that are the product of sex discrimination. To fail to do so is to deny the right of the individual woman involved to trial by the same rules that are applicable to male defendants.

The court also noted that women "suffer from a conspicuous lack of access to training in and the means of developing those skills necessary to effectively repel a male assailant without resorting to the use of deadly weapons."

Imminent Versus Immediate

Traditionally, self-defense required that the danger be immediate (at that very moment) to justify the use of force. Accepting "imminent" (about to occur) danger as a justification permits the jury to understand the social circumstances of a battered woman's behavior. A history of abuse explains why a defendant might react to the threat of violence more quickly than a stranger would in the same circumstances. The Washington Supreme Court, in *Wanrow*, found that, when the jury considered a woman's actions based on "immediate" danger, they were required to focus only on the time immediately before the defendant's actions. "It is clear that the jury is entitled to consider *all* of the circumstances surrounding the incident in determining whether [the] defendant had reasonable grounds to believe grievous bodily harm was about to be inflicted."

Lenore Walker, as a frequent expert witness for battered women, notes that it is often hard for a jury to understand how a woman can be continuously afraid of a man she lives with. Walker insists, however, that most battered women have a constant underlying fear of the man's potential for violence even when the woman has learned coping skills to permit her to continue living with him. Walker's research found that 85 percent of the 400 battered women interviewed felt that they could or would be killed at some time by their assailants.

Juries and Expert Testimony

Whether a woman will be convicted often depends on the jury's attitude (or the judge if it is not a jury trial) and the amount of background and personal history of abuse that the jury is permitted to hear. Juries not presented with expert witnesses and the "battered woman syndrome" (BWS) theory (see Chapter IV) are often unsympathetic to women who kill their spouses.

Regina Schuller et al. ("Jurors' Decisions in Trials of Battered Women Who Kill: The Role of Prior Beliefs and Expert Testimony," *Journal of Applied Psychology*, vol. 24, no. 4, 1994) discussed the influence of expert testimony on mock jurors' decisions in cases of women who killed their spouses. Jurors who received information on BWS through expert testimony were more likely to believe that the woman feared for her life, that she was in danger, and that she was trapped in the relationship. Furthermore, this knowledge was more likely to lead to a decrease in murder convictions, compared to the decisions of a control group of jurors who were not given this additional information.

The researchers examined whether a person's belief in a "just world" influenced how they received expert testimony. A strong belief in a just world says that a person deserves his or her fate. In other words, bad things happen to bad people. Therefore, if a woman is abused, she must be responsible for the beating in some way or she must deserve the outcome, and the husband is not the only guilty party. The study found that women who did not accept the concept of a just world were especially open to and influenced by expert testimony. Men, however, were more resistant to the influence of expert witnesses.

Lenore Walker believes that an expert witness can be extremely helpful in educating a jury on issues that they cannot normally be expected to understand. But it is often up to the judge's discretion whether an expert's testimony will be permitted. In Walker's experience, when an expert witness is not allowed to testify before the jury, a woman will not be acquitted on grounds of self-defense.

The risk with an expert witness is that he or she will tell the jury what to think. In some states, an expert witness is only permitted to speak generally on the phenomenon of battered woman syndrome and not about the individual woman on trial. On the other hand, other states permit the expert to express an opinion on the ultimate question — whether the battered defendant's behavior was reasonable for the conditions.

State v. Norman

In the case of *State v. Norman* (89 NC App. 384, 366 S.E. 2d 586, 1988), Judy Norman shot her husband to death while he slept. The North Carolina Court of Appeals overturned a lower court's verdict of voluntary manslaughter because the original court had failed to instruct the jury on self-defense. In the final appeal, however, the North Carolina Supreme Court reversed that opinion and reaffirmed the validity of the first court's traditional objective standard of self-defense (324 NC at 254, 378 S.E. 2d at 9, 1989).

Judy Norman had been continually abused during her 25-year marriage to her husband, J. T. He had beaten her with every available weapon, had forced her to prostitute herself and earn at least $100 a day, had required her to eat dog food from a bowl on the floor, had thrown her down the stairs when she was pregnant with their youngest child, causing a premature birth, and often threatened to "cut her heart out." Dr. Tyson, an expert witness at the trial, characterized her situation as "torture, degradation, and reduction to an animal level of existence, where all behavior was marked purely by survival."

On this final occasion, Mr. Norman had been arrested for drunk driving and, on his release from jail, had come home to vent his anger on his wife, beating her for 36 hours. In the past, Mrs. Norman had sought help from the Mental Health Services and the Department of Social Services. Mr. Norman, however, had always come to get her, reaffirming her belief that her husband was invulnerable to the law and social service agencies. In her mind, the only choices left to her were to kill him or die.

The defense relied heavily on the battered spouse syndrome and the theory of learned helplessness. (See Chapter IV.) Susannah Marie Bennett (see above), in her analysis of *State v. Norman,* applauded the Appeals Court's decision to accept the special circumstances of a battered woman.

> By recognizing that self-defense was a proper issue, the court of appeals answered affirmatively and endorsed the view that one *may* reasonably fear imminent death or harm from a sleeping person. According to the court, the existence of reasonable, deadly fear is not only hypothetically possible, but is viable, and may have existed in Mrs. Norman's mind.

But Bennett argued that the Court of Appeals was wrong to claim that "therefore, a battered spouse who kills a passive abuser *can* satisfy the traditional elements of self-defense under an objective analysis." (Italics used by Bennett; underlining used by editor.) Bennett pointed out that

> the imminency requirement may prevent the woman from exercising the right of self-defense at the only time it would be effective — when the abuser is passive. Instead, the rule mandates that the woman wait until she may be completely defenseless — during or immediately before a battering incident — before she can justifiably save her life.... Thus, in essence, the court recognized that the requirement of imminent danger may be met by events outside of an actual attack or threat of attack, but only in the special circumstances of battered spouses. This recognition is certainly a momentous exception to the general principle of self-defense.

By accepting this definition of self-defense, the court cannot claim to have used an objective standard. Bennett suggests that the reason the North Carolina Supreme Court overturned the Appeals Court decision was because the Appeals Court may have tried to mask its move to subjectivity, and it would have been better off to admit that "it was relaxing its objective standard in order to accommodate those killings that do not objectively comport with traditional self-defense notions." Bennett concluded,

> Rather than clinging to antiquated notions and strict interpretation regarding self-defense, the [Appeals] court made an honest effort to cope with the legal ramifications of spousal abuse. The court exhibited great insight in recognizing the predicament facing some victims of battered spouse syndrome — a dilemma created because of the lethal combination of characteristics of the syndrome and strict judicial adherence to standards that never contemplated such predicaments. Accordingly the court responded with a compassionate and insightful opinion, albeit imprecise and confusing, that is part of a growing trend in self-defense law.

On July 7, 1989, Governor James G. Martin commuted (changed) Mrs. Norman's six-year manslaughter sentence to time served.

Should the Law Be Changed?

By acknowledging the differences between women and men, the courts are coming closer to providing two standards of justice. A woman can be permitted to use a gun in self-defense in cases where a man could not, and she may need the extra help of an expert witness to explain her motivation to a jury. Is this a step in the right direction for the courts? Are the courts only now incorporating changes needed to deal with previously unconsidered situations? Have women been discriminated against throughout history and society is only now righting the wrongs?

Those opposed to changing the law claim that many domestic disputes are more complicated than they are portrayed by battered women's advocates. Sonny Burmeister, president of the Georgia Council for Children's Rights (an organization that lobbies for equal treatment for men in custody cases) believes that women are trying to write a customized set of laws. "We paint men as violent and we paint women as victims, removing them from the social and legal consequences of their actions. I don't care how oppressed a woman is; should we condone premeditated murder?"

Incorrect Assumptions

There are those who object to revising the law, claiming that this will permit women to kill their husbands indiscriminately and that by allowing this change, the law is sending a message to society that revenge and vigilantism (taking the law in your own hands) is acceptable, even sanctioned (permitted) under the law. Holly Maguigan, defense attorney and law professor, in "Battered Women and Self-Defense: Myths and Misconceptions in Current Reform Proposals" (*University of Pennsylvania Law Review*, vol. 140, no. 2, 1991), argues that the law does not need to be changed; the law needs to be properly applied.

According to Maguigan, the effort to change the law is based on two incorrect assumptions. The first is that juries convict battered women for killing in nonconfrontational circumstances (during a lull in the violence or while the man is sleeping). The second is that the current definitions of self-defense apply only to men of roughly equal size and power. Some insist that the law ignores the social context of the battered woman's act. Maguigan counters that reformers have not carefully examined the law as it stands and that when the reformers explain what they mean by a "fair trial," they are referring to a not-guilty verdict.

Studies show that a large majority of women kill their abusers during a confrontation and not during a break in the attack. Angela Browne (*When Battered Women Kill*) estimated that at least 70 percent of women killed their abusers during confrontations. Other researchers have estimated that as many as 90 percent of women kill under confrontational circumstances. Maguigan examined 223 cases and found that 75 percent involved confrontations, 4 percent were contract killings, and 8 percent involved "sleeping-man" situations. In 8 percent of the cases, the defendant was the aggressor in a lull in the violence, and in the remaining 5 percent, there was not enough background in the court opinions to know.

Regarding equal force, Maguigan points out that nearly every jurisdiction decides questions of equal force on a case-by-case basis and does not ban a woman from using a weapon against an unarmed man.

Courts have recognized for years that when a battered woman uses a weapon against an unarmed man, it is not necessarily disproportionate. In 1940, in *Kress v. State* (144 S.W. 2d. 735), the Tennessee Supreme Court reversed the conviction of a woman who shot her husband in the midst of an attack. "Where great bodily violence is being inflicted, or threatened, upon a person, by one much stronger and heavier, with such determined energy that the person assaulted may reasonably apprehend death or great bodily injury, he is justifiable in using a deadly weapon...."

Furthermore, the law in every state permits a history of past abuse to be presented in court. Cases of abused women who have killed their partners and who have claimed self-defense are not new. They date back at least to 1902, long before the theory of the battered woman's syndrome. Maguigan agrees that jurisdictions which accept imminent danger as opposed to immediate danger are more likely to present the history of abuse to the jury to explain the reasonableness of the woman's conduct.

A Misapplication of the Law

Maguigan's analysis revealed that convictions of battered women usually resulted from a misapplication of the law, not from the unjust structure of the law. She found that 40 percent of the guilty verdicts were later reversed in higher courts, a rate significantly higher than the national average rate of reversal of 8.5 percent in homicide cases in general. Problems arise when trial court judges interpret the woman's act as vigilantism and do not permit instruction to the jury on self-defense or history-of-abuse evidence. In *State v. Branchal* (684 P.2d 1163, NM, 1984), the trial judge commented that the court "did not want to condone spousal retaliation for past violence."

Maguigan concluded,

In the majority of jurisdictions, it is not the definition of self-defense jurisprudence that prevents battered women from receiving fair trials. Rather, the failure of trial judges to apply the generally applicable standards of self-defense jurisprudence in cases where the defendants are battered women is to blame. Problems that result from a refusal to apply the law will not be remedied by either current proposals for legal redefinition or by the creation of separate standards.

When legal exceptions are made, the danger arises that trial judges will apply the law too strictly, perhaps excluding some women. For example, a trial judge in Missouri made a decision (later reversed on appeal) that the defendant was not eligible for "battered spouse syndrome" testimony because she was not married to her abuser.

When the law attempts to define a special group of people, it serves to eliminate others, in this situation potentially denying expert witnesses or special instructions on self-defense to those who do not fit the rigidly drawn-up definition of a battered woman.

Maguigan suggests that flexibility and general terms are more beneficial to women. She cited the proposed rule of evidence for the New York state courts as an example. "If scientific, technical, or other specialized knowledge will assist the trier of fact to understand the evidence or to determine a fact in issue, a witness qualified as an expert by knowledge, skill, experience, training, or education, may testify."

According to Maguigan, the laws to provide a woman with a fair trial are already in place. What is needed is for jurisdictions to understand and accept the legal precedents of imminent rather than immediate danger and to allow evidence of a history of battering and expert testimony to explain the reasonableness of a battered woman's reaction.

CHAPTER IX

VIOLENCE AGAINST THE ELDERLY

HISTORY

Family violence against the elderly did not begin in the past 15 years, just as child abuse did not begin in the 1960s, nor spouse abuse in the 1970s. Since the 1981 milestone report from the House Select Committee on Aging, *Elder Abuse: An Examination of a Hidden Problem*, Americans have become more aware of the problem of elder abuse. However, the reluctance to report a problem so alien to "the American ideal" and the limited federal and state resources in the field of elder abuse present barriers to making progress in overcoming the problem. In addition, experts cannot agree on the definitions of elder abuse, which vary from state to state and researcher to researcher, nor on the causes or the steps needed to prevent abuse.

Although some think that elder abuse is a current problem and that it was not as prevalent in the past when it was the norm for several generations to live together in the same house, this is probably not correct. Suzanne Steinmetz, an expert in elder abuse, concluded from her research, "The romantic view of close-knit, multigenerational families of yesteryear is a mythical representation rather than an accurate account of family life in the past."

In pre-industrial Europe, and even well into the nineteenth century, many elderly found themselves forced out of their homes into poorhouses and hospitals by their grown children, despite community values advocating that the family take care of them. Historians believe that the witchcraft mania of the sixteenth and seventeenth centuries was fueled, in part, by a dislike among many for older women. In

sixteenth century Germany, at least 100,000 women and children were said to have been accused of and executed for sorcery.

Until the industrial revolution in the late eighteenth century, power and wealth were based on agricultural production, which, in turn, was based on land ownership. In those days, it was not unusual for a landowner to be murdered by a grown child who would not wait for the parent to die a natural death in order to inherit. Such murders were less common in North America, where there was plenty of land available.

Recent Financial and Social Changes

Over the past two generations, other major changes have occurred in the relationship between the older and younger generations. Social Security and private pensions have increased economic security for some older persons. Before World War II, most Americans feared retirement, but since the 1950s and until recently, retirement appeared attractive to those elderly who were well provided for through insurance, pensions, and savings. These older people rarely live with a child, and if they can afford it, some buy a retirement home in a warm climate.

For some older Americans, however, the future is looking less bright than they had expected. Health care costs, a major source of concern, have risen dramatically. If long-term nursing care is required, the older person may be financially ruined. Advances in health care mean that Americans are living longer, but not necessarily healthier, lives.

Heart, stroke, and cancer (the three primary killers of the elderly) patients often live longer today and require high levels of care.

More and more elderly are turning to their children for help and care just when the offspring of the adult child may either need expensive financing to complete a college education or may be returning home because his/her job does not pay well enough to finance independent living. The middle-age adults in this situation are often called the "sandwich generation," caught between supporting both their parents and their children.

Many women enter the job market in order to supplement the family income or to provide all of the family income if the woman is a single mother. Working outside the home makes it harder for a woman to take care of elderly parents, as women had traditionally done. In addition, with increased financial responsibility and independence, many women no longer think it is solely their duty to care for elderly parents.

With Americans living longer and the baby boom generation approaching retirement, the nation is becoming more aware of the problems of the elderly and the difficulty in resolving them. Today, with social security expenses spiraling, politicians have raised the very sensitive issue of increasing taxes or limiting social security benefits — a government entitlement that has until recently been considered untouchable. Issues such as adequate retirement income and health care for the aged have become crucial. Elderly abuse has become a concern as parents live longer and run the risk of being abused by their children, their spouses, or the growing number of institutions developed to care for them.

The Government's Role

The British recognized the problem of elder abuse as a public issue before the Americans. In 1975, G. R. Burston, in "Granny-Battering," published in the *British Medical Journal* (September 6, 1975), publicized the problem for the first time.

Suzanne K. Steinmetz, in "The Politics of Aging, Battered Parents" (*Society*, July-August 1978) and in testimony before the House of Representatives Select Committee on Aging, made Americans aware of the problem. This committee, chaired by the late Representative Claude Pepper (D-FL) (himself an active elderly person), coined the term "elder abuse."

Despite the government's awareness, the problem still did not get much attention. *The Attorney General's Task Force on Family Violence* (Washington, DC, 1984) hardly considered elder abuse and then only to indicate the difficulties in getting any information on the subject. The government report *Elder Abuse: A Decade of Shame and Inaction* (Washington, DC, 1990) highlighted the extraordinarily small amounts of money that were spent on the problem.

Through the Family Violence Prevention and Services Act of 1992 (PL 102-295), Congress mandated a study of the national incidence of abuse, neglect, and exploitation of elderly persons. The U.S. Department of Health and Human Services funded the *National Elder Abuse Incidence Study* (NEAIS), a four-year study conducted by the National Center on Elder Abuse. The NEAIS (see below) was published in 1998, challenging policy makers, service providers, researchers, advocates, and the society as a whole to use the information to better the lives of many of America's elderly.

WHAT IS ELDER ABUSE?

One of the major problems in discussing and researching elder abuse is that there is no agreed-upon definition. Not only elder abuse but also most other aspects of elderly life are relatively unexplored areas of research. When researchers first studied elder abuse, comparisons to child abuse were often made, based on the similarity in apparent dependency of both the young and the elderly. It soon became clear, however, that while parents have a legal responsibility to care for their children, most adult children do not have a legal responsibility to their parents. Older persons have the right to be independent, responsible individuals and are, therefore, in a very different structural relationship with their caregivers.

Elder abuse cannot be easily compared to other forms of abuse ("a part of a spectrum of domestic violence which affects all ages" — the British Department of Health). For one thing, unlike other forms of domestic violence, there may not be a clear victim or perpetrator. In "Issues Involved in Identifying and Intervening in Elder Abuse," *Elder Abuse: Practice and Policy*, Filinson and Ingram, eds., Human Sciences Press, New York City, 1989), Linda Phillips asked,

> Is it the responsibility of an adult child to enforce rules of cleanliness on a legally competent elder when the elder does not want to be clean? Who is the victim and who is the perpetrator in situations where a legally competent elder refuses to act in his or her own best interests? And perhaps even more basic than any of these is the question of how can responsibility be assigned in a society that has yet to establish clear criteria regarding the minimum material and emotional rights to which every individual in society is entitled?

Cases of elder abuse are often a combination of acts of omission (not doing), acts of commission (doing), and situations in which elders may themselves be partly responsible for the abuse.

Types of Abuse

Over the past decade, researchers have identified various types of abuse: physical, sexual, psychological, material, and financial abuse; violation of civil rights; active neglect; passive neglect; psychological neglect; self-neglect; and poor residential environment. Individual definitions vary dramatically. What one researcher calls passive neglect is psychological neglect to another, and what is material abuse to one is a violation of rights for another. All agree that hitting elderly persons,

threatening them with a knife or gun, not giving them food, or stealing their money is elder abuse. Determining precise definitions, however, is necessary for legal purposes, the ability to compare research, and uniformity in reporting.

SOME DEFINITIONS

The Pennsylvania Task Force's Definition

While researchers have attempted to write all-encompassing, simple definitions, the complexity of the situation frustrates these efforts. The (Pennsylvania) Attorney General's Family Violence Task Force, in *Violence Against Elders* (Harrisburg, Pennsylvania, 1988), defined "elder abuse" as

> any of several forms of mistreatment of an elder by a person with whom the elder victim has a special relationship. The forms of mistreatment include **physical abuse** (non-accidental physical force that results in injury), **sexual abuse** (non-consensual sexual contact), **psychological abuse** (infliction of mental anguish by threat, intimidation, humiliation, or other such conduct), **financial abuse** (unauthorized use of funds or property), and **neglect** (failure to fulfill a caretaking obligation). Some of the literature and statutes on elder abuse distinguish among several types of neglect. The types include **active neglect** (willful failure to provide care), **passive neglect** (non-willful failure to provide care resulting, for example, from inadequate knowledge or infirmity of the caretaker), and **self-neglect** (failure of the elder, usually as a result of physical or mental impairment, to care adequately for himself or herself).

The Task Force noted that elder abuse may or may not be a crime. Most physical, sexual, and financial abuses are crimes. Depending on the conduct and the consequences, some psychological abuses can be crimes. Neglect, under certain conditions, can be a crime, while self-neglect is never a crime.

Elder abuse can further be classified as "institutional elder abuse" or "domestic elder abuse." The Pennsylvania Task Force defined these terms by the relationship between the abuser and the elder victim, not the physical location where the abuse took place. "Institutional elder abuse" is committed by a person who has undertaken a contractual obligation to provide care to the elder victim. "Domestic elder abuse" applies to a person who has volunteered to provide care to the elder victim or who otherwise has a special relationship with the victim. Although the Pennsylvania Task Force believes "the relationship between the abuser and the abused is a more important distinction than the site of the abuse," many researchers consider "institutional elder abuse" only that which is committed in an institution.

The Structure of Mistreatment

Elder abuse expert Rosalie Wolf, in testimony before Congress, addressed the problem of definition ("Elder Abuse and Family Violence: Testimony Presented Before the U.S. Senate Special Committee on Aging," *Journal of Elder Abuse & Neglect*, vol. 8, no. 1, 1996). An act considered abuse in one state may not be in another, which creates problems of data collection and prevention. Self-neglect is especially difficult to define; if a person chooses to live in a certain manner (perhaps unclean or inadequately nourished), is it someone else's right or responsibility to require, or force, the elder to change?

Wolf presented a five-level structure of mistreatment that includes the concepts of abuse and neglect (presented by Margaret F. Hudson in "Elder Mistreatment: A Taxonomy with Definitions by Delphi," *Journal of Elder Abuse & Neglect*, vol. 3, no. 2, 1991). The main classification is "violence involving older adults" (Level I). Level II classifies mistreatment in terms of the relationship between victim and perpetrator: self-mistreatment, elder mistreatment, and crime by strangers. Elder mistreatment is further subdivided into the relationship between victim and perpetrator (family member, health-care provider, or business relation-

ship). Level III determines whether the act is one of omission (neglect) or commission (abuse). Both neglect and abuse may be either intentional or unintentional (Level IV) and may include any of the Level V behaviors (physical, psychological, social, and financial). (See Figure 9.1.)

Other researchers have questioned the entire basis of elder abuse, suggesting that the elder person's perception of the behavior is the only basis for identification and intervention. Others have expanded this, noting the importance of cultural values, attitudes, and traditions in defining unacceptable behavior within the family.

Characteristics of Abuse: How Are the Elderly Abused?

Physical Abuse and Neglect

Physical and passive abuse often occurs together. Passive abuse, generally called neglect, includes the withholding of medication, medical care, food, and personal care necessary for the well-being of the elderly person. This is not to be confused with self-neglect (neglect by the elderly themselves) or passive neglect (where a caregiver is incapable of taking care of an elderly person but is not maliciously neglecting that person).

Elderly parents living with adult children who are drug and alcohol abusers or have serious psychological problems are at risk for this abuse. Many of these adult children are also financially dependent on their parents. A Texas woman was living with her son, who was armed, dangerous, and often on drugs. The 94-year-old mother was in such bad condition and her skin had broken down so badly that she had to be transferred to the hospital in a body bag (a plastic bag for transporting dead bodies). Her son objected to her removal saying, "Then who will pay the utility bills here?" The woman died two weeks later, and the son was convicted under the Texas Penal Code for "willful neglect to an elderly individual causing physical harm."

119

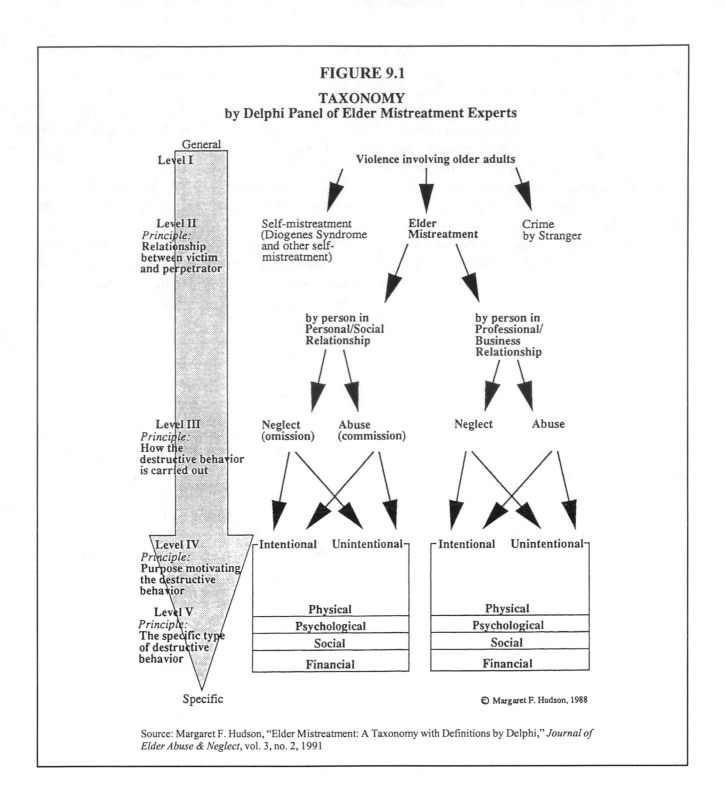

FIGURE 9.1

TAXONOMY
by Delphi Panel of Elder Mistreatment Experts

Source: Margaret F. Hudson, "Elder Mistreatment: A Taxonomy with Definitions by Delphi," *Journal of Elder Abuse & Neglect*, vol. 3, no. 2, 1991

Financial Abuse

Financial abuse involves the theft of money or anything of value belonging to the elderly by their relatives or caretakers. Sometimes this theft is accomplished by threats and/or force, and other times it is carried out through deceit and fraud. The elderly can often be convinced to sign over their as-

sets and legal rights in exchange for promises of housing and care. On the other hand, some elderly are declared incompetent and committed to public institutions so that the family can obtain their property.

In some cases, relatives will not permit an elderly person to be admitted to a nursing facility because then the facility will receive the elder's financial resources and Social Security payments. In Louisiana, a woman's son cashed all her Social Security checks and used them for himself, leaving the mother alone and malnourished. The social worker reported, "He was her representative payee for Social Security — Social Security here thinks that all relatives who agree or request to be appointed payees will act in the person's interest. No investigation done or questions asked." In some cases, adult children leave their parents in unheated homes without food and medication in order to obtain the maximum amount of money for their own personal use.

Psychological Abuse

Psychological abuse cannot be defined by specific behaviors, but rather by the effect it has on the elderly victim. It is a systematic effort to dehumanize the elderly, sometimes with the goal of driving a person to insanity or suicide. Psychological abuse usually exists with other forms of abuse. The abuse can be small things, such as refusing to give the elder person his or her glasses or hearing aid, or more overt actions, such as threatening the person with a gun.

Self-Neglect

Self-neglect sometimes stems from diminished physical and/or mental capabilities. It may also result from a loss of desire to live. Sometimes economic conditions force an elderly person to make hard decisions about what is necessary and what can be skipped. According to the U.S. Bureau of the Census, in 1996 10.8 percent of all elderly (those over 65 years of age) lived in poverty. The poverty level was defined as $7,740 a year for a single elderly person and $10,360 for a married couple, usually not enough to cover food, living, and medical expenses. Elderly females are more likely to be poor than elderly males.

An elderly woman in New Jersey with terminal cancer refused to see her doctor because she owed him $190 and could not pay. The case studies frequently reveal elderly people living in de-plorable squalor and filth but refusing to seek help or leave their homes.

Sexual Abuse

Sexual abuse is the least common form of elder abuse, and case studies show that where it does exist, it is most likely a continuation of the abuse a husband has committed throughout the marriage. Occasionally, a nonrelative or a child will force sex on an elder, but this is rare. Cases of a son abusing a mother usually originated with an incestuous relationship established by the mother when the son was a boy. In addition, alcohol abuse often plays a role in sexual abuse.

Difficulties with Definitions

Problems with definitions often arise when they are applied to specific cases. Tanya Johnson, in "Critical Issues in the Definition of Elder Mistreatment" (in *Elder Abuse — Conflict in the Family*, edited by Karl Pillemer and Rosalie Wolf, Auburn House, Dover, Massachusetts, 1986), discussed some of the problems that can develop:

Does the act of tying the older person to a chair constitute elder mistreatment? What if tying the older person to a chair is a method to protect the older person from injury due to falling? What about the older person who is malnourished because of the poor eating habits of the caregiving family? Can we say that a family is neglectful of the older member's nutritional needs if they apply the same standards to themselves? Is the older person who appears anxious signaling mistreatment from others or a personality characteristic peculiar to that individual? The inclusion of intent to harm in definitions of elder mistreatment raises a number of questions that have no easy answers. Should families who are unaware that they are being neglectful be counseled by professionals in the same way as those who have knowingly left the older person unattended? If the effect is elder neglect, how important is the cause?

Johnson prefers a definition based on the suffering ("intense and sustained pain and anguish") of the victim. This would eliminate the isolated incident of shoving or occasional "slanderous" name-calling that may come out of a fit of frustration. Nonetheless, Johnson recognizes that even her definition runs into serious problems. "For some older persons, teasing may cause mental anguish; for others it may be the usual mode of interaction." Some families have shouted at each other all their lives, and it indicates no abuse, while for others it might involve considerable suffering. Each case must be handled in the context of that individual relationship.

FIGURE 9.2

Iceberg theory of elder abuse

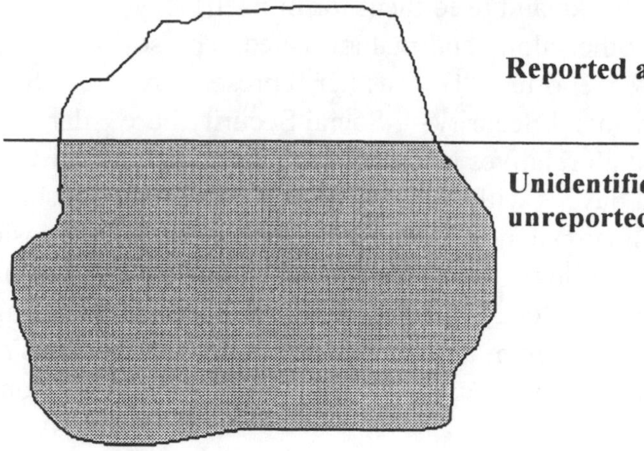

Reported abuse

Unidentified and unreported abuse

Source: *National Elder Abuse Incidence Study*, National Center on Elder Abuse, Washington, DC, 1998

PROBLEMS OF REPORTING

Not having consistent definitions of elder abuse affects reporting laws and data collection. Although there are mandatory reporting laws, the states vary widely in their definitions, the standards they provide for reporting, the penalties for failure to report, and the types of immunity provided for those who do report abuse. For this reason, it is impossible to gather national data from state-compiled statistics on the extent and types of abuse that exist. It also prevents developing an effective prevention program.

Unlike child abuse, where the victim is usually in constant contact with teachers, doctors, and others who might recognize the results of abuse, the elderly are often isolated and do not come into contact with those who might recognize the symptoms of violence. Caregivers can attribute bruises and broken bones to a fall. An elderly victim might not be believed because of his or her confusion or senility.

A significant difficulty in gathering information from the elderly is their frequent reluctance to either report or prosecute the crime. Margaret Hudson, in "Elder Mistreatment: Current Research" (Chapter VI in *Elder Abuse*), wrote that the elderly often deny (consciously or unconsciously) that the abuse is taking place for several reasons:

- Fear of retaliation, abandonment, or being removed from the home or family setting.

- Belief that the abuse was deserved.

- Sense that there is nowhere else to go or that nothing can be done to help.

- Shame in admitting such treatment by one's own children. Elders wish to protect their image as good parents. If their children have abused them, then, as some elders believe, it must have been their own fault.

Most elderly are afraid to go to nursing homes. Many would rather stay at home and be mistreated than be institutionalized. Since social workers cannot force an elderly person to report an abuser, they must honor each person's right to choose. Sometimes, even though the cases involve serious violence or neglect, the authorities are unable to take any action.

Fear of isolation, loss of support, and great embarrassment resulting from the revelation that their own children would abuse them is often greater than the fear of continued abuse. Usually, a neighbor or another relative reports the abuse. Elderly cooperation in the prosecution of the crime is just as unusual. As a result, the statistics used in earlier studies on elderly abuse, ranging from 1 to nearly 10 percent of the study samples, must be seen as indicative of the reality, but not the reality itself. The assumption that officially reported cases of abuse represent only the "tip of the iceberg" is widely accepted. Figure 9.2 depicts the iceberg theory of elder abuse.

HOW FREQUENT IS ELDER ABUSE?

Karl Pillemer and Jill Suitor, in "Prevention of Elder Abuse" (*Treatment of Family Violence*, Robert Ammerman and Michael Hersen, eds., John Wiley and Sons, New York, 1990), pointed out that very few scientifically valid studies of elder abuse have been conducted. Some experts have characterized elder abuse as being in the situation that child abuse was in 20 years ago. S. Powell and R. Berg ("When the Elderly Are Abused: Character-istics and Intervention," *Educational Gerontology*, vol. 13, 1987) observed that, "Lack of quality data has led to statements presented as facts that have no scientific foundation but are used to frame both policy and programs to treat and prevent the abuse of older persons."

An American Large Random Survey

Karl Pillemer and David Finkelhor, authorities in the field of abuse and members of the Family Research Laboratory at the University of New Hampshire, completed the only American large-scale, random sample survey of elderly abuse. One of the main objectives was to generate a national prevalence rate of domestic elder abuse. Between September 1985 and February 1986, the Center for Survey Research at the University of Massachusetts interviewed 2,020 elderly households in the Boston metropolitan area regarding their experience of physical violence, verbal aggression, and neglect. Elderly in institutions were not included in this survey. Pillemer and Finkelhor published their conclusions in "The Prevalence of Elder Abuse: A Random Sample Survey" (*Gerontologist*, vol. 28, no. 1, 1988).

TABLE 9.1
Perpetrator — Victim Relationship
(Including Proxy Respondents, unweighted data)

	All types*	Physical violence	Chronic verbal aggression	Neglect
Husband to wife	14 (22%)	7 (17%)	7 (27%)	2 (29%)
Wife to husband	23 (36%)	17 (43%)	7 (27%)	—
Son to mother	5 (8%)	4 (10%)	2 (8%)	—
Son to father	5 (8%)	3 (7%)	3 (11%)	—
Daughter to mother	4 (6 %)	1 (3%)	2 (8%)	2 (29%)
Daughter to father	1 (2%)	1 (3%)	—	—
Other	11 (18%)	7 (17%)	5 (19%)	3 (42%)
Total	63	40	26	7

*The total number of cases in specific categories exceeds the All Type category, because more than one type of abuse was sometimes present.

Source: Karl Pillemer and David Finkelhor, "The Prevalence of Elder Abuse: A Random Sample Survey," *Gerontologist*, vol. 28, no. 1, p. 54, 1988. Copyright © The Gerontological Society of America

Pillemer and Finkelhor found that of the 2,020 persons interviewed, 63 persons, or 32 per 1,000 elderly, had been mistreated. Based on the population of Boston, where the survey was taken, Pillemer and Finkelhor estimated that between 8,646 and 13,487 elderly Bostonians suffered abuse. If this rate is projected to the United States, between 701,000 and 1,093,560 older Americans have possibly been abused. (For various methodological reasons, Pillemer and Finkelhor believe they might have undercounted, to some extent, the number of abused. Also, they did not count financial abuse.)

The most commonly cited statistics for the rate of elder abuse range between 500,000 and 2.5 million cases per year. The upper estimate, however, is generally considered to be a distortion of Pillemer's work, which concluded that no more than 1.1 million older Americans had *ever* been abused.

Most Elderly Abused by the Elderly

Unlike most other studies, Pillemer and Finkelhor found that spouses committed most of the violence done to the elderly. They reported that almost three-fifths (58 percent) of the abusers were spouses, compared to 24 percent of the cases that involved abuse by a child of the victim. (See Table 9.1.) The researchers found little difference between minority and White elderly, the older old (over 75) and younger old (65 to 74), and no significant differences based on religious, economic, or educational background. Most earlier studies had found a higher rate of elderly abuse among the older elderly and the more economically disadvantaged. The researchers believe the higher rate among these two groups might be accountable not to "a greater risk for abuse but from the greater visibility of the very old and disadvantaged to potential reporters of abuse."

On the other hand, they found those living alone had much lower rates of abuse. This was to be expected since simply being in constant contact with another person naturally increases the chances of violence. Consequently, those living alone, such as widows, divorcees, and those never married, suffered less abuse. Those in poor health were more likely to suffer from neglect than were those in good health, as were those with no caretaker.

Spousal Abuse

Until research began to show otherwise, the generally accepted stereotype of elder abuse had been that of a mentally or physically dependent parent moving in with a child, who, overwhelmed by the situation, strikes out in some way against the parent. In Pillemer and Finkelhor's survey, however, spousal abuse appeared to be more common. This was not because the elderly are any more violent than their children are. Rather, since spouses are more likely to live in the same household than are the children, the opportunity for spousal violence is greater. "If more elderly lived with their children," noted Pillemer and Finkelhor, "there would probably be more child-to-elder violence." The spousal abuse may well be a continuation of a long-established pattern of behavior in the marriage.

Pillemer and Finkelhor pointed out that some earlier studies had found spousal abuse to be a major factor in elderly abuse, but that this had been played down. They attributed this to the desire of those trying to gain sympathy for the abused elderly to put the issue in the most compelling light. The image of an adult child abusing a dependent, weak, elderly parent is more likely to raise sympathy, while the image of one elderly person hitting another is less likely to do so.

A Canadian Survey

A Canadian study of service providers (unpublished data by Connie Chapman for the Elder Abuse Community Development Project, titled *Learning from Service Providers Working with Abused Seniors*, 1994) found that 38 percent of 176 actively abused elderly were emotionally abused, 31 percent suffered financial or material abuse, and 23 percent were physically abused. In the 73 cases of suspected abuse, about one-third (31 percent) were thought to be emotionally

TABLE 9.2

KIND OF ABUSE	ACTIVE INVOLVEMENT		SUSPECTED	
	Number	Percentage	Number	Percentage
Emotional	67	38%	23	31%
Material/Financial	54	31	26	37%
Physical	40	23	0	0
Sexual	0	0	0	0
Neglect	12	7	12	16%
Self-Neglect	3	2	6	8%
Abuse Unknown	0	0	6	8%
TOTALS	176	101.00	73	100.00

Source: Connie Chapman, *Learning from Service Providers Working with Abused Seniors*, prepared for the Elder Abuse Community Development Project, North Shore Community Services, April 1994

abused, more than one-third (37 percent) were financially abused, and 16 percent were neglected. There were no cases of suspected physical abuse. (See Table 9.2.)

One-third of confirmed abuse was perpetrated by the husband, compared to only 3 percent by wives. More than half (51 percent) the abusers were sons or daughters or their spouses (Table 9.3). The majority of seniors were abused by only one person (70 percent), although 23 percent of victims were abused by two people and 7 percent were abused by three people. Most research does not ask how many perpetrators are involved in each

TABLE 9.3

RELATIONSHIP OF ABUSER TO VICTIM	ACTIVE INVOLVEMENT		SUSPECTED	
	Number	Percentage	Number	Percentage
Husband	41	33%	12	19%
Wife	4	3	1	2
Son	20	16	11	17
Daughter-in-law	19	15	5	8
Son-in-law	11	9	5	8
Daughter	14	11	11	17
Grandson	2	2	0	0
Granddaughter	6	5	1	2
Other relative	3	3%	14	22
Neighbour	3	3%	2	3
Abuser unknown	0	0	2	3
TOTALS	123	100.00	64	101.00

Source: Connie Chapman, *Learning from Service Providers Working with Abused Seniors*, prepared for the Elder Abuse Community Development Project, North Shore Community Services, April 1994

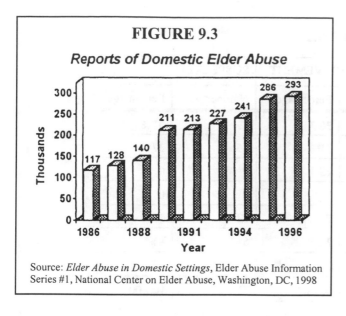

FIGURE 9.3

Reports of Domestic Elder Abuse

Source: *Elder Abuse in Domestic Settings*, Elder Abuse Information Series #1, National Center on Elder Abuse, Washington, DC, 1998

case of elder abuse, and it is usually assumed that it is a one-on-one phenomenon. There may be, however, a significant number of elderly who are abused by several people.

ELDER ABUSE AND THE GOVERNMENT

Elder abuse first became a public issue in 1978. In 1981, the late Claude Pepper (D-FL) chaired the Select Committee on Aging, the committee responsible for the first report, *Elder Abuse: An Examination of a Hidden Problem*. Ten years later, a government study on domestic elder abuse, "Elder Abuse: A Decade of Shame and Inaction" (Washington, DC, 1990), revealed in its title how little had been accomplished.

The first report recommended legislation identical to the Child Abuse Prevention and Treatment Act of 1974 (PL 93-247; see *Child Abuse: A Betrayal of Trust*, Information Plus, Wylie, Texas, 1999) as a step towards controlling violence against the elderly. Since then, every Congress has supported this legislation, prompting the majority of the states to pass elder abuse protection statutes. Prior to 1980, only 16 states had adult protective service laws; by 1995, with the passage of New Jersey's statute, all 50 states and the District of Columbia had passed legislation, including mandatory reporting provisions for the elderly.

Without funding, however, the laws have not had much effect. In 1988, Congress passed legislation to provide assistance to the states, but funds were never appropriated (allocated). The states, until recently financially strained and having received nothing from the federal government, have also failed to fund programs for the elderly abused. In addition, critics have begun to question the usefulness of approaching elder abuse from the child abuse model. Not all abused elders want the government to interfere in their lives in a process that frequently ends up with victims being placed in nursing homes. Some experts feel that putting money into solid preventive programs such as in-home care and psychological counseling would yield better results.

At present, the only federal program that specifically addresses elder abuse is the Elder Abuse Prevention Program under Chapter 3, Title VII of the Older Americans Act (PL 95-478). Though this act has not been reauthorized since 1992, programs for the elderly have been extended through continuing resolutions in Congress. The $4.7 million appropriation for the Elder Abuse Prevention Program extends through fiscal year 1999. The Older Americans Act also provides states with funding for their Long-Term Care Ombudsman programs, which handle complaints, including maltreatment, made by or on behalf of residents of long-term care facilities. For 1999, Congress authorized $7.4 million, a significant increase from the $4.4 million authorized in 1997.

A STUDY OF
ADULT PROTECTIVE SERVICES

The National Center on Elder Abuse (NCEA) has been collecting data on domestic elder abuse since 1986. National summaries from the results of surveys of state adult protective service agencies and state units on aging indicate a 150 percent increase in elder abuse reports from 1986 to 1996. In 1996, there were 293,000 reports of domestic elder abuse, compared to 117,000 reports in 1986. (See Figure 9.3.) These counts may be

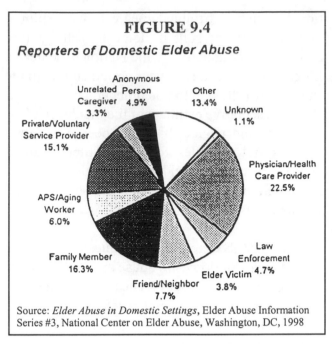

FIGURE 9.4

Reporters of Domestic Elder Abuse

Anonymous Unrelated Person 4.9%
Caregiver 3.3%
Other 13.4%
Private/Voluntary Service Provider 15.1%
Unknown 1.1%
APS/Aging Worker 6.0%
Physician/Health Care Provider 22.5%
Family Member 16.3%
Law Enforcement 4.7%
Friend/Neighbor 7.7%
Elder Victim 3.8%

Source: *Elder Abuse in Domestic Settings*, Elder Abuse Information Series #3, National Center on Elder Abuse, Washington, DC, 1998

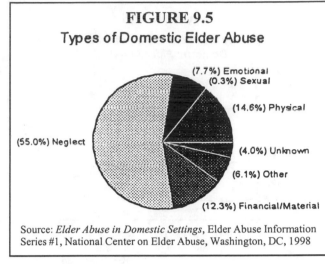

FIGURE 9.5

Types of Domestic Elder Abuse

(7.7%) Emotional
(0.3%) Sexual
(14.6%) Physical
(4.0%) Unknown
(6.1%) Other
(12.3%) Financial/Material
(55.0%) Neglect

Source: *Elder Abuse in Domestic Settings*, Elder Abuse Information Series #1, National Center on Elder Abuse, Washington, DC, 1998

duplicated; in other words, more than one report may have been filed for one victim or one report may represent more than one victim.

Adult protective service (APS) professionals believe that elder abuse is a widespread problem, and some estimate that as few as one case in 14 comes to the attention of the authorities. The true prevalence of elder abuse is unknown, and the APS data can be used only as an indicator.

In all but eight states, certain types of professionals are designated as mandatory reporters of domestic elder abuse, required by law to report suspected cases of abuse, neglect, and exploitation. Reports from physicians and health care providers comprised the largest proportion of reports of domestic elder abuse, 22.5 percent in 1996. Family members were the next most likely to report abuse (16.3 percent). Another 15.1 percent came from service providers. (See Figure 9.4.)

All reports of elder abuse are investigated and a decision is made whether to substantiate (confirm) the report. Close to two-thirds of the reports in 1996 were substantiated. Of those reports, about one-quarter were for abuse by others, while 32 percent were for self-neglect. Most of the substan-

tiated abuse was described as neglect (55 percent). The next most common forms of abuse were physical (14.6 percent) and financial abuse (12.3 percent). (See Figure 9.5.)

In 1996, the ratio of male perpetrators to female perpetrators dropped to the point that there was no significant difference between the two genders. The reports showed that 47.4 percent of abusers were male, compared to 48.9 percent female. Over one-third of the perpetrators were the adult children of elderly victims. This category from the total reports increased the most, from 30.1 percent in 1990 to 36.7 percent in 1996. Spouses and other relatives were the next most likely to be reported for abuse (12.6 and 10.8, respectively, in 1996). (See Figure 9.6.)

The victims of abuse were mainly female (67 percent in 1996) and older elderly (40.5 percent over age 80). In 1996, the median age of elder abuse victims was 77.9 years, excluding self-neglecting elders. About two-thirds were White, and close to 19 percent were Black. Proportionally, Blacks were overrepresented in the abuse reports because they make up only about 13 percent of the population as a whole. Hispanic victims accounted for about 10 percent of domestic elder abuse, while the proportions of Native Americans and Asian Americans/Pacific Islanders were each less than 1 percent.

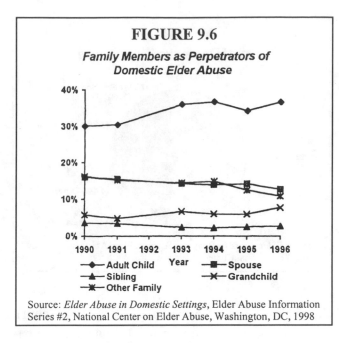

FIGURE 9.6

Family Members as Perpetrators of Domestic Elder Abuse

Source: *Elder Abuse in Domestic Settings*, Elder Abuse Information Series #2, National Center on Elder Abuse, Washington, DC, 1998

NATIONAL ELDER ABUSE INCIDENCE STUDY

The *National Elder Abuse Incidence Study* (NEAIS), mandated by Congress to study the na-tional incidence of abuse, neglect, and exploitation of elderly persons in domestic settings (see above), was conducted by the National Center on Elder Abuse over a four-year period ending in the summer of 1997. Up to this time, no large, nationally representative estimate of the incidence of elder abuse and neglect had ever been calculated. This research provides, for the first time, national incidence estimates of elder abuse, which can serve as a baseline for future research and service interventions.

The NEAIS asked the basic question: What is the incidence of domestic abuse and elder neglect in the United States today? The term "incidence," in public health and social research, means the number of new cases occurring over a specific time period. For example, how many new cases occurred in 1996? "Prevalence," in contrast, is similar to a census and refers to the total number of ongoing cases in a given population at a designated point of time. For example, what is the total number of

TABLE 9.4

National estimates of the incidence of abuse, neglect, and self-neglect of persons 60 years and older, 1996 (unduplicated)

	Estimated Number of Elderly[1]			
	(1) Reported by Sentinels	(2) Reported to APS	(3) Reported to APS: Substantiated Only	(4) Total: Columns (1) and (3)
Total Abuse, Neglect and Self Neglect (Standard error)	435,901 (114,887)	236,479 (34,298)	115,110 (20,326) *48.7%*	551,011 (118,008)
Total Abuse and Neglect (Standard error)	378,982 (117,758)	151,408 (18,999)	70,942 (11,881) *46.9%*	449,924 (119,512)
Abuse (Standard error)	355,218 (116,875)	95,761 (15,579)	47,069 (9,814) *49.2%*	402,287 (116,084)
Neglect[2] (Standard error)	147,035 (52,290)	85,143 (12,966)	35,333 (6,706) *41.5%*	182,368 (58,743)
Self-Neglect (Standard error)	81,635 (21,966)	113,573 (28,907)	57,345 (15,350) *50.5%*	138,980 (24,232)

[1] Subtotals do not add to totals because more than one type of abuse was reported for some cases.

[2] Includes abandonment.

Source: *National Elder Abuse Incidence Study*, National Center on Elder Abuse, Washington, DC, 1998

ongoing cases of elder abuse right now? The NEAIS examined the incidence of newly filed reports of abuse and neglect among those age 60 and above in 1996.

The study gathered data on domestic elder abuse, neglect, and self-neglect through a nationally representative sample of 20 counties in 15 states. Data came from two sources: (1) reports from the local adult protective services (APS) responsible for receiving and investigating reports in each county and (2) reports from "sentinels," specially trained individuals in a variety of community agencies having frequent contact with the elderly.

The sentinel data collection approach, used earlier for federally supported national incidence studies of child abuse and neglect, has been accepted as a less costly alternative to a general population survey. In addition to collecting data from local APS agencies, the NEAIS used over 1,000 trained "sentinels" to observe and document incidents of elder abuse. Many sentinels were mandatory or voluntary reporters of elder abuse as defined by state laws and were employed by such organizations as hospitals and clinics, elder care providers, law enforcement agencies, and financial institutions.

Definitions of Elder Maltreatment

In the NEAIS, the phrase "elder maltreatment" refers to the seven types of abuse and neglect measured in the study: physical abuse, sexual abuse, emotional or psychological abuse, financial or material exploitation, abandonment, neglect, and self-neglect. The following are the standardized abuse and neglect definitions used in the study:

- **Physical abuse**—the use of physical force that may result in bodily injury, physical pain, or impairment. Physical abuse may include but is not limited to such acts of violence as striking (with or without an object), hitting, beating, pushing, shoving, shaking, slapping, kicking, pinching, and burning. The unwarranted administration of drugs and physical restraints,

force-feeding, and physical punishment of any kind also are examples of physical abuse.

- **Sexual abuse**—nonconsensual sexual contact of any kind with an elderly person. Sexual contact with any person incapable of giving consent also is considered sexual abuse; it includes but is not limited to unwanted touching, all types of sexual assault or battery such as rape, sodomy, coerced nudity, and sexually explicit photographing.

- **Emotional or psychological abuse**—the infliction of anguish, emotional pain, or distress. Emotional or psychological abuse includes but is not limited to verbal assaults, insults, threats, intimidation, humiliation, and harassment. In addition, treating an older person like an infant; isolating an elderly person from family, friends, or regular activities; giving an older person a "silent treatment"; and enforced social isolation also are examples of emotional or psychological abuse.

- **Neglect**—the refusal or failure to fulfill any part of a person's obligations or duties to an elder. Neglect may also include a refusal or failure by a person who has fiduciary responsibilities to provide care for an elder (e.g., failure to pay for necessary home care service, or the failure on the part of an in-home service provider to provide necessary care). Neglect typically means the refusal or failure to provide an elderly person with such life necessities as food, water, clothing, shelter, personal hygiene, medicine, comfort, personal safety, and other essentials included as a responsibility or an agreement.

- **Abandonment**—the desertion of an elderly person by an individual who has assumed responsibility for providing care or by a person with physical custody of an elder.

- **Financial or material exploitation**—the illegal or improper use of an elder's funds, property, or assets. Examples include but are not limited to cashing checks without authorization or permission; forging an older person's signature; misusing or stealing an older person's money or possessions; coercing or deceiving an older person into signing a document (e.g., contracts or a will); and the improper use of conservatorship, guardianship, or power of attorney.

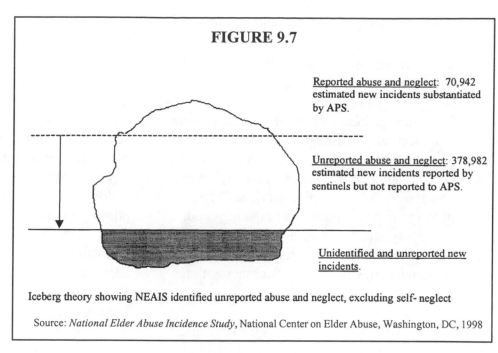

FIGURE 9.7

Reported abuse and neglect: 70,942 estimated new incidents substantiated by APS.

Unreported abuse and neglect: 378,982 estimated new incidents reported by sentinels but not reported to APS.

Unidentified and unreported new incidents.

Iceberg theory showing NEAIS identified unreported abuse and neglect, excluding self-neglect

Source: *National Elder Abuse Incidence Study*, National Center on Elder Abuse, Washington, DC, 1998

- **Self-neglect**—characterized as the behaviors of an elderly person that threaten his/her own health or safely. Self-neglect generally manifests itself in an older person's refusal or failure to provide himself/herself with adequate food, water, clothing, shelter, safety, personal hygiene, and medication (when indicated). For the purpose of this study, the definition of self-neglect **excludes** a situation in which a mentally competent older person (who understands the consequences of his/her decisions) makes a conscious and voluntary decision to engage in acts that threaten his/her health or safety.

Cases that did not meet the study definitions were excluded from the database.

Estimated Incidence of Domestic Elder Abuse and/or Neglect in 1996

According to the *National Elder Abuse Incidence Study* (NEAIS), the "best national estimate" of elder abuse and neglect, including self-neglect, in domestic settings in 1996 was a total of 551,011 elderly persons, ages 60 and over. Of this total, 21 percent (115,110) were reported to and substantiated by adult protective services (APS) agencies, while the remaining 79 percent (435,901) were not reported to APS. (See Table 9.4.) Almost four times

as many new incidents of abuse, neglect, and/or self-neglect were unreported, compared to the reported and substantiated cases.

Excluding self-neglect, the "best national estimate" of elder abuse and/or neglect in domestic settings in 1996 was 449,924 elderly persons, ages 60 and over. Of this total, 16 percent (70,942) were reported to and substantiated by APS agencies; the remaining 84 percent (378,982) were not reported to APS. (See Table 9.4.) This indicated that over five times as many new incidents of abuse and neglect were unreported, compared to the reported and substantiated cases.

The impact of the NEAIS estimates on the "iceberg" theory of elder abuse (see above) is shown in Figure 9.7. A significant area of previously unidentified and unreported elder abuse has been exposed and estimated. However, the NEAIS researchers acknowledge that not all elder abuse, due primarily to the isolation of so many of the elder population, can be identified and reported. Hence, a submerged core of abuse and neglect remains unidentified, unreported, and inestimable at this time.

The elder abuse victims reported to APS agencies are similar in characteristics to those identified by sentinel agencies. Female elders are abused

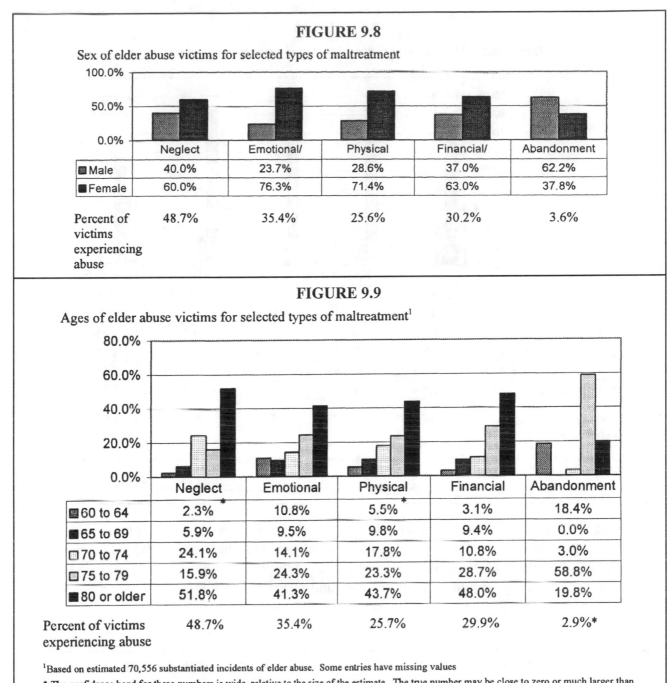

FIGURE 9.8

Sex of elder abuse victims for selected types of maltreatment

	Neglect	Emotional/	Physical	Financial/	Abandonment
Male	40.0%	23.7%	28.6%	37.0%	62.2%
Female	60.0%	76.3%	71.4%	63.0%	37.8%
Percent of victims experiencing abuse	48.7%	35.4%	25.6%	30.2%	3.6%

FIGURE 9.9

Ages of elder abuse victims for selected types of maltreatment[1]

	Neglect	Emotional	Physical	Financial	Abandonment
60 to 64	2.3%*	10.8%	5.5%*	3.1%	18.4%
65 to 69	5.9%	9.5%	9.8%	9.4%	0.0%
70 to 74	24.1%	14.1%	17.8%	10.8%	3.0%
75 to 79	15.9%	24.3%	23.3%	28.7%	58.8%
80 or older	51.8%	41.3%	43.7%	48.0%	19.8%
Percent of victims experiencing abuse	48.7%	35.4%	25.7%	29.9%	2.9%*

[1] Based on estimated 70,556 substantiated incidents of elder abuse. Some entries have missing values

* The confidence band for these numbers is wide, relative to the size of the estimate. The true number may be close to zero or much larger than the estimate.

Source of both figures: *National Elder Abuse Incidence Study*, National Center on Elder Abuse, Washington, DC, 1998

at a higher rate than males, even after accounting for their larger proportion in the aged population. In APS reports, women represent from 60 percent to 76 percent of elder abuse victims in each category of abuse and neglect except abandonment, even though women represent 58 percent of the elderly population (over 60 years of age). (See Figure 9.8.) Emotional or psychological abuse was the category of greatest disparity between men and women. Three-fourths of the incidences in this form of abuse were women. In sentinel reports, from 67 percent to 92 percent of those reported as abused were female, depending on the type of abuse. The greatest difference between men and women in the sentinel reports was in the rates of financial abuse; 92 percent of the victims were women.

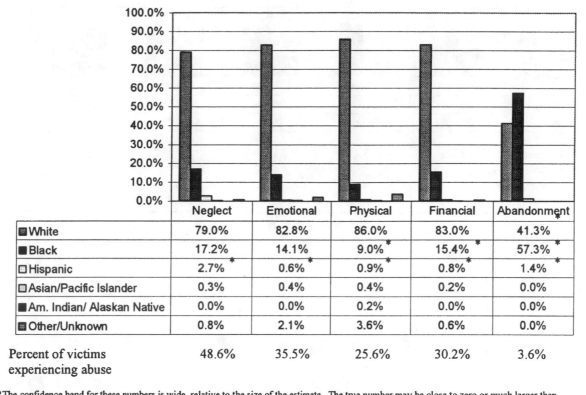

FIGURE 9.10

Race/ethnicity of elder abuse victims for selected types of maltreatment

	Neglect	Emotional	Physical	Financial	Abandonment
White	79.0%	82.8%	86.0%	83.0%	41.3%
Black	17.2%	14.1%	9.0% *	15.4% *	57.3% *
Hispanic	2.7% *	0.6% *	0.9% *	0.8% *	1.4% *
Asian/Pacific Islander	0.3%	0.4%	0.4%	0.2%	0.0%
Am. Indian/ Alaskan Native	0.0%	0.0%	0.2%	0.0%	0.0%
Other/Unknown	0.8%	2.1%	3.6%	0.6%	0.0%
Percent of victims experiencing abuse	48.6%	35.5%	25.6%	30.2%	3.6%

*The confidence band for these numbers is wide, relative to the size of the estimate. The true number may be close to zero or much larger than the estimate.

Source: *National Elder Abuse Incidence Study*, National Center on Elder Abuse, Washington, DC, 1998

The oldest elders, those 80 years and over, were abused and neglected at a rate of two to three times their proportion of the elderly population. APS reports indicated that 52 percent of neglect victims were over age 80 (Figure 9.9). Sentinels found 60 percent in this oldest age group. APS reports also show that this age group was disproportionately subjected to physical abuse, emotional abuse, and financial exploitation.

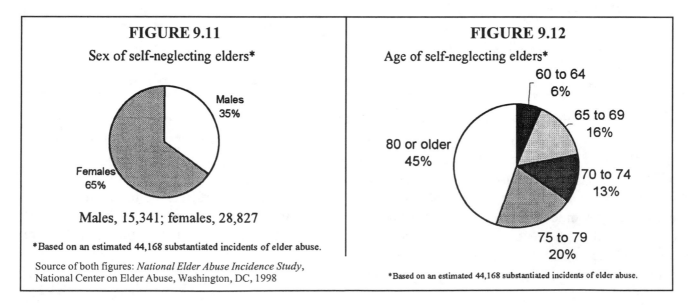

FIGURE 9.11

Sex of self-neglecting elders*

Males 35%
Females 65%

Males, 15,341; females, 28,827

*Based on an estimated 44,168 substantiated incidents of elder abuse.

Source of both figures: *National Elder Abuse Incidence Study*, National Center on Elder Abuse, Washington, DC, 1998

FIGURE 9.12

Age of self-neglecting elders*

60 to 64 6%
65 to 69 16%
70 to 74 13%
75 to 79 20%
80 or older 45%

*Based on an estimated 44,168 substantiated incidents of elder abuse.

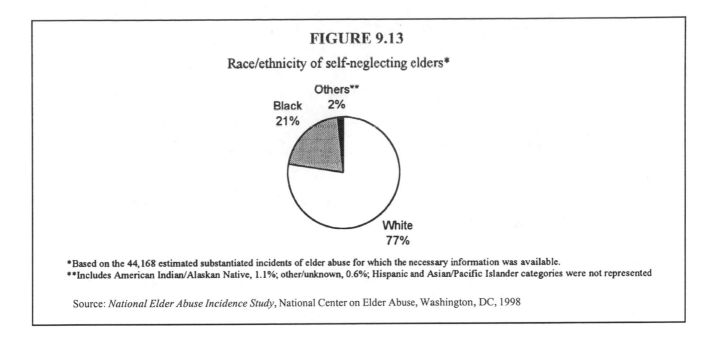

FIGURE 9.13

Race/ethnicity of self-neglecting elders*

Others** 2%

Black 21%

White 77%

*Based on the 44,168 estimated substantiated incidents of elder abuse for which the necessary information was available.
**Includes American Indian/Alaskan Native, 1.1%; other/unknown, 0.6%; Hispanic and Asian/Pacific Islander categories were not represented

Source: *National Elder Abuse Incidence Study*, National Center on Elder Abuse, Washington, DC, 1998

In 1996, White elders comprised 84 percent of the total elder population, while Black elders were 8.3 percent and Hispanic elders were 5.1 percent of the population. Though sentinel data show that fewer than 10 percent of minority elders (including Blacks, Hispanics, Asians, Pacific Islanders, and others) were subjected to any form of abuse, APS agencies report higher proportions of Black victims. Black victims of elder abuse accounted for 9 percent of physical abuse cases, 14.1 percent of emotional abuse cases, 15.4 percent of financial abuse reports, 17.2 percent of neglect cases, and 57.3 percent of abandonment cases. Only small proportions, 3 percent or less, of other minorities were represented in most categories of abuse reported to APS. (See Figure 9.10.)

Self-neglect among the elderly is a serious problem, with about 139,000 new unduplicated incidences reported in 1996. About two-thirds of these were women (Figure 9.11), and 45 percent were over the age of 80 (Figure 9.12). Self-neglecting elders were predominately White (77 percent), but 21 percent were Black. (See Figure 9.13.) The

Black elderly were two and a half times more likely to be self-neglecting than their proportion of the elderly population. Not surprisingly, most self-neglecting elders (93.3 percent) have difficulty caring for themselves. In addition, many are confused and/or depressed.

According to the APS reports, men outnumbered women as perpetrators by at least 3 to 2, except in the category of neglect, where 52 percent of the abusers were women. Sentinel data show male perpetrators outnumbering female perpetrators by 1.8 to 1.

Most perpetrators were younger than their victims. About 65 percent were under the age of 60. However, APS agencies report that the perpetrators of financial abuse were younger — 45 percent were age 40 or under, and another 40 percent were between 41 and 59 years old. Data show that relatives or spouses of the victims commit approximately 90 percent of domestic elder abuse. Adult children were the largest category of abusers.

CHAPTER X

CAUSES AND ISSUES OF ELDER ABUSE

I know I push her sometimes, but she is always there. — A daughter explaining the repeated bruising of her mother

Growing old has turned into a humiliating and isolated journey with the spirit broken long before the body. We seem to forget that these people we are tossing into the corner are, in fact, our future selves. — Robert Butler, former director of the National Institute on Aging, from "Ageism's Angry Critic," *Human Behavior*, 1979

Many theories have been proposed to explain the causes of elder abuse. Some of these have included drug and alcohol abuse, chronic medical problems, financial problems, dependency of the victim, provocation by the victim, dependency of the caregiver, and social isolation. Because elder abuse is relatively unexplored, there is considerable disagreement over how well each of these theories explains the causes of abuse.

Abuse has no single explanation, and each case reflects the personal problems in a relationship. Trends and potential risks can be identified, however, and they can help alert caregivers and the elderly to dangerous situations. None of the theories discussed below are mutually exclusive (accepting one theory does not mean that you cannot accept the others), so two or three, or all of them, may apply to any given situation without being inconsistent.

PHYSICAL DISABILITY AND DEPENDENCY

The theory of dependency proposes that the neediness of the elder, often because of physical or mental impairments, contributes to elder abuse. This is probably the most widely held belief. In general, researchers have found that elders in poor health are more likely to be abused than those in good health. How-

ever, several recent studies have questioned this theory, proposing that the crucial factor is the dependency of the abuser, not the elderly victim.

Elder abuse was assumed to be the result of the stress of having to care for a needy elder. According to a recent study by the U.S. General Accounting Office (*Time South Pacific*, Issue 31, August 3, 1998), approximately 80 percent of the estimated 6 million dependent elders in the United States are cared for at home. The caregiver may lack the skill to care for the elder and may not have support from other family members. There is often no respite in the care of dependent elders and frequently no visible benefit for all the effort that is expended.

Michael Nolan ("Carer-Dependent Relationships," *The Mistreatment of Elderly People*, Decalmer and Glendenning, eds., Sage Publications, London, England, 1993) found that, in surveys of caregivers, one of the most frequently voiced sources of stress was feeling manipulated by a dependent. Manipulative behavior was especially destructive to the relationship when such behavior was interpreted as willful and deliberate. A lack of appreciation and "not trying" often went along with manipulative behavior, and when this occurred, it increased the caregiver's feelings of anger. A frustrated caregiver complained,

Sometimes Mother just sits there demanding attention and wanting it there and then. I wouldn't mind so much but some of the things she could do herself if only she'd try. In any case no matter what I do it never seems good enough and she never says thank you. Things would be so much better if just once in a while at the end of a meal, she said "Thank you, that was very nice."

The dependence of the abused elder appears to be a logical risk factor, especially since it is consistent with similar interpretations of child abuse, another situation involving dependency. Furthermore, it is easy to imagine someone reacting this way to the stress of caregiving. Expert Suzanne Steinmetz has been a proponent of this view, arguing that the "generational inversion" (the once-dependent child becomes the caretaking adult, and the parent becomes as dependent as a baby) leads to increased stress. The caregiver then begins to see the relationship as unfair, which sometimes results in abuse.

Dependency of the Caregiver

Some experts have disagreed on the question of whose dependency is the major cause of abuse. Karl Pillemer's research has found that the crucial factor was not the ill health or frailty of an elderly person, but the caregiver's dependence on the elder for financial support and/or housing. In 1989, Pillemer found that 64 percent of abusers were financially dependent on their victims, and 55 percent were dependent for housing. Drug and alcohol abusers and adult children with mental disorders, often dependent on elders for support, were also more likely to be abusive caretakers.

According to Pillemer, power appears to be the key to abuse. Acts of abuse "seem to be acts carried out by abusers to compensate for their perceived lack or loss of power." In "Prevention of Elder Abuse" (*Treatment of Family Violence*, Robert Ammerman and Michael Hersen, eds., John Wiley and Sons, New York City, 1990), Pillemer and Jill Suitor pointed out that abuse in younger populations (spouse and child abuse) often stems from either a sense of powerlessness or parental inadequacy.

The feeling of powerlessness experienced by an adult child who is still dependent on an elderly parent may be especially acute because it goes so strongly against society's expectations for normal adult behavior. This perceived power deficit appears to be a better explanation for elder abuse than the notion that the abuser holds too much power in the relationship.

In Pillemer's original study of elder abuse ("The Dangers of Dependency: New Findings on Domestic Violence Against the Elderly" *Social Problems*, vol. 33, no. 2, 1985), caregivers' mental or emotional problems appeared to contribute to violence. About 79 percent of the abused thought their caregiving relatives suffered from mental health problems (compared to only 24 percent of the control group). Indeed, Pillemer noted, "We can speculate that mental disorder may be one factor in the continuing dependence of the abusers on their victims." Pillemer further observed that their relatives' mental health problems were a major reason why many elderly chose not to leave their abusive situations. They feared no one would be able to take care of their (in most cases) son or daughter.

Pillemer believes the typical abused elder is

an older woman supporting a dependent child or, to a lesser extent, a physically or mentally disabled spouse. The victims perceived themselves as on the losing end of the exchange, as giving much and receiving little. Most felt trapped by a sense of family obligation and therefore did not leave the situation.

Pillemer claims that his findings, unlike the "previous research that has attributed abuse to the demands of the older individual [which] tends to blame the victim," focus attention on the abuser, where it belongs.

Whose Dependency: The Victim's?

Steinmetz and Pillemer debated the question of dependency in *Current Controversies on Family Violence* (Gelles and Loseke, eds., Sage Publications, Newbury Park, California, 1993). In "The Abused Elderly Are Dependent," Steinmetz attributed the differences in results to differences in research. Pillemer's elderly subjects were generally younger and less dependent than the elderly in Steinmetz's research. In addition, Pillemer's caregivers were also younger (an average age of 38), 73 percent had never married, and two-thirds had never left home. This sample, according to Steinmetz, represented adults who had not achieved the independence normally expected of grown children and might suggest that they were more psychologically troubled than normal.

In contrast, Steinmetz's sample represented families in which a dependent elder was forced to move in with the adult child and the family was forced to accommodate the dependent in the home. The average age of Steinmetz's caregivers was 52.

Steinmetz believes Pillemer is mistaken when he measures the caregiver's dependency by ability to perform the tasks of daily living (washing, dressing, toileting) that the elderly person is no longer able to do independently. In her opinion, "If one defines dependency in terms of the number of responsibilities that the caregiver has to fulfill and the inability to be relieved of these responsibilities..., then a relationship between dependency and abuse is found." In other words, this measure of dependency, according to Steinmetz, shows the dependency of the elder.

Or the Caregiver's?

Pillemer ("The Abused Offspring Are Dependent") charged that the impulse to blame an elders' dependency for abuse is motivated by society's perceived need to provide assistance to the weak and helpless. "Our society is seen as morally obligated to provide for these elders, because they, like children, cannot fend for themselves." Pillemer claims that Steinmetz's interpretation of extreme dependency of the elderly as the root of abuse is a form of ageism. The elderly are equated with children in that they need protection simply because of their age.

Instead, according to Pillemer, "All studies that have addressed this issue [of dependent caregivers] have been unequivocal in their assessment: elder abus-

ers — rather than being stable, well-intentioned caregivers — tend to suffer from a variety of mental health, substance abuse, and stress-related problems." In addition, researchers have found that many of these abusers were violent in other contexts, have been arrested, and have been hospitalized for psychiatric reasons. Pillemer points out this data cannot be compared to Steinmetz's work because she never asked questions about this type of behavior.

Pillemer thinks it is important to focus the attention on the dependency of the caregiver. Blaming the dependency of the elderly person unintentionally blames the victim in the same way that battered wives have been blamed for their abuse because they may have nagged or been unpleasant. Furthermore, by focusing on the stress imposed on the caregiver, funding is directed toward services such as support groups and home care when the money might be better spent elsewhere.

Causes May Differ by Type of Abuse

Rosalie Wolf ("Victimization of the Elderly: Elder Abuse and Neglect," *Reviews in Clinical Gerontology*, vol. 2, 1992) has proposed that different types of abuse are caused by different types of abusers. An analysis of 328 model project cases found that there were three profiles of abuse. Many cases represented more than one form of abuse, and the categories, therefore, overlapped.

The first profile represented physical and psychological abuse, and the perpetrators were more likely to have a history of psychological trouble and to be financially dependent on the victim. This abuse was usually conducted by close family members, and a past history of poor family relations was likely.

The second profile described a victim who was likely to be widowed and very old and to have few social supports. This elderly victim was usually mentally and physically dysfunctional. In these cases, the abuse appeared to stem from the caregiver's stress of supporting a dependent elder, and not caregiver dependency.

Financial abuse represented the third profile. The victim's physical and mental state was unimportant in these cases. The perpetrators had financial problems and histories of substance abuse. The motivating factor in these cases had no relation to dependency; it was greed.

INTERGENERATIONAL TRANSMISSION OF VIOLENT BEHAVIOR

When I was a laddie,
I lived with my granny,
And many a hiding [spanking] *me granny gi'ed me.*
Now I am a man,
And I live with my granny.
And I do to my granny,
What she did to me. — English rhyme

The theory of intergenerational violence is linked to the generally accepted theory of child and spousal abuse, which holds that a child learns violent behavior growing up in a violent family. When a child's father or mother responds to a situation with violence, a child learns that this is acceptable behavior. As an adult, when he or she becomes frustrated or angry, he or she may also react violently. This theory has led to the idea of the "cycle of violence." The abused child abuses his or her own child or the child who has seen the father beat the mother engages in spouse abuse or accepts being beaten as an adult. At least some of the caregivers who abuse their elderly family members were either abused as a child by the care recipient or witnessed someone else being abused by other family members.

Adult children who were abused by a parent and, in turn, abuse that parent when he or she has become old is not the same as abuse against children or spouses, cautions Pillemer. "[T]he cycle becomes more direct: the formerly abused child strikes out at his or her own abuser. This involves a different psychological process—one with elements of retaliation as well as imitation."

Jill Korbin et al., in "The Intergenerational Cycle of Violence in Child and Elder Abuse" (*Journal of Elder Abuse & Neglect*, vol. 7, no. 1, 1995), con-ducted a small survey of abusing adults reported to adult protective services to test the theory of the cycle of violence. The authors found that child-abusing parents were significantly more likely than elder-abusing adult children to have been severely abused in childhood (based on the Conflict Tactics Scale — see Chapter II). Two-thirds of child-abusing parents reported severe violence from their parents, compared to one-quarter of elder-abusing adult offspring.

Korbin suggests that a possible reason for the weaker link between adult children abusing elders than between parents abusing children may be related to the age of the perpetrators. The elder abusers were an average of 48 years old and may have considered the physical punishment they may have received as children to be normal. The child abusers were 29 years old on average and grew up with a greater awareness of child abuse (child abuse became a social issue in the early 1960s). They may, therefore, have been more likely to perceive and report their childhood experiences as abusive.

In addition, the better known a problem is, the more it is recognized and reported. Child abuse is far better known than elder abuse, and intergenerational abuse of children has been researched much more thoroughly than elder abuse.

Korbin notes that her sample was small, that it was based on personal memory, and only the perpetrators of violence were interviewed. Furthermore, the data does not reflect differences in the frequency of violent behavior. In this study, a one-time violent event has the same weight as repeated violence.

SPOUSE ABUSE

Spouse abuse is one of the more common forms of elder abuse, but little is known about its causes. It may be a continuation of abuse that began earlier in a marriage, or it may begin as a result of age-related stresses, such as retirement, failing health, caregiver burdens, or increased dependency. Public services for abused elderly are largely health-related, and there is scant help available for the elderly trapped in abusive relationships.

Sarah Harris, in "For Better or for Worse: Spouse Abuse Grown Old" (*Journal of Elder Abuse & Neglect*, vol. 8, no. 1, 1996), used the 1985 *Family Violence Survey* (see Chapter II) to compare data from respondents who were under 60 years old and those over 60 years old. Although the incidence of spouse abuse in older couples was significantly less than that of younger couples, many of the risk factors for violence were the same. Not surprisingly, abuse occurs most often in situations where there is a high degree of conflict.

The factors associated with older couple violence included lower education levels, lower family income, verbal aggression, drug abuse, depression, perceived stress, low use of reasoning tactics, and marital conflict. Racial/ethnic group also played a part: Blacks and Hispanics in the younger group and Blacks in the over-60 group were more likely to experience couple violence. When violence was reported for more than the previous 12 months, intergenerational violence and poor physical health were also found to be significant.

Harris found that different factors supported different theories of abuse. Low income, poor health, verbal aggression, and low marital agreement were linked to perceived stress, supporting the theory that stress causes domestic violence.

High use of verbal aggression in the elders' relationships can be interpreted as support for the dynamic model of abuse. According to the dynamic model, batterers blame their abuse on their partner's behavior. Verbal abuse, such as nagging or name-calling, can provoke abusive behavior from a person who has learned violence from his or her family.

Low income and racial/ethnic group factors support the theory that a subculture of violence causes abuse. That is, violence is considered more normal in some cultures and is therefore more prevalent in certain ethnic and lower income groups.

Harris concluded that these older couples were independent adults who had chosen to remain in their relationship despite the violence. To stop the abuse, social, legal, and psychological help is needed.

EXTERNAL STRESS

Problems of Caring for Elderly Parents

External stress has been determined to play some role in child and wife abuse and may have significance, as well, in the case of elder abuse. According to the American Medical Association's 1991 Congressional Report on elder abuse, 63 percent of reported abuse cases cite caregiver stress as a factor. There are a wide variety of problems associated with taking care of an elderly parent. As the older person becomes more frail, as disabilities develop, and as he or she is less able to care for himself, the caregiver role can become overwhelming.

Richard L. Douglass, of the American Association of Retired Persons (AARP), outlined the difficulties. "Few families are prepared to provide adequate supervision or personal care without professional help. Many probably don't realize that the average length of home care for a severely dependent person who is over 70 is between five and six years."

It should not be forgotten that the caregiver is also growing older and may become less able to perform many of the tasks required. In some cases, caregivers neglect themselves as they care for their elderly charges. Experts on aging point out that options other than home care, including group housing designed for the elderly, and even institutional care, may be better for both the caregiver and the receiver of care.

Although many families assume that home care is the "best" care, they may be offering it out of a sense of duty or guilt rather than as a logical choice made from the available options. This decision should be made early on, because once the individuals choose family care, the decision to discontinue it is extremely difficult to make. "Acknowledging the need to institutionalize a frail dependent after a period of home care is commonly viewed as an admission of failure, and some caregivers tend to avoid or defer remedial action, even when the situation imposes an overwhelming burden on them. This situation has high potential for unintentional or passive neglect."

Nursing Home Versus Home Care

Douglass notes that well-trained nursing home staff may be superior to well-intentioned but untrained family care. Although the belief that all nursing homes are "bad" is widespread, "home care is not necessarily superior or even equal to nursing home care for patients needing high levels of care. Families who avoid placement, while well-meaning, may be unintentionally shortchanging their loved ones and themselves." If a caregiver does not know how to turn and bathe a bed-bound person without hurting him or her, to feed a very weak person, to help with bodily functions without causing embarrassment, "abilities [which] are neither obvious nor instinctive, passive neglect is virtually inevitable as the recipient of care grows more frail over time." (See below for abuse in nursing homes.)

Other Stresses

Emotional separation from a parent is common, and when it is compounded by geographic separation, it can lead to almost no contact between parent and child. When the elderly in this position can no longer live independently, they may reunite with their children after many years. The sudden appearance of a dependent parent, with all the responsibilities involved, can cause stress and frustration. Without the love and friendship necessary to balance the new, often difficult, responsibilities of the adult children, the relationship can become overwhelming. The adult child may resent the elderly parent as an intruder, resulting in abuse.

Fundamental parent-child conflicts that may have never been resolved often reappear. The additional financial burden may be too much for the children to handle, coming at a time, as it often does, when the children must pay for their own children's education. The adult children may even be saving and planning for their own retirement. Medical bills are an ever-increasing expenditure for elderly Americans as they and their children find that medical costs are frequently not compensated or are undercompensated by federal and private health insurance.

Sharing the home with an elderly person can also reduce privacy. Individual freedom may become limited as the children are often reluctant to go out and leave an invalid parent unattended. Conflicts frequently develop between generations on how households should be run and children raised. Young children, in fact, may vie for attention with the grandparents, leading to further tension. A wife who wants to return to work or continue her career finds her future threatened because it is usually the woman who cares for the aged parent. Older parents often feel frustrated that they are no longer able to take care of themselves alone and, in many instances, pay for their own support. They may feel guilty that they have become a burden to their children.

The Effect of Stress

The *National Family Violence Surveys* (see Chapter III) studied the connection between stress and child and spousal abuse. No similar study has yet been completed for the elderly, but experts believe that the same risks exist. Stressful changes in the family that are perceived to be negative (job loss, retirement, the main caregiver returns to school) are often associated with lower levels of marital adjustment. Sugarman and Hotaling (Chapter III) found that the most consistently reported risk factor for spouse abuse was marital strife; similarly, it is possible that discord in the household caused by external stresses can lead to a greater risk of elder abuse.

The problems associated with increased stress are compounded by the likelihood that there are few places to turn for help. Maggie Kuhn, until her death a leading figure in the Gray Panthers, an organization founded to promote the rights of the elderly, had observed that even the best parent-child relationships can deteriorate as the burden of care stretches over a long time. According to Steinmetz, "the bottom line is that if you increase the stress on family members without adding supports to help them cope with it, you increase the likelihood of violence because a person and a family can handle only so much." *The Attorney General's Task Force on Domestic Violence* (Washington, DC, 1984) agreed that "the stress of full-time care of an elderly person can be overwhelming," a factor that can not only threaten the elderly person, but the well-being of the entire family.

While stress may be a contributing factor, it cannot be a complete explanation of abuse. As in the case of child and wife abuse, millions of families are placed in situations of severe stress, yet the parents do not beat their children, the husband does not hit his wife, and the adult child does not abuse his or her elderly parent. In fact, abuse occurs only in a small proportion of families in which an elderly person is part of the family.

ALZHEIMER'S DISEASE

Alzheimer's disease (AD), characterized by a gradual loss of mental ability, sinking into dementia, poses special problems for caregivers. Once thought to be rare, today an estimated 3 to 4 million Americans are affected by a dementing disease at a yearly cost to society of $80 billion, more than three times the costs associated with heart disease and cancer combined. (Cited in Halley and Caledon, "Alzheimer's Disease: Special Issues in Elder Abuse and Neglect," *Journal of Elder Abuse & Neglect*, vol. 4, no. 4, 1992.) Experts estimate that 80 percent of dementia is caused by AD. Fifteen percent is caused by small strokes that lead to progressive deterioration of cognitive function. Less common causes are Parkinson's, Pick's, and Huntington's diseases.

The needs of an elderly AD patient change as the disease progresses. Initially, the caregiver is required for financial, transportation, and shopping tasks. As the disease progresses, more basic needs must be addressed, such as dressing and feeding. In the middle phase of the illness, potentially dangerous and disruptive behaviors begin. These are particularly stressful for a caregiver because they are unpredictable and the patient must be constantly supervised. In the latter phases of the disease, these behaviors diminish and care becomes full-time nursing care, followed by death.

Halley and Caledon point out that AD patients change personality; once mild-mannered people become aggressive and abusive. They cited a survey of 342 AD caregivers, one-third of whom had been physically abused by their patients, in contrast to 12 percent of caregivers who admitted to similarly abusing the AD patient. AD patients are also a safety risk to themselves. They may forget to turn off the stove or to take their medications. These patients need help, but they may refuse as part of their progressing illness. Appropriate care of demented patients may include coercion and force that would be intolerable in the case of a mentally healthy older person. Patients may need to be locked in to prevent wandering, cabinets must be locked to prevent the patient from ingesting household poisons, and medication and hygiene may need to be forced on a reluctant patient.

Caregivers of AD patients are at high risk of abusing their charges. Research shows that AD patients are twice as likely to be physically abused than elderly persons without the disease. In addition, AD caregivers show high levels of emotional, physical, and mental exhaustion, as well as high levels of hostility. AD patients can be irritating and anger-provoking. In one case, a husband insisted on calling his second wife by the name of his first wife, insisting she was the only woman he could ever love.

ABUSE IN NURSING HOMES

The Office of Inspector General of the U.S. Department of Health and Human Services has identified seven types of abuse that can occur in nursing homes (reported in *The Family Therapy Letter*, vol. 3, no. 10, 1991):

- Physical abuse: the infliction of pain or injury. Examples include pushing, slapping, or intentionally inflicting harm.

- Verbal/emotional abuse: the infliction of mental or emotional suffering. Examples include making demeaning statements, harassing, threatening, humiliating, or intimidating the residents.

- Misuse of restraints: the chemical or physical control of a resident beyond physician's orders or not in accordance with accepted medical practice (see below).

- Physical neglect: a disregard for necessities of everyday living. Examples include failing to provide necessary food, clothing, clean linens, or daily care, such as helping with a bath or brushing a resident's hair.

- Medical neglect: a lack of care for existing medical problems. Examples include ignoring a special diet, not calling a physician when necessary, not being aware of negative effects of medication, or not taking action on medical problems.

- Verbal/emotional neglect: a failure to foster esteem. Examples include not considering a patient's wishes, restricting contact with family members, friends, or other residents, and ignoring the resident's need for verbal and emotional contact.

- Abuse of personal property: the illegal or improper use of a resident's property by another person for personal gain. Examples include stealing a resident's private television, clothing, or jewelry.

The Inspector General's office found that the most common types of abuse are physical neglect, emotional neglect, and verbal abuse. The primary abusers are orderlies and aides, but some family members, friends, and other staff members also contribute to the abuse. Abuse is more likely to occur in facilities with inadequate supervision, high staff turnover, low staff-to-resident ratio, and staffers who have not been trained to handle stressful situations.

Characteristics and Consequences of Nursing Home Abuse

Brian Payne and Richard Cikovic examined 488 cases of nursing home abuse reported to Medicaid Fraud Control Units ("An Empirical Examination of the Characteristics, Consequences, and Causes of Elder Abuse in Nursing Homes," *Journal of Elder Abuse & Neglect*, vol. 7, no. 4, 1995). Forty-two states have Medicaid Fraud Control Units, which are responsible for detecting, investigating, and prosecuting Medicaid fraud and abuse.

Most (84.2 percent) of the abuse was physical, including slapping; hitting with an object, such as a hairbrush, toilet plunger, spatula, or wet towel; kick-

---

TABLE 10.1

Occupations of Nursing Home Personnel Accused of Abuse

Occupation	n	%
Nurses' Aide	302	61.9
Licensed Practical Nurse	32	6.6
Direct Care Worker	15	3.1
Supervisor	15	3.1
Certified Nurse's Technician	11	2.3
Registered Nurse	9	1.8
Maintenance/Housekeeping	7	1.4
Orderly	6	1.2
Resident Counselor	6	1.2
Mental Health Caseworker	5	1.0
Licensed Caretaker	4	0.8
Human Service Worker	2	0.4
Developmental Trainer	2	0.4
Other/Missing	72	14.8
Total	**488**	**100.0**

Source: Brian K. Payne and Richard Cikovic, "An Empirical Examination of the Characteristics, Consequences and Causes of Elder Abuse in Nursing Homes," *Journal of Elder Abuse and Neglect,* vol. 7, no. 4, 1995, pp. 61-74. Copyright © 1995, Haworth Press, Inc., Binghamton, New York.

---

ing; and spitting. The remaining acts were sexual (8.8 percent), monetary (1.4 percent), or duty-related, in which the employee misperformed specific duties (for example, a nurse daily removed bandages with a sharp instrument).

Although nurses' aides comprised the largest group of abusers (62 percent), this does not mean that they were the most likely to be abusive, simply that they represented the largest occupation group employed in nursing homes. (See Table 10.1.)

Of the 488 incidents, nearly two-thirds (63 percent) involved a male employee. Males were also slightly more likely to be victims (57 percent) than fe-

---

TABLE 10.2

Gender of the Accused by Gender of the Victim

Gender of Victim	Gender of Accused			
	Male		Female	
	n	%	n	%
Male	126	(66.0)	48	(41.4)
Female	65	(34.0)	68	(58.6)
Total	**191**		**116**	

chi-square 17.66, phi = .24, p = .01

Source: Brian K. Payne and Richard Cikovic, "An Empirical Examination of the Characteristics, Consequences and Causes of Elder Abuse in Nursing Homes," *Journal of Elder Abuse and Neglect,* vol. 7, no. 4, 1995, pp. 61-74. Copyright © 1995, Haworth Press, Inc., Binghamton, New York.

males, although more females are employed in nursing homes and more residents are female. Male employees were more likely to abuse male residents, while female employees tended to have abused female victims (Table 10.2).

In response to these reports of abuse, the criminal justice system convicted 335 abusers and sentenced 295 offenders. Probation was the most common sentence (69 percent), while only 18 percent served any jail time (Table 10. 3). Sexual abusers were more likely to receive prison sentences than other abusers.

Offenders justified their behavior by claiming stress and provocation. Employees, however, receive little or no training in stress management or in ways to deal with violent impulses. It is recognized that nurses' aides are perhaps more likely to commit abuse because there are so many more aides than nurses, and they spend more time with the residents. It is also possible that inadequate training contributes to the abuse.

General Accounting Office (GAO) Report to the Senate Committee on Aging

Following up on a story that appeared in *Time* magazine in the fall of 1997, the GAO studied California nursing homes and found that close to 1 in 3 had been cited by state inspectors for "serious or potentially life-threatening care problems." The study also indicated that the same problems probably exist across the nation. The continuing growth of the elderly population will likely put even greater pressure on the nation's nursing homes, which, according to the GAO report (*Time South Pacific*, Issue 31, August 3, 1998), are understaffed and underregulated.

In its report to the Senate Special Committee on Aging, the GAO also observed that more than half (34 of 62) the suspicious deaths studied in the California nursing homes were probably due to malnutrition, dehydration, or other forms of neglect. Applying this percentage of negligent deaths to the nation's nursing home population as a whole suggests that approximately 200,000 nursing-home residents are dying prematurely or in unnecessary pain, or both.

Senator Charles Grassley, the Republican chairman of the Committee on Aging, blames the federal government for nursing home problems, saying, "It's been too permissive and too forgiving in its enforcement." Since July of 1998, enforcement has begun to tighten following a Clinton Administration crackdown on nursing home violators and on states that do a poor job of regulating them.

Physical Restraints

Many elderly are physically tied to chairs and beds to prevent them from falling and wandering. A restrained person does not have to be supervised and can be left alone for hours. H. Terri Brower, in "Physical Restraints: A Potential Form of Abuse" (*Journal of Elder Abuse & Neglect*, vol. 4, no. 4, 1992), analyzed the problem.

The first recorded testimony on the problems of restraining patients was in 1974 before the U.S. Senate Subcommittee on Long-Term Care. The federal government established rules requiring that restraint be authorized only by a physician and prohibiting it for

TABLE 10.3

Criminal Justice System's Response to the Abuse

Sentence	n	% *	Average	Range
Community Service	38	12.9	100.9 hours	15-350 hrs
Prison	14	4.7	4.0 years	0.5-15 yrs
Probation	203	68.8	19.9 months	0.25-10 yrs
Fine	177	60.0	402.5 dollars	$10-$8,300
Jail	54	18.3	5.5 months	1 day-4 yrs
Total	295			

* Some offenders were given more than one sentence. Therefore, the percentages do not add up to 100 percent.

Source: Brian K. Payne and Richard Cikovic, "An Empirical Examination of the Characteristics, Consequences and Causes of Elder Abuse in Nursing Homes," *Journal of Elder Abuse and Neglect,* vol. 7, no. 4, 1995, pp. 61-74. Copyright © 1995, Haworth Press, Inc., Binghamton, New York.

staff convenience. Restraints were to be used only to prevent injury. According to Brower, the rules were ineffective, and the use of restraints increased. In 1988, 2 out of every 5 residents were physically or mechanically restrained. In 1991, an estimated half a million Americans, including one-third of the nursing home population, were restrained with belts, vests, jackets, and other devices.

Based on the number of citations for violations, the best nursing homes restrained about 6.5 to 44 percent of the patients. The worst homes used restraints on 70 to 95.5 percent of their patients. Restraining nursing home residents inhibits circulation and contributes to conditions such as pneumonia, bed sores, incontinence, and depression. Immobilizing people makes them dependent, and they lose their will to take care of themselves. They also are more likely to become confused and agitated.

The use of restraints raises serious ethical questions, including human rights, the quality of life, dignity, a sense of control — and even the right to fall, with its potential for injury. How are health care providers to decide between protecting the patients from harm and preserving their independence and dignity? Legally, patients have the right to make their own decisions about patient care; however, many of the elderly in nursing homes are suffering some degree of dementia and are no longer competent to make their own decisions.

Medical experts estimate that between 70 and 200 deaths each year are caused by restraints, usually by strangling — more than the number of deaths from any other modern medical device.

The final rules on long-term care in the Omnibus Budget Reconciliation Act of 1989 (PL 101-103, 101-239, 101-508) required nurses to document what other interventions they had tried without success before resorting to restraints. Some states objected, claiming that this would only make for more paperwork. Five states refused outright to follow the guidelines. The guidelines were changed in 1992, replacing most of the "musts" in the original language of the document to "should." In some states, misuse of restraints is considered a form of elder abuse, and failure to report an incident is criminally punishable.

MORTALITY RISK FROM ELDER ABUSE

Older adults who have been mistreated are at a significantly greater risk for death than nonabused older persons. Beginning in 1982, researchers from Cornell and Yale conducted a study of 2,812 community-dwelling adults older than 65 years. The study found that those subjected to abuse or neglect were three times more likely than their peers to die during the 13-year follow-up period, even after adjusting for other factors, such as injury and chronic illness. The study population consisted of 1,643 women and 1,169 men, 593 of whom were nonwhite. After initial interviews and comprehensive assessments, participants were interviewed in person every three years and by telephone every year.

The study designated three groups of subjects: those who had been abused or neglected by another person, those suffering from self-neglect, and those who had no contact with elderly protective services. In the first five years, the survival rate was similar. By the end of the follow-up, those seen for abuse and/or neglect had far poorer survival rates (9 percent) than either those seen for self-neglect (17 percent) or those who had no contact with protective services for the elderly (40 percent).

SELF-NEGLECT

Self-neglect occurs when an elderly person is unable to care for him/herself. According to the National Association of Adult Protective Service Administrators,

Self-neglect is the result of an adult's inability, due to physical and/or mental impairments or diminished capacity, to perform essential self-care tasks including: providing essential food, clothing, shelter, and medical care; obtaining goods and services necessary to maintain physical health, mental health, emotional well-being and general safety; and/or managing financial affairs.

Although all states have some legislation to deal with elder abuse, only 13 have laws that recognize self-neglect, and 15 have administrative policies covering self-neglect. Studies have found that self-neglect represents 50 to 70 percent of the cases brought to the attention of Adult Protective Services (APS).

John F. Longres compared information from the Wisconsin Elder Abuse Reporting System on elders receiving services for self-neglect with those who were treated for maltreatment by others ("Self-Neglect Among the Elderly," *Journal of Elder Abuse & Neglect*, vol. 7, no. 1, 1995).

Abuse investigators described the typical self-neglecting elder as a person who lived alone, isolated from family, with few or no friends, and very little involvement in community activities. Although 72 percent of the self-neglected lived alone at the time of the reported incident, about 21 percent of those maltreated by others also lived alone. Self-neglect cases were more likely to involve elderly with dementia, mental illness, and drug and alcohol problems. On the other hand, the self-neglected were not significantly more likely than other abused elders to be impaired, have medical problems, or be physically frail. (See Table 10.4.)

TABLE 10.4

Type of Maltreatment by Demographic, Impairment, and Case Characteristics: Substantiation Cases (n = 2989)

	Self-Neglect Only (n = 1500)	Self/ Other (n = 161)	Maltreatment by Others (n = 1328)
Demographic Characteristics			
mean age (years)	77.2	75.8	75.4**
% male	37.0	45.3	28.0**
% white	92.6	91.3	86.7**
Impairment Characteristics			
% no impairments	2.3	1.9	13.0**
% medical problems	43.1	43.5	36.1**
% frail/physically disabled	62.3	57.8	62.0
% developmental disability	1.0	2.5	2.1*
dementia	32.3	29.2	18.5**
% mental illness	13.3	13.0	3.5**
% alcohol/drug problem	17.0	21.1	7.2**
Case Characteristics			
% formal referral source	74.2	74.5	64.8**
% incident at residence	95.6	96.9	93.3*
% living in own home/ alone	72.2	43.5	20.6**
% prior report	24.0	27.3	23.6
% life threatening incident	19.9	16.8	12.6**

** = categories significantly differ at p = .01.
 * = categories significantly differ at p = .05.

Source: John F. Longres, "Self-Neglect Among the Elderly," *Journal of Elder Abuse and Neglect,* vol. 7, no. 1, 1995, pp. 69-86. Copyright © 1995, Haworth Press, Inc., Binghamton, New York.

One woman reported to Wisconsin APS was a 93-year-old obese woman whose leg had been amputated and who was unable to prepare meals. The woman wanted "no interference from nobody" but finally accepted help because her only friend, her cat, was slowly dying because it was not being fed.

The self-neglecting elderly not only live alone, but they are cut off from immediate family attachments. Some have no family, while others have either purposely cut off or been cut off from any family connection. One elder abuse investigator explained, "A lot of those families have just terrible dynamics. We're never going to change that." The family conflict was usually long-term, and the elderly were so estranged from their children, they preferred to see themselves as childless. Investigators pointed out that it was not always the children who had been at fault for the conflict. Some of these elderly parents had been abusive or had driven away their children by being "too rigid and demanding."

IMPORTANT NAMES AND ADDRESSES

American Association of Retired
Persons (AARP)
601 E St. NW
Washington, DC 20049
(202) 434-2222
FAX (202) 434-6466

American Public Welfare
Association
810 First St., Suite 500
Washington, DC 20002
(202) 682-0100
FAX (202) 289-6555

Center for the Prevention of
Sexual and Domestic Violence
936 N. 34th St., Suite 200
Seattle, WA 98103
(206) 634-1903
FAX (206) 634-0115

Center for Women Policy Studies
1211 Connecticut Ave. NW, #312
Washington, DC 20036
(202) 872-1770
FAX (202) 296-8962

Domestic Abuse Intervention
Project
202 E. Superior St.
Duluth, MN 55802
(218) 722-2781
FAX (218) 722-0779

Family Research Laboratory
University of New Hampshire
126 Horton Social Science Center
Durham, NH 03824
(603) 862-1888
FAX (603) 862-1122

Family Violence Prevention Fund
383 Rhode Island St., Suite 304
San Francisco, CA 94103-5133
(415) 252-8900
FAX (415) 252-8991

Gerontological Society of
America
1030 15th St. NW, Suite 250
Washington, DC 20005
(202) 842-1275
FAX (202) 842-1150

National Association of State
Units on Aging
1225 I St. NW, Suite 725
Washington, DC 20005
(202) 898-2578
FAX (202) 898-2583

National Clearinghouse for the
Defense of Battered Women
125 S. 9th St., Suite 302
Philadelphia, PA 19107
(215) 351-0010
FAX (215) 351-0779

National Coalition Against
Domestic Violence
P.O. Box 18749
Denver, CO 80218
(303) 839-1852
FAX (303) 831-9251
Hot Line (800) 799-7233

National Committee for the
Prevention of Elder Abuse
c/o Institute on Aging
UMass Memorial Health Care
119 Belmont St.
Worcester, MA 01605
(508) 793-6166
FAX (508) 793-6906

National Council of Juvenile and
Family Court Judges Family
Violence Project
University of Nevada, Reno
P.O. Box 8970
Reno, NV 89507
(775) 784-6012
FAX (775) 784-6628

National Council on Child Abuse
and Family Violence
1155 Connecticut Ave. NW, #400
Washington, DC 20036
(202) 429-6695
FAX (202) 467-4924

National Institute of Justice
810 7th St. NW
Washington, DC 20531
(202) 307-2942
FAX (202) 307-6394

National Resource Center on
Domestic Violence
Pennsylvania Coalition Against
Domestic Violence
6400 Flank Dr., Suite 1300
Harrisburg, PA 17112
(800) 537-2238
FAX (717) 671-8149

Older Women's League
666 11th St. NW, Suite 700
Washington, DC 20001
(202) 783-6686
(800) 825-3695
FAX (202) 638-2356

Self-Help Clearinghouse
St. Clare's Health Services
25 Pocono Rd.
Denville, NJ 07834
(973) 625-7101
FAX (973) 625-8848

Sexual Assault Recovery
Anonymous Society (SARA)
P.O. Box 16
Surrey, British Columbia
V3T 4W4 Canada
(604) 584-2626
FAX (604) 584-2888

RESOURCES

When spouse abuse first became a public issue, during the 1970s and 1980s, a number of studies were conducted. More recently, however, there has been almost no government-funded statistical research on domestic violence. As a result, the work done by the Family Research Laboratory at the University of New Hampshire, Durham, New Hampshire, has become a major source of studies on domestic violence.

Murray Straus, Richard Gelles, David Finkelhor, Suzanne Steinmetz, and others who have been associated with the laboratory have done some of the most informative and scientifically rigorous work in the field of abuse. Studies released by the Family Research Laboratory investigate all forms of domestic violence, many based on their two major surveys — *The National Family Violence Survey, 1975* and *The National Family Violence Resurvey, 1985*. Murray Straus and Glenda Kaufman Kantor have published more current data in "Changes in Spouse Assault Rates from 1975 to 1992: A Comparison of Three National Surveys in the United States" (1994).

Much of the Family Research Laboratory research has been gathered into *Physical Violence in American Families: Risk Factors and Adaptions to Violence in 8,145 Families,* edited by Richard Gelles and Murray Straus (Transaction Publishers, New Brunswick, New Jersey, 1990). Straus and Gelles have also published their research for the general public in *Intimate Violence: The Definitive Study of the Causes and Consequences of Abuse in the American Family* (Simon and Schuster, New York, 1988). Information Plus is grateful for permission to reproduce tables from both books. Also useful was Straus's "State-to-State Differences in Social Inequality and Social Bonds in Relation to Assaults on Wives in the United States," published by the *Journal of Comparative Family Studies* (1994).

The World Health Organization granted permission to use a map from its booklet *Female Genital Mutilation.* Some private sources on abuse include the *Commonwealth Fund Survey of Women's Health* (Commonwealth Fund, New York, 1993) and the World Bank's *Violence Against Women: The Hidden Health Burden* by Lori Heise (World Bank Discussion Papers, Washington, DC, 1994). Information Plus thanks them for their permission to reproduce a number of graphics.

Useful books that contributed to this publication include *Terrifying Love: Why Battered Women Kill and How Society Responds* by Lenore Walker (Harper and Row, New York, 1989); *When Battered Women Kill* by Angela Browne (Free Press, New York, 1987); *Current Controversies on Family Violence,* edited by Richard

Gelles and Donileen Loseke (Sage Publications, Newbury Park, California, 1994); *Legal Responses to Wife Assault,* edited by Zoe Hilton (Sage Publications, Newbury Park, California, 1993); *Wife Rape* by Raquel Kennedy Bergen (Sage Publications, Newbury Park, California, 1996); *The Batterer: A Psychological Profile* by Donald Dutton (Basic Books, New York, 1995); *Women at Risk* by Evan Stark and Anne Flitcraft (Sage Publications, Newbury Park, California, 1996); *Do Arrests and Restraining Orders Work?,* edited by Eve and Carl Buzawa (Sage Publications, Newbury Park, California, 1996); and *Abused Men: The Hidden Side of Domestic Violence* by Philip W. Cook (Praeger Publishers, Westport, Connecticut, 1997).

The federal government's Bureau of Justice Statistics in Washington, DC, in its compilation of crime data, has provided information on intimate violence in *Violence by Intimates: Analysis of Data on Crimes by Current or Former Spouses, Boyfriends, and Girlfriends* (Lawrence Greenfeld et al., 1998), *Murder in Families* by John Dawson and Patrick Langan (1994), and *Spouse Murder Defendants in Large Urban Counties* (1995).

In addition to its *National Violence Against Women Survey,* the National Institute of Justice in Washington, DC, published *Stalking in America: Findings from the National Violence Against Women Survey* (1998), *Batterer Intervention: Program Approaches and Criminal Justice Strategies* (1998), and *Civil Protection Orders: The Benefits and Limitations for Victims of Domestic Violence* (1997).

The U.S. Merit Systems Protection Board, an agency of the federal government, examined sexual harassment in *Sexual Harassment in the Federal Workplace* (1995), which provided data on trends and responses to harassment.

Many journals publish useful articles on abuse. Some of the journals used here include *Family Relations, The Psychology of Women Quarterly, Journal of Marriage and the Family, Violence Against Women, Violence and Victims, Journal of Comparative Family Studies, Journal of Research in Crime and Delinquency,* and *The Journal of Interpersonal Violence.* Information Plus thanks those that gave permission to reproduce graphics.

Information Plus would like to thank the National Center on Elder Abuse for permission to reproduce graphics from its 1996 statistical data summarized in *Elder Abuse in Domestic Settings* and *The Journal of Elder Abuse & Neglect,* a useful source of current re-

INDEX

147

INDEX (Continued)